C000152266

C. Brad Faught is Associate Professor of History and Chair of
the Arts Division at Tyndale University College in Toronto. A
graduate of the Universities of Oxford and Toronto, he is a
Fellow of the Royal Historical Society and a Senior Fellow of
Massey College at the University of Toronto. He is the author
of *The Oxford Movement: A Thematic History of the Tractarians
and Their Times* (2003); *Gordon: Victorian Hero* (2008); and the
forthcoming *Into Africa: The Imperial Life of Margery Perham*.

To my brother, Wylam
and to my sisters, Julie and Josie

C. Brad Faught

The New
A–Z of Empire

A Concise Handbook
of British Imperial History

I.B. TAURIS

PUBLISHERS

Published in 2011 by I.B.Tauris & Co. Ltd
6 Salem Road, London W2 4BU
175 Fifth Avenue, New York NY 10010
www.ibtauris.com

Distributed in the United States and Canada Exclusively by Palgrave Macmillan
175 Fifth Avenue, New York NY 10010

ISBN: 978 1 84511 870 9 (hb)
ISBN: 978 1 84511 871 6 (pb)

A full CIP record for this book is available from the British Library
A full CIP record is available from the Library of Congress

Library of Congress Catalog Card Number: available

Typeset in Minion Pro by Ellipsis Books Limited, Glasgow
Printed and bound in Great Britain by TJ International Ltd, Padstow, Cornwall

Contents

Preface

Set in this Stormy Northern Sea,
Queen of these restless fields of tide,
England! What shall men say of thee,
Before whose feet the worlds divide?

Oscar Wilde

Imperialism is not a word for scholars, a scholar reputedly once said. Nor, for at least the last fifty years, has it been a word for much anyone else. A term derived from *Imperator*, used by its classic Roman progenitors to describe a general authorized by the Senate to expand the borders of the republic, Imperialism had lived for a good part of the twentieth century in the shadows of a deep disparagement. Recently, however, this situation has changed. Over the last ten years or so, Imperialism has re-entered afresh both scholarly discourse and, to some extent, popular conversation, sometimes even in a positive manner. In numerous academic books and articles, as well as in film and fiction, the time and tide of the world's great empires – especially the British – have received a renewed and sustained examination. Works by Niall Ferguson, for example, and John Darwin, come immediately to mind. Of course, with the exception of the United States, where a mostly unacknowledged approximation of old-style Imperialism continues, empire as an organizing principle for international relations remains roundly denounced as immoral by most, and unsustainable by the rest. But even where Imperialism is denounced, what *has* changed in recent years is its overt inclusion as a means by which to understand more fully – sometime even sympathetically – the forces that have shaped the contemporary world.

This book aims to contribute to the burgeoning historiography on the topic by offering itself as a compendium of all things British Imperial. To do so, some 400 entries – in the main, persons, places, and events, each accompanied by a brief bibliography – have been given essential definitions that describe their importance to the history of the British Empire in its last and greatest phase, from around 1780 until 1980. The majority of the entries speak, naturally, to aspects of the British Empire during its nineteenth-century height, but there is, of course, coverage on either side of the cardinal Victorian era.

Setting out to cover the history of what is usually called the Second British Empire (that period of British Imperial history commencing with the revolt of the American colonies in 1776 and running down to the years following the Second World War) requires a close exercise in distillation. Apart from the chronology as outlined above, I have attempted in the book to concentrate on those things that can bear scrutiny as being truly 'things' of empire; that is, those events, passages, and persons for which the term 'British Empire' would have been commonly understood to mean empire of rule, including the colonies of settlement. By definition, such a restriction eliminates the later transition to Commonwealth, although one hopes the border will be seen as porous to some degree. To that end, included are some items that properly speaking belong to the Commonwealth, that twentieth-century organic successor to the British Empire, which continues to exist as a kind of intergovernmental club made up of its former members. Throughout the book, however, my intention has been to concentrate on the so-called high noon of empire, which the advent of the First World War began to eclipse.

Additionally, the later distinction brought to Imperial studies between 'formal' and 'informal' empire, while provocative and of necessary use as an instrument of historical investigation and broader understanding, is not especially useful for the purposes of a prescriptive dictionary-handbook. Hence, as examples, neither Argentina nor King Leopold of the Belgians appears as discrete entries, even though their impact on the British Empire was significant.

The New A-Z of Empire: A Concise Handbook of British Imperial History is thus intended as a reference companion for all those – scholar, student, or general reader – interested in the history of that period of time when Britain came to rule some one-quarter of the earth's surface along with an equal proportion of its people. Compared to the Roman Empire, or to others such as the Russian or the Chinese, Britain's intense foray into contemporary Imperialism was relatively short: just 131 years separates the Treaty of Paris that formally ended the American War of Independence in 1783 with the outbreak of war in Europe in 1914. But a generation before the Empire's demise, its chief chronicler, Rudyard Kipling, was already predicting that such an event would soon come to pass. In 'Recessional' (1897), he spoke of the British Empire becoming one 'with Ninevah and Tyre.' He was right about that, of course, as those who predict the end of empires always are right. What this book hopes to provide are points of entry into a vanished world, a world whose existence did much to shape the age in which we live now and whose residue is part of the cultural, social, religious, and political fabric of hundreds of millions of people today.

Acknowledgements

I would like to thank those who have helped *The New A-Z of Empire* see the light of day. The book owes its genesis to Dr Lester Crook, Senior History Editor at I.B.Tauris, who first suggested that such a work would be a useful and necessary addition to the historiography of the British Empire. He has guided it every step of the way. In this regard too, I would like to thank Joanna Godfrey, also a history editor at I.B.Tauris, as well as those in production and marketing and to Amy Wright and Ellipsis Books. My thanks to Tyndale University College in Toronto, where I teach, for support in writing this book, and to my students whose interest in and questions about British Imperial history help to keep my own interest in the subject current and keen. Thanks, also, to Katie Carline for fact-checking the text. All errors, of course, are my own.

I first started studying the British Empire as an undergraduate at Calgary, where I was well-taught in this regard by the late Professor R.A.M. Shields. Later, at Oxford, I had the pleasure of working under the late Professor Ronald E. Robinson and the current Beit University Lecturer in the History of the British Commonwealth, Dr John Darwin. To them, I offer my sincere thanks. I would like to acknowledge also A.H.M. Kirk-Greene, Emeritus Fellow of St Antony's College, Oxford, an outstanding scholar of colonial Africa and a constant inspiration and help. Finally, to my wife Rhonda, and our children, Claire and Luke, I extend my heartfelt thanks for (most of the time!) putting up with my historical obsessions. As Claire said recently, as we began to play yet another round of 'dinnertime trivia': 'No more British history allowed!'

Timeline

Timeline

1867	Confederation of Canada
1869	Suez Canal opens
1875	Disraeli purchases for the British government 45 per cent of Suez Canal Company
1877	Queen Victoria proclaimed Empress of India
1879	Zulu War
1881	First Boer War
1882	British occupation of Egypt
1885	General Gordon dies at Khartoum
1895	Jameson Raid
1899–1902	Second Boer War
1901	Queen Victoria dies
1901	Commonwealth of Australia proclaimed
1902	Cecil Rhodes dies
1910	Union of South Africa proclaimed
1914–18	First World War
1921	Cairo Conference on the future of the Middle East
1922	Chanak Crisis
1924–5	British Empire Exhibition at Wembley Stadium, London
1926	Balfour Definition of Dominion status
1931	Statute of Westminster
1939–45	Second World War
1947	India gains independence
1956	Suez Crisis
1956	Sudan gains independence
1957	Ghana gains independence
1960	Nigeria gains independence
1961	Tanganyika gains independence
1962	Uganda gains independence
1963	Kenya gains independence
1980	Southern Rhodesia (Zimbabwe) gains independence
1982	Falklands War
1994	Apartheid ends in South Africa
1997	Reversion of Hong Kong to the People's Republic of China

A

Abdul Rahman, Tunku, Putra al-Haj (1903–90). As a nationalist leader in Malaya* beginning in the mid-1940s, Abdul Rahman helped bring about Malayan independence in 1957. He served as Prime Minister until 1961 and then, as chief architect of the federation of Malaysia*, remained in the same office until retiring in 1970.

Further Reading

Putra Al-Haj Abdul Rahman Tunku (1984). *Malaysia: The Road to Independence* (Petaling Jaya, Pelanduk Publications)

A.J. Stockwell, ed. (2004). *Malaysia* (London, Stationery Office)

Abdullah bin al-Husayn (1882–1951). Emir of Jordan from 1921 to 1946 under a British mandate, Abdullah subsequently became King of Jordan after its independence in the latter year. A controversial figure in the Arab world for his apparent pro-Western views and his willingness to discuss the partition of Palestine*, Abdullah was assassinated in 1951 by a disaffected Palestinian.

Further Reading

Joab B. Eilon (2007). *The Making of Jordan: Tribes, Colonialism and the Modern State* (London and New York, I.B.Tauris)

Mary C. Wilson (1990). *King Abdullah, Britain and the Making of Jordan* (Cambridge, Cambridge University Press)

Aboukir Bay, Battle of. In 1798, Napoleon exported French Revolutionary fervour to Egypt in an attempt to use the country as a staging base to launch an invasion of British India. Nelson* – ennobled later that year and rising fast in the estimation of his countrymen – attacked the French fleet at Aboukir Bay, just off Alexandria. Here, in August, his captains, or 'Band of Brothers,' routed the French, with just two of their thirteen vessels escaping destruction. Nelson's sole captain lost was George Blagdon Westcott of HMS *Majestic*. The short-lived French occupation of Egypt ended formally in 1802.

Further Reading

Robert Gardiner, ed. (1997). *Nelson Against Napoleon: From the Nile to Copenhagen, 1798–1801* (London, Chatham)

Andrew Lambert (2004). *Nelson: Britannia's God of War* (London, Faber and Faber)

Achebe, Chinua (1930–). One of the first African writers to be known in Britain, Achebe was born in colonial southern Nigeria*, the son of a teacher at an Anglican Church Missionary Society school. He earned a BA at University College, Ibadan, and not long afterwards, in 1958, published his first novel, *Things Fall Apart*. The book was an indictment of the impact of British Imperialism on his Ibo (Igbo) people, which proved especially resonant in the run-up to Nigerian independence two years later. The book proved to be perhaps the most important text in early African nationalist literature.

Further Reading

Chinua Achebe (2006). *Things Fall Apart* (London, Penguin)

Catherine L. Innes (1990). *Chinua Achebe* (Cambridge, Cambridge University Press)

Aden. An ancient port at the entrance to the Red Sea, Aden became the most important coaling station on the route to India* following the opening of the Suez Canal* in 1869. Located directly across the Gulf of Aden from the Horn of Africa, the port functioned also as an important trade entrepot and jumping-off point for expeditions to the interior of the African continent. Controlled by Britain from 1839 as part of India, it became a Crown Colony in 1937. Thirty years later the British pulled out in the face of a protracted insurgency.

Further Reading

Peter Hinchcliffe (2006). *Without Glory in Arabia: The British Retreat from Aden* (London and New York, I.B.Tauris)

Roxani Eleni Margariti (2007). *Aden and the Indian Ocean Trade: 150 Years in the Life of a Medieval Arabian Port* (Chapel Hill, University of North Carolina Press)

Afghan Wars. Three wars fought over a span of about eighty years in the nineteenth and early twentieth centuries, at the conclusion of which Afghanistan achieved independence. Remote and mountainous, Afghanistan nonetheless was at the centre of the so-called Anglo-Russian Great Game*. Ever concerned about the security of India, Britain was especially aware of the exposed Northwest Frontier and the possibility of a Russian incursion there. Successive Afghan governments were measured by the strength of their pro-British stance, and when found wanting, intervention was the result. The first of these took place from 1839 until 1842. The second and most famous of the Afghan wars occurred during 1879–80 and made the reputation of General Frederick Roberts*. Finally, in 1919 and following the unrest of the recent Russian Revolution, the British intervened a third time. In 1921, a definitive treaty was signed, which settled Afghanistan's borders and recognized its independence.

Further Reading

Edward Ingram (2001). *The British Empire as a World Power* (London, Frank Cass)

Karl E. Meyer (1999). *Tournament of Shadows: The Great Game and the Race for Empire in Central Asia* (Washington, DC, Counterpoint)

African National Congress. Founded in 1912 by John Dube and Solomon Plaatje, among others, the ANC developed into the chief political voice of black South Africans, achieving national power ultimately in 1994. After the National Party's victory in the 1948 election, the ANC committed itself to fighting apartheid* at home and endorsing democratic socialism abroad. Nelson Mandela* had helped form the ANC Youth League in 1944. Fifty years later in post-apartheid South Africa*, he was elected the first black President in the country's history. During those years the ANC had carried out domestic resistance in the face of severe repression, doing so with the assistance of an influential international campaign to discredit and boycott the white South African regime. In 1992, apartheid was ended and two years later, multi-racial elections were held.

Further Reading

Saul Dubow (2000). *The African National Congress* (Stroud, Sutton)

Morgan Norval (1993). *Politics by other Means: the ANC's War on South Africa* (Washington, DC, Selous Foundation Press)

Alberta. Named for a daughter of Queen Victoria, Alberta, located in Canada's west, was made a province within the Canadian Confederation in 1905. Alberta's territory first belonged to the Hudson's Bay Company under its 1670 Royal Charter. Beginning in 1870, the Canadian government controlled it as part of the Northwest Territories until the attainment of full provincial status thirty-five years later. The building of the Canadian Pacific Railway* opened up Alberta to agricultural production from the 1890s, a thriving economic base buttressed by the discovery of oil in 1914 and later natural gas. Its scenic beauty of rolling grassland and craggy mountains, along with abundant natural resource wealth, made Alberta one of the most desirable and prosperous provinces in Canada by the second half of the twentieth century.

Further Reading

J.F. Conway (2006). *The West: The History of a Region in Confederation* (Toronto, James Lorimer)

Donald G. Wetherell (2000). *Alberta's North: A History, 1890–1950* (Edmonton, University of Alberta Press)

All India Muslim League. The principal nationalist organ for Muslims within British India, it was founded in Dhaka (located today in Bangladesh) in 1906, initially as a body concerned with the protection of Muslim rights. Gradually the League's purpose changed to one of Indian independence, first in cooperation with the Indian National Congress*. Muhammad Ali Jinnah* became the League's President in 1916, but after increasing strain with Mohandas Gandhi* he broke with Congress in 1920. In the 1920s and 1930s various attempts were made to encourage Hindu-Muslim amity, especially as Britain began to devolve power. In 1940, the League's Lahore Resolution made clear its commitment to an independent Muslim state of Pakistan. Gandhi disagreed wholly with a two-state solution, but the British became convinced that Partition was the only way forward that would satisfy Jinnah and the League, and at Indian independence in 1947 such was achieved.

Further Reading

Ayesha Jalal (1994). *The Sole Spokesman: Jinnah, the Muslim League and the Demand for Pakistan* (Cambridge, Cambridge University Press)

Nadeem Shafiq Malik, ed. (1997). *The All India Muslim League: 1906–47* (Lahore, National Book Foundation)

Allenby, Edmund H.H., 1st Viscount Allenby (1861–1936). A soldier and administrator, Allenby gained fame for his command of British forces in the Middle East, beginning in 1917. Born in Suffolk, he was educated at Haileybury* and Sandhurst and then served in Africa, including as a cavalry commander in the Second Boer War*. During the First World War* Allenby was given command of the Egyptian expeditionary force charged with rooting out the Turks and putting an end to the Ottoman Empire's control of Palestine*. A bear of a man, he proved himself highly skilled at directing mobile warfare and captured Jerusalem in December 1917. Subsequent victories over the Turks enabled the success of the Arab Revolt, whose leading inspiration was Colonel T.E. Lawrence*, and the eventual imposition of Anglo-French Imperial rule in the region. Promoted Field Marshal in 1919, he was appointed High Commissioner in Cairo that same year, remaining in the position until his retirement in 1925.

Further Reading

Matthew Hughes (1999). *Allenby and British Strategy in the Middle East, 1917–1919* (London, Frank Cass)

Lawrence James (1993). *Imperial Warrior: The Life and Times of Field-Marshal Viscount Allenby, 1861–1936* (London, Weidenfeld & Nicolson)

Amery, Leopold (Leo) C.M.S. (1873–1955). An Imperial statesman of firm views and pugnacious style, Amery was born in India and educated at Harrow and Oxford*, after which he became a barrister. The Boer War* galvanized his interest in Empire and he became a great admirer of Viscount Alfred Milner* and a member of his 'kindergarten' of Imperial thinkers and men on the spot. Amery gained a public profile by editing and contributing much of the content of *The Times History of the War in South Africa* (1900–9), and shortly thereafter in 1911 was elected to Parliament as a Conservative where he would serve for the next thirty-four years. As a member of the Cabinet Secretariat, Amery's drafting of the Balfour Declaration* in 1917 on the establishment of a Jewish 'national home' in Palestine marked the beginning of a sustained period of close involvement in Imperial questions. As First Lord of the Admiralty (1922), Colonial Secretary (1924–9), Secretary of State for Dominion Affairs (1925–9), and Secretary of State for India* and Burma* (1940–5), Amery established a reputation as a strong advocate of the Empire's gradual transition to Commonwealth, symbolized by India's move to independence, which culminated in 1947.

Further Reading

John Barnes and David Nicholson, eds (1980). *The Leo Amery Diaries*. 2 vols (London, Hutchinson)

Wm. Roger Louis (1992). *In the Name of God, Go! Leo Amery and the British Empire in the Age of Churchill* (New York, Norton)

Amin, Idi (*c.*1925–2003). One of the most brutal of post-colonial African leaders, Amin ruled Uganda* from 1971 to 1979. Born around 1925, probably in Kampala, Amin was raised a Muslim. In 1946, he joined the King's African Rifles* as a cook. He rose through the ranks, a trajectory that continued after Ugandan independence in 1962. In 1968, he was promoted to major general, and soon thereafter President Milton Obote* appointed him Commander-In-Chief of the armed forces. A rift between Amin and Obote sparked a coup in January 1971. Obote's regime was toppled and Amin embarked on a mostly scandal-ridden eight years of tyranny during which it is estimated 300,000 Ugandans died. Forced from power in 1979 – largely through the intervention of Julius Nyerere* of Tanzania* – Amin spent most of his remaining years in exile in Saudi Arabia, dying in ignominy in Jeddah in 2003.

Further Reading

Tony Avirgan (1982). *War in Uganda: The Legacy of Idi Amin* (Westport, CT, L. Hill)

Bob Measures and Tony Walker (1998). *Amin's Uganda* (London, Minerva Press)

Amritsar Riots. Site of the Golden Temple, the holiest shrine in the Sikh religion, Amritsar was situated within British India's Punjab province (in today's Pakistan). In 1919, India* experienced severe rioting, which was linked to emergent nationalism. At Amritsar in April a large crowd gathered in protest even though political demonstrations were prohibited. The unarmed crowd was fired upon at the command of the dyspeptic Brigadier-General Reginald E.H. Dyer. Almost 400 protestors were killed and more than 1,200 wounded. The episode became instantly notorious, and in the minds of nationalists such as Gandhi*, evidence of British Imperial oppression. Dyer was later censured officially and resigned his commission.

Further Reading

N.A. Collett (2005). *The Butcher of Amritsar: General Reginald Dyer* (London, Hambledon and London)

Denis Judd (2004). *The Lion and the Tiger: The Rise and Fall of the British Raj* (Oxford, Oxford University Press)

Anderson, Sir H. Percy (1831–96). A civil servant, Anderson was educated at Marlborough College and Christ Church, Oxford*. Appointed Junior Clerk, Foreign Office, in 1852, he developed an expertise in African affairs and from 1883 was head of the African Department. A member of the British delegation to the Berlin West Africa Conference* of 1884–5, he was the best-informed British official there and was a critical presence then and in later European negotiations during the partition of Africa. He insisted that Britain's strategic interests in the East depended upon a strong position in Africa, and he consistently attempted to use King Leopold of the Belgians to advance the British cause against the French. Appointed KCB in 1890 and Assistant Under-Secretary in 1894, he died two years later.

Further Reading

Wm. Roger Louis (2006). 'The Scramble for Africa: Sir Percy Anderson's Grand Strategy', in *Ends of British Imperialism: the Scramble for Empire, Suez and Decolonization* (London and New York, I.B.Tauris), 51–74

Thomas Pakenham (1991). *The Scramble for Africa: White Man's Conquest of the Dark Continent from 1876 to 1912* (New York, Avon Books)

Anglo-Irish War. In the same month that the world focused its attention on the Paris Peace Conference, the final violent encounter between Britain and Ireland commenced. Agitation for Irish independence had continued from the Rising in 1916 and in January 1919 the Dail issued a declaration of independence. Violence soon became endemic between the recently formed Irish Republican Army* – especially its 'Flying Columns' – and the Royal Irish Constabulary, along with the Auxiliaries and the 'Black and Tans,' the latter an ill-disciplined and infamously brutal force established by Colonial Secretary Winston Churchill*. The guerilla conflict was made official in March 1921 when the Dail – still unrecognized by Westminster – issued a formal declaration of war. Amid increasing bloodshed and mutual atrocities, a truce was reached in July, which in turn led to the signing of the Anglo-Irish Treaty on 6 December and the establishment of the Irish Free State*. The war made it clear that Irish political and military leadership revolved around two charismatic figures, Eamon de Valera* and Michael Collins*.

Further Reading

Roy Foster (1990). *Modern Ireland: 1600–1972* (London, Penguin)

William H. Kautt (1999). *The Anglo-Irish War, 1916–1921: A People's War* (Westport, CT, Praeger)

Anguilla. A tiny Caribbean island inhabited by English settlers from 1650. The Treaty of Utrecht (1713) recognized it as a British possession. Linked constitutionally for many years to St Kitts and Nevis*, since 1980 Anguilla has been a British Overseas Territory and thereby one of the last outposts of Empire.

Further Reading
Brian Dyde (2005). *Out of the Crowded Vagueness: A History of St Kitts, Nevis & Anguilla* (Oxford, Macmillan Caribbean)
Simon Winchester (2004). *Outposts: Journeys to the Surviving Relics of the British Empire* 2nd edn (London, Harper Perennial)

Antigua. An island in the Caribbean Leeward chain, Antigua was colonized by the English beginning in 1632, some 140 years after being claimed for Spain by Columbus. Slave plantation sugar cane dominated its economy from the latter seventeenth century until the 1834 abolition of slavery* throughout the British Empire. Antigua served as an important Royal Navy base in the eighteenth century and was used by Nelson* many times, the last coming in 1805 not long before the Battle of Trafalgar*. Later part of two successive island federations, Antigua gained its complete independence from Britain in 1981.

Further Reading
Brian Dyde (2000). *The History of Antigua: The Unsuspected Isle* (London, Macmillan Caribbean)
J.R. Ward (1988). *British West Indian Slavery, 1750–1834: The Process of Amelioration* (Oxford, Oxford University Press)

Apartheid. An Afrikaans word meaning 'apartness,' apartheid was used by the mainly Afrikaner* National Party to define its policy in the 1948 South African election campaign in which it came to power. Laws entrenching racial segregation along the lines of what was customary in the Transvaal were passed progressively by the new government and implemented nation-wide. Beginning in the 1950s, apartheid was condemned internationally. In 1961, Commonwealth Prime Ministers led by John Diefenbaker of Canada* publicly opposed the policy and demanded that it be modified. In response, South African Prime Minister Hendrik Verwoerd vowed to remove the country from the Commonwealth, which took place later that year. The apartheid laws remained in force until 1992.

Further Reading

T.R.H. Davenport (1995). *South Africa: A Modern History* (Toronto, University of Toronto Press)

Roland Oliver and Anthony Atmore (2004). *Africa Since 1800* (Cambridge, Cambridge University Press)

Arabi Pasha (Ahmed Urabi) (1841–1911). The leader of the revolt against Khedivial Egypt, which led to the British bombardment of Alexandria in the summer of 1882 and the country's subsequent occupation. Born into a family of means and university educated, Arabi later entered the Egyptian army where he rose through the officer class and was known as both a fiery orator and a strong Egyptian nationalist who despised the Turkish and European presence in his country. In 1879, Egypt's protracted financial crisis caused the Anglo-French backers of the Khedive Ismail's regime to depose him from power and replace him with his son, Tawfiq. Meanwhile, the Prime Minister, Nubar Pasha, was an Armenian Christian, and other ministerial posts were likewise occupied by foreigners. Egyptian nationalists, Arabi among them, bridled at these foreign intrusions. In October 1881, Colonel Arabi led a massive street demonstration in Alexandria denouncing the manipulation of Egypt by foreigners. The British and the French waited to respond until January 1882, when they threatened Arabi and his supporters that should the disturbances continue they would intervene militarily on behalf of the Khedive's embattled regime. Arabi was unintimidated by the Anglo-French threat. Tensions rose apace. The British Mediterranean Fleet arrived off Alexandria in July just in time to be told that fifty Europeans had been slaughtered in the city by Arabi-inspired nationalists. Citing the massive financial investments in Egypt and the security of the Suez Canal, the Gladstone government acted, authorizing an attack on Alexandria. In the ensuing bombardment over 1,000 Egyptians were killed. Arabi fled, but in September he was engaged at his main base of Tel-el-Kebir, where his forces were decisively defeated. He was sent into exile in Ceylon* for the next nineteen years, before being allowed to return to Egypt in 1901, where he died ten years later.

Further Reading

Peter Mansfield (1971). *The British in Egypt* (London, Weidenfeld & Nicolson)

Thomas Mayer (1988). *The Changing Past: Egyptian Historiography of the Urabi Revolt, 1882–1883* (Gainesville, FL, University of Florida Press)

Arden-Clarke, Sir Charles N. (1898–1962). Colonial governor. Arden-Clarke presided over the Gold Coast*, which, as Ghana*, was the first British African colony to gain independence, in 1957. Arden-Clarke was born in India*, the son of a Church of England missionary. Educated at the Rossall School in the tradition of colonial service made aspirational by fellow alumnus Lord Lugard*, Arden-Clarke served in the First World War* – including a stint fighting against the Communists in Russia. Afterwards, he declined a scholarship to read classics at Cambridge and, in 1920, joined the Colonial Service*. He served as a district officer in Northern Nigeria* and then in the secretariat in Lagos before being trans-ferred to Bechuanaland* where he became resident commissioner in 1937. Five years later he took up a similar appointment in Basutoland*. In 1946, Arden-Clarke was knighted and sent to Sarawak* as governor. Three years later he was appointed governor of the Gold Coast. He served in this capacity until its independence in 1957. These eight years saw Arden-Clarke reach the summit of his gubernatorial career, embodying the modern colonial administrator who was increasingly conversant with (African) nationalism and able to work well with those – especially Kwame Nkrumah* – who agitated for independence. When it came, such was the respect accorded Arden-Clarke by the new Ghanaian government, he was asked to become the country's first Governor-General. Temperamentally unsuited to the job, however, he served only briefly before retiring to England where he became a well-consulted advisor on African and colonial affairs in the years prior to his death in 1962.

Further Reading

A.H.M. Kirk-Greene (1999). *On Crown Service: A History of HM Colonial and Overseas Civil Services, 1837–1997* (London and New York, I.B.Tauris)

David Rooney (1982). *Sir Charles Arden-Clarke* (London, R. Collings)

Ashanti. Owing to its key position along the main trade routes through West Africa to the Gold Coast, this area and its Asante-speaking people were known to the British since the eighteenth century. Invaded by a British force fighting under Sir Garnet Wolseley* in 1873 in order to stamp out slavery and human sacrifice, the Ashanti were temporarily defeated. British interest was renewed in the 1890s by the outbreak of a gold rush. A British Protectorate was proclaimed in 1896 and the Ashanti king, Pempeh I, exiled. In 1900, a revolt was precipitated when the British governor, Sir Frederick Hodgson, made an ill-advised demand to sit upon the Ashanti's revered symbol of kingship, the Golden Stool. The revolt was put down, however, and the Ashanti kingdom was incorporated into the Gold Coast colony, and then after independence in 1957 as a province of Ghana.

Further Reading

Robert B. Edgerton (1995). *The Fall of the Asante Empire: The Hundred Year War for Africa's Gold Coast* (New York, The Free Press)

Alan Lloyd (1964). *The Drums of Kumasi: The Story of Ashanti Wars* (London, Longmans)

(Webster-) Ashburton Treaty. Named for Alexander Baring, 1st Baron Ashburton, the treaty ended some of the disharmony in Anglo-American relations remaining from the War of 1812*. In 1842, the new British Prime Minister, Sir Robert Peel, dispatched Ashburton as a special envoy to the United States. He negotiated an end to the right of maritime search – about which the Americans had objected vociferously – and, among other things, the treaty signed that year set the border between the USA and Canada* as the forty-ninth parallel.

Further Reading

Howard Jones (1977). *To the Webster-Ashburton Treaty: A Study in Anglo-American Relations, 1783–1843* (Chapel Hill, University of North Carolina)

H.V. Nelles (2004) *A Little History of Canada* (Toronto, Oxford University Press)

Attlee, Clement, 1st Earl Attlee (1883–1967). The first British Labour Prime Minister to hold office with a Parliamentary majority, Attlee governed from 1945 to 1951, during which time he oversaw India's independence. Born in London and educated at Haileybury* and Oxford*, Attlee became a barrister, served in the First World War, and then in 1922 was elected Labour MP. He served in Parliament for the next thirty-two years. From early in his Parliamentary career Attlee took a strong interest in Imperial affairs, and in 1935, after becoming Labour Party leader, began to champion the cause of Dominion* status for India.* From 1942 to 1943 he served as Dominions Secretary in Churchill's* wartime coalition government, and the experience of it made plain to him the necessity of India's independence. Once in power he guided the Indian Independence Bill through Parliament and in 1947 appointed Lord Mountbatten* Viceroy in order to supervise Britain's withdrawal from India, which culminated on 15 August. To his critics, Attlee was never sufficiently committed to the British Empire. He responded that in the age of the airplane it was simply no longer possible to maintain a sea-based Empire. He argued, instead, for a Commonwealth* of loosely joined states with the British sovereign as 'Head'. In 1949, such a plan was formalized in the London Declaration*.

Further Reading

Jerry H. Brookshire (1995). *Clement Attlee* (Manchester, Manchester University Press)

R.D. Pearce (1997). *Attlee* (London, Longman)

Auchinleck, Sir Claude J.E. (1884–1981). Field Marshal, and the penultimate British Commander-in-Chief of the Indian Army*, Auchinleck was a career soldier who began his service in the Punjab in 1904. During the First World War* he served in the Middle East, and then between the wars returned to India* where he was an instructor at the Staff College at Quetta and in 1938 chaired a committee that formed the basis of the Chatfield Report, which re-made and enlarged the British Indian Army. Service in the Middle East and North Africa followed during the Second World War*, as did brief service in 1941 as Commander-in-Chief of the Indian Army. A severe disagreement with Churchill* in 1942 over his strategy in North Africa led to Auchinleck's return to India and the next year his re-appointment as Commander-in-Chief of the Indian Army. Auchinleck objected strongly to the policy of partition adopted by Lord Mountbatten*, the last Viceroy, and in protest resigned from his command just months before Indian independence in 1947.

Further Reading

Niall Barr (2004). *Pendulum of War: The Three Battles of El Alamein* (London, Jonathan Cape)

John Keegan, ed. (1991). *Churchill's Generals* (London, Cassell)

Australia. The first Englishman to sight what was later named Australia was Captain James Cook* in 1770. In 1788, the First Fleet arrived at Botany Bay in order to establish a British penal colony and European settlement of the island continent commenced. Annexation by Britain occurred in 1817. The exploration of Australia continued apace, as did agricultural production, especially sheep farming, and the exploitation of gold. In 1850, the Australian Colonies Act gave effective self-government to the colonies of New South Wales*, South Australia*, and Van Diemen's Land* (Tasmania). Federation, modelled on the Canadian example of 1867 and spurred by French, German, and US Imperialism in the South Pacific, arrived in 1901 when the original three 'states' were joined by Western Australia*, Victoria*, and Queensland*. Canberra was agreed as the federal capital in 1909. The Northern Territory* became a federal responsibility in 1911, remaining so until achieving self-government in 1978. Australia gained autonomy within the Empire through the Statute of Westminster* in 1931. The last constitutional vestiges of the country's colonial past were removed in 1986 with the passage of the Australia Acts.

Further Reading

Geoffrey C. Bolton, et al. (1986–90). *The Oxford History of Australia*, 5 vols (Melbourne, Oxford University Press)

Deryck M. Schreuder and Stuart Ward, eds (2008). *Australia's Empire* (Oxford, Oxford University Press)

B

Baden-Powell, Robert S.S., 1st Baron Baden-Powell (1857–1941). Soldier, hero of Empire, and founder of the Boy Scouts, Baden-Powell joined the 13th Hussars in India in 1876, and then moved onto Africa where he fought in the Zulu War* of 1879. Further service in Southern Rhodesia* followed, and then against the Ashanti* in 1896. Widespread fame met his 217-day defence of the siege of Mafeking* in 1899–1900 during the Second Boer War*. Promotion to Major-General and appointment to Inspector-General of Cavalry capped his military career. Baden-Powell retired in 1910 in order to devote his time to the expansion of the Boy Scouts movement, which he had established in 1907 and which under his guidance as Chief Scout flourished. He died at his home in Kenya and is buried there. In recent years Baden-Powell has been portrayed by some biographers in a controversial light. But his reputation remains mostly intact and his legacy the millions of boys worldwide who retain membership in the Boy Scouts.

Further Reading
Tim Jeal (1989). *Baden-Powell* (London, Hutchinson)
Robert H. MacDonald (1993). *Sons of the Empire: The Frontier and the Boy Scout Movement* (Toronto, University of Toronto Press)

Bahadur Shah Zafar II (1775–1862). The nominal King of Delhi, and the last of a long line of Mughal emperors, Bahadur acceded to the throne in 1837. For the next twenty years until the Mutiny* in 1857, he lived lavishly in Delhi's Red Fort supported by an enormous pension provided by the British, which stemmed from a treaty made with his Mughal forebears. At the outbreak of the Indian Mutiny* he was induced by Muslim rebels to lend them his support. A dreamy, contemplative man, his putative spiritual leadership of the Delhi mutineers ended quickly, and in September 1857 he was captured by the British, charged with rebellion, and imprisoned. He died in exile in Rangoon.

Further Reading

Syed Z. Ahmed (1996). *Twilight of an Empire* (Lahore, Ferozsons)

William Dalrymple (2007). *The Last Mughal: The Eclipse of a Dynasty, Delhi 1857* (London, Bloomsbury)

Bahamas. A chain of islands in the Atlantic near Florida, the Bahamas saw its first English settlers arrive in 1629. The Treaty of Paris (1783) confirmed Bahamian sovereignty as British and it was duly made a Crown Colony, a status maintained until 1964 when the Bahamas became self-governing. Complete independence with continued membership in the Commonwealth came in 1973.

Further Reading

Michael Craton (1986). *A History of the Bahamas*, 3rd edn (Waterloo, ON, San Salvador)

_____ (1997). *Empire, Enslavement, and Freedom in the Caribbean* (Oxford, James Currey)

Baker, Sir Herbert (1862–1946). Architect and keen Imperialist, Baker made his reputation in South Africa during the 1890s. Cecil Rhodes* commissioned him to remodel his Cape Town home, Groote Schurr, and henceforth Baker-designed buildings would come to be found in Pretoria, Salisbury (Harare), Nairobi, London, and Oxford*, in the aptly named Rhodes House, home of the Rhodes Trust*, and elsewhere. Knighted in 1926, Baker's most famous work is India's Parliament House in New Delhi, on which he worked closely with the doyen of Imperial architects, Sir Edwin Lutyens*.

Further Reading

Doreen E. Greig (1970). *Herbert Baker in South Africa* (Cape Town, Purnell)

Robert G. Irving (1981). *Indian Summer: Lutyens, Baker and Imperial Delhi* (New Haven, Yale University Press)

Baker, Sir Samuel W. (1821–93). An explorer and Imperial administrator, Baker became famous in mid-Victorian Britain for his intrepid ways and exotic 'Gypsy' second wife, Florence. Eight years as a pioneer settler cultivating tea in Ceylon* was followed by an intensive period of Nilotic exploration in the 1860s, capped in 1869 with his appointment by the Khedive Ismail* of Egypt* as Governor-General of Equatoria in southern Sudan*. He was paid exceedingly well for the job, one that required an attempt to eradicate the Omani slave trade. After four years of negligible success, however, Baker retired to the comfortable life of a country squire and Imperial pundit in Devon.

Further Reading

Michael Brander (1982). *The Perfect Victorian Hero: Samuel White Baker* (Edinburgh, Mainstream)

Brian Thompson (2001). *Imperial Vanities: The Adventures of the Baker Brothers and Gordon of Khartoum* (London, HarperCollins)

Balewa, Sir Abubakar Tafawa (1912–66). A leading figure in Nigerian government and politics during the last years before the colony's independence in 1960, Balewa then held the position of Federal Prime Minister from 1957 until 1966. As a Hausa and a Muslim he worked in constructive tension with Ibo, Yoruba, Christian, and animist government colleagues from all over the country. In January 1966, his government was overthrown and he was assassinated during a military coup, an event that heralded the secession of Biafra in 1967 and the ensuing years of Nigerian instability, violence, and military rule.

Further Reading

Abubakar Tafawa Balewa (1967). *Shaihu Umar* (London, Longman)

Trevor Clark (1991). *A Right Honourable Gentleman: The Life of Alhaji Sir Abubakar Tafawa Balewa* (Lagos, Hudahuda)

Balfour Declaration (2 November 1917). In the penultimate year of the First World War* and at the behest of British Zionists, Foreign Secretary Arthur Balfour pledged British support for a Jewish 'national home' in the post-war settlement to come. As part of the pledge, Balfour insisted that this new 'Palestine' must provide for the rights of non-Jews. The Lloyd George* government's position on Palestine was supported by the major allied powers in 1919–20 and it laid the foundations of the modern state of Israel.

Further Reading

R.J.Q. Adams (2007). *Balfour: The Last Grandee* (London, John Murray)

Jonathan Schneer (2010). *The Balfour Declaration: The Origins of the Arab-Israeli Conflict* (New York, Random House)

Banana, Canaan S. (1936–2003). The first president of Britain's last colony in Africa, Zimbabwe* (Southern Rhodesia), Banana was a Methodist minister who entered politics as a moderate. In 1976, the Rhodesian People's Movement made him its publicity secretary. During the waning years of Ian Smith's* white government he was imprisoned. In 1980, at the conclusion of the Lancaster House process that determined the conditions of Southern Rhodesian independence, Banana was chosen as Zimbabwe's President, a largely ceremonial post. He retained the position until 1987, when the constitution was altered to make the presidency an executive office, henceforth occupied by the former Prime Minister, Robert Mugabe*.

Further Reading

Canaan S. Banana, ed. (1989). *Turmoil and Tenacity: Zimbabwe 1890–1990* (Harare, College Press)

Michael O. West (2002). *The Rise of an African Middle Class: Colonial Zimbabwe, 1898–1965* (Bloomington, Indiana University Press)

Banda, Hastings (1898–1997). A medical doctor turned President of Malawi*, Banda was born in Nyasaland*, mission-educated by the Church of Scotland, and received the assistance of Methodists in gaining a medical education in the United States and Scotland. He practised in London in the late 1940s and early 1950s, becoming a nationalist at the same time in concert with other future African leaders such as Kwame Nkrumah* and Jomo Kenyatta*. After five years in Kenya he returned home in 1958, plunging into politics. Upon Nyasaland receiving self-government in 1963 he became Prime Minister, a position he held through Malawi's* independence the next year and far beyond. In 1966, after constitutional changes, he became President, inaugurating a dictatorship that lasted until 1994, a period marked by violence and political assassination.

Further Reading

John Lloyd (1993). *Kamuzu Banda of Malawi: Study in Promise, Power and Paralysis (Malawi under Dr Banda, 1961–1993)* (Glasgow, Dudu Nsomba)

Philip Short (1974). *Banda* (London, Routledge & Kegan Paul)

Bangladesh. A state in Southeast Asia surrounded mostly by India*. Historically part of Bengal* in British India, at Indian independence in 1947 its territory was partitioned with the western part going to India and the eastern portion becoming a province in Pakistan* called East Bengal, and later East Pakistan. The site of a number of famines during the British period, including that in 1943 during which over 3 million people died, the territory was controversially and unsuccessfully divided by the British along Hindu-Muslim lines between 1905 and 1911. Never satisfied with being subordinate to Pakistan after 1947, in 1971 East Pakistan declared and then won its independence as Bangladesh.

Further Reading

A.F. Salahuddin Ahmed (2001). *India, Pakistan, Bangladesh: Perspectives on History, Society, and Politics* (Kolkata, Readers' Service)

Roedad Khan, ed. (2002). *The British Papers: Secret and Confidential, India, Pakistan, Bangladesh Documents 1958–1969* (Karachi, Oxford University Press)

Banks, Sir Joseph (1743–1820). Probably the best-known English botanist of his age, Banks sailed to the South Pacific in 1768 with Captain James Cook*, giving Botany Bay its name. Born into wealth and educated at Eton and Christ Church, Oxford* (he left without a degree), Banks was a precocious student of the natural world who gained election to the Royal Society when he was just twenty-three years of age. In 1778, he became its President, a post he held for forty-two years until his death. During this period Banks was a leading figure in the fields of natural history and science, as well as a prominent voice in advocating for the colonization of Australia and, through the Africa Association – the forerunner of the Royal Geographical Society* – the exploration of the so-called Dark Continent.

Further Reading

Neil Chambers (2007). *Joseph Banks and the British Museum: The World of Collecting, 1770–1830* (London, Pickering & Chatto)

Patrick O'Brian (1989). *Joseph Banks: A Life* (London, Harvill)

Barbados. A teardrop island of just 166 square miles located in the southern reaches of the Caribbean Sea, Barbados was first seen by an Englishman in 1625. Uninhabited at that time, eighty English settlers arrived two years later and by the middle of the century sugar plantations had emerged as the dominant industry on the island. Crown Colony status was granted in 1662, which was around the same time that the importation of African slaves began. The plantocracy, slavery, and the Church of England (its Codrington College was founded as early as 1710) defined Barbadian history until well into the nineteenth century. In the twentieth, post-Second World War Barbadian nationalism led to internal self-government in 1961 and independence five years later.

Further Reading

Hilary Beckles (2007). *A History of Barbados: From Amerindian Settlement to Caribbean Single Market*, 2nd edn (Cambridge, Cambridge University Press)

Larry D. Gragg (2003). *Englishmen Transplanted: The English Colonization of Barbados, 1627–1660* (Oxford, Oxford University Press)

Baring, Evelyn, 1st Baron Howick of Glendale (1903–73). A British colonial governor, first in Southern Rhodesia* from 1942 until 1944 and then in Kenya* from 1952 until 1959, Baring presided over the latter colony during its violent Mau Mau* period. Born the youngest child of his namesake father, also known as the Earl of Cromer*, long-time Agent and Consul-General of Egypt*, Baring's career was nowhere near as storied as the elder Baring's and its Kenya period continues to be controversial. His handling of the Mau Mau crisis, particularly the establishment of internment camps where thousands of suspected Mau Mau oath takers and sympathizers were summarily held, as well as many tried and executed, is the subject of fierce contemporary debate.

Further Reading

David Anderson (2005). *Histories of the Hanged: Britain's Dirty War in Kenya and the End of the Empire* (London, Weidenfeld & Nicolson)

Charles Douglas-Home (1978). *Evelyn Baring: The Last Pro-Consul* (London, Collins)

Barnato, Barney (1852–97). Born an impoverished Jew in London's East End, Barnato became a millionaire South African Randlord. Following the lead of his brother, he went out to the Cape Colony in 1873 to join in the diamond frenzy at Kimberley. Success came quickly. He formed the Barnato Diamond Mining Company and used it to consolidate his holdings to the point where his only serious rival for control of the diamond business in South Africa was Cecil Rhodes*. After vigorous competition he was later bought out by Rhodes, who wrote him a then record-sized cheque of some £4 million. Subsequently, Barnato turned his attention to politics and was elected to the Cape Parliament in 1889, sitting for Kimberley until his early death eight years later.

Further Reading

James Leasor (1997). *Rhodes & Barnato: The Premier and the Prancer* (London, Leo Cooper)

Geoffrey Wheatcroft (1985). *The Randlords* (London, Weidenfeld & Nicolson)

Basutoland (see Lesotho)

Beaconsfield, Earl of (see Disraeli, Benjamin)

Bechuanaland (see Botswana)

Beit, Alfred (1853–1906). Another of the so-called Randlords, Beit, a German Jew, arrived in Kimberley, South Africa* in 1875 in order to buy diamonds for his Dutch firm, Jules Porges & Cie. He quickly fell in with Rhodes* and together they formed an irresistible duo buying up digging ventures and gaining control over principal diamond-mining claims like De Beers. After gold was discovered on the Witswatersrand in 1885, Beit turned much of his attention to deep-level mining. He formed the firm Wernher, Beit & Co. and in 1888 was a leader in the founding of the British South Africa Company*. Despite his move to London that same year, Beit and Rhodes remained tightly bound financially and politically. Both attributes came to the fore in 1895 when Beit helped to plan and finance the disastrous Jameson Raid*, designed to spark a rebellion in the Transvaal* which would potentially topple the government of the stern Afrikaner leader, Paul Kruger*. Beit's part in the Raid was made clear through a House of Commons inquiry and as punishment he was required to resign from the board of the BSAC. In his declining years he became a generous benefactor and his will set out the terms of the Beit Trust.

Further Reading

George S. Fort (1932). *Alfred Beit: A Study of the Man and His Work* (London, Nicholson)

C.W. Newbury (1989). *The Diamond Ring: Business, Politics, and Precious Stones in South Africa, 1867–1947* (Oxford, Clarendon Press)

Belize. Located on the Yucatan Peninsula between Mexico and Guatemala, Belize saw the arrival of its first English settlers in the 1650s. A British government presence was established in 1780, and status as the colony of British Honduras* was proclaimed in 1862. The colony's geographical location and its rich and abundant forests – especially of mahogany – meant ongoing tension over natural resources with neighbouring Guatemala. In 1964, self-government was achieved, followed in 1971 with a name change to Belize. Independence came in 1981.

Further Reading

Debra A. Miller (2005). *Belize* (Detroit, Lucent Books)

P.A.B. Thomson (2004). *Belize: A Concise History* (Oxford, Macmillan Caribbean)

Bell, Gertrude L.B. (1868–1926). A leading Arabist and one of the most important British advisors on the Middle East during and after the First World War*, Bell was born into a wealthy family in Durham and read modern history at Lady Margaret Hall, Oxford, becoming the first woman to achieve first-class honours in the subject, even though upon completion of the course in 1888 women were not yet awarded degrees. A peripatetic and independent life of travel, archaeology, and mountaineering followed until 1900, when she settled more or less permanently in the Middle East. During the First World War she was attached to the Arab Bureau in Cairo, before moving on to Mesopotamia (Iraq*). She took up residence in Baghdad in 1917 as Oriental Secretary to the British governor, and never left. Bell was an integral presence at the Cairo Conference* of 1921 where the future of Mesopotamia was considered, and later helped to form the Hashemite Kingdom of Iraq under Faisal I*. She founded the National Museum of Iraq in 1923, but her political influence soon began to wane. Three years later she died, almost certainly by committing suicide, and is buried in Baghdad.

Further Reading

Georgina Howell (2006). *Daughter of the Desert: The Remarkable Life of Gertrude Bell* (London, Macmillan)

Liora Lukitz (2006). *A Quest in the Middle East: Gertrude Bell and the Making of Modern Iraq* (London and New York, I.B.Tauris)

Bengal. A cornerstone province in the history of British India, Bengal saw the establishment of East India Company* factories in 1633. By the end of the seventeenth century the EIC's Bengal Presidency had been formed, centred on Calcutta. Mughal territorial suzerainty eroded steadily until the local nawab, Suraj-al Dowlah, launched an attack on the EIC's Fort William at Calcutta in 1756. The British retaliated under Robert Clive* the next year, with his victory at Plassey* proving to be decisive.

In the years after 1757 Bengal and its contiguous territories became part of an EIC Empire, which was transferred to the Crown in 1858. In that year the first Viceroy arrived, making Calcutta the capital of the British Raj until 1912, when the capital shifted to New Delhi. At Indian independence in 1947 the Presidency of Bengal was partitioned into the separate country of East Bengal/Pakistan (Bangladesh*) and the Indian province of West Bengal.

Further Reading

Lawrence James (1997). *Raj: The Making and Unmaking of British India* (London, Little, Brown & Co.)

Robert Travers (2007). *Ideology and Empire in Eighteenth Century India: The British in Bengal, 1757–93* (Cambridge, Cambridge University Press)

Berlin (West Africa) Conference. Organized by German Chancellor Otto von Bismarck and held from late 1884 until early 1885, the Conference was an attempt to delimit the competing claims of the Great Powers in Africa, particularly those pertaining to the Congo River basin. Fourteen European nations, including Britain, were represented in Berlin and they agreed on a number of guiding principles. One of the most important of these was the Principle of Effectivity, which made it incumbent upon the occupying European power to sign treaties with the local people and to organize an administration of the putative colony. If such were not done then the territory – even if claimed – would remain free for rival occupation. The Conference had the effect of speeding up the Scramble for Africa and by 1895 virtually the entire continent was under some form of European rule.

Further Reading

Sybil E. Crowe (1981). *The Berlin West Africa Conference, 1884–1885* (New York, Longman, Green)

Stig Forster, Wolfgang J. Mommsen and Ronald E. Robinson, eds (1988). *Bismarck, Europe, and Africa: The Berlin Africa Conference 1884–1885 and the Onset of Partition* (Oxford, Oxford University Press)

Bermuda. Located in the Caribbean north, Bermuda was visited by the Spanish as early as 1503, before the English began to frequent it a century later. Controlled initially by the Virginia Company and then, beginning in 1615, the Somers Isles Company, Bermuda became a Crown Colony in 1684, a status held for successive centuries. In 1968, Bermuda received a new constitution in which control over only foreign relations, defence, and internal security remained with Britain. Located some 900 kilometres east of North Carolina, Bermuda has always had close ties with the American South, but it is Britain's oldest and most populous remaining Overseas Territory.

Further Reading

John J. Jackson (1988) *Bermuda* (Newton Abbot, David & Charles)
W.S. Zuill (1983). *The Story of Bermuda and Her People* (London, Macmillan)

Besant, Annie (1847–1933). A social disturber whose manifest energies found their most important impact in British India*, Besant lived much of the last forty years of her life there, where the one-time Victorian social reformer transformed herself into a virulent critic of the Empire, which, she said in her 1917 address as newly elected President of the Indian National Congress*, had made India the 'crucified among Nations'. Born in London, she was sent away to Dorset to be educated privately by an evangelical spinster. In 1867, she married the Revd Frank Besant, but the death of one of their children and a consequent loss of faith brought about divorce and in 1874 she embarked on a life of free-thinking and reform that led ultimately to a new faith, that of theosophy. Founded only a short while before in 1875 by a Russian mystic and an American ex-military officer, theosophy was headquartered in Madras, to which Besant decided to go in 1893. As a practiced civic reformer and public campaigner, she plunged quickly into Indian politics, soon taking up the cause of Indian nationalism. Her timing could not have been better. The INC had developed steadily from its 1885 roots as a tea-drinking social club into a much stronger vehicle for political change. Gandhi* was an admirer of Besant, having first met her in London at the home of Madame Blavatsky, theosophy's founder, in 1888, and was well pleased when she arrived in India and 'captivated the country'. The problem, politically speaking, for the kinetic Besant, however, was that the gradualist approach of Gandhi and the INC smacked of a deference that long ago she had abandoned. Gandhi, for example, during the First World War, agreed that he and his colleagues would temporarily cease their public opposition to the Raj to makes things easier for Britain. Besant, however, paid this gentleman's agreement no heed. In August 1914 she proclaimed provocatively 'England's need is India's opportunity,' and in December of that year she became the first woman President of the INC. In the meantime, Besant built on her reputation as India's champion and saw her influence peak. Gandhi, by this time, however, was beginning to steadily assert himself as the moral leader of the Indian nationalist movement and under his leadership, as well as that of Nehru*, the final years of the Raj unfolded. Besant died in India.

Further Reading

Arthur H. Nethercot (1963). *The Last Four Lives of Annie Besant* (Chicago, University of Chicago Press)

Anne Taylor, ed. (1992). *Annie Besant: An Autobiography* (Oxford, Oxford University Press)

Blackfoot Nation. A confederacy of three Native Indian tribes in western Canada and the northern United States, the Blood, Peigan, and Blackfoot were considered 'British' Indians in the period of exploration and settlement in the nineteenth century. Blackfoot culture was based almost entirely on the plentiful existence of the Plains Bison, whose rapid culling after about 1850 is linked causally to their decline. In 1877, the Canadian government and representatives of the Blackfoot led by the great Chief Crowfoot signed Treaty No.7, which signalled the end of the old nomadic life and the start of that lived on the reservation known as Blackfoot Crossing located in east-central Alberta*.

Further Reading

Hugh A. Dempsey (1976). *Crowfoot, Chief of the Blackfoot* (Edmonton, Hurtig Publishers)

Amelia M. Paget (2004). *People of the Plains* (Regina, Canadian Plains Research Centre)

Black Hole of Calcutta. An infamous event in the history of the British in India, the 'Black Hole' was an episode in the struggle between the British and the French for control over Bengal* in the mid-eighteenth century. On the night of 20–21 June 1756, the Nawab of Bengal and a client of the French, Suraj-ud-Dowlah, attacked the East India Company's* Calcutta trading station. He promptly had its British population of about 150 traders and soldiers imprisoned in a tiny basement cell measuring only some 250 square feet. When the prisoners were finally released the next morning after a sweltering night, only twenty-three of them remained alive. The EIC's outrage over the incident was embodied by Clive*, who exacted revenge by defeating Suraj at the Battle of Plassey* the next year.

Further Reading

Noel Barber (1965). *The Black Hole of Calcutta: A Reconstruction* (London, Collins)

Jan Dalley (2006). *The Black Hole: Money, Myth, and Empire* (London, Penguin)

Bligh, William (1754–1817). (In)famous in his time and today as the disciplinarian 'captain' of HM Armed Vessel *Bounty* who lost his ship to mutineers, Bligh was a lifetime mariner who was signed up for the Royal Navy at the tender age of seven. Hailing from Cornwall, he rose through the ranks and in 1776 accompanied Captain Cook* on his third and final Pacific voyage. In 1787, as Commanding Lieutenant of the *Bounty*, he sailed to Tahiti to obtain breadfruit trees for transport to the Caribbean, where their suitability as food for slaves was to be tested. The voyage proved interminable, held up by bad storms and slow-ripening breadfruit, and the small crew became increasingly disaffected with Bligh's command, which while highly strict was not violent. Intensely frustrated nonetheless, Fletcher Christian, Master's Mate, led the bloodless mutiny in April 1789, setting Bligh and his loyalists adrift in a launch. In a virtuoso display of seamanship, Bligh then navigated his tiny craft over 6,000 kilometres to Timor. In 1790, he was exonerated of any blame in the mutiny and continued his career in the Navy, fighting with Nelson at Copenhagen in 1801, and later becoming Governor of New South Wales from 1806 until 1808. Appointed

Vice Admiral in 1814, he died in London a few years later. Though his post-*Bounty* career was long and respected, his reputation never recovered fully from the events of 1789.

Further Reading

Caroline Alexander (2004). *The Bounty: The True Story of the Mutiny on the Bounty* (London, Penguin)

Gavin Kennedy (1978). *Bligh* (London, Duckworth)

Boer Wars. Two late-nineteenth-century wars fought between the original, mostly Afrikaner (Boer), settlers of South Africa* and the British. In 1881, in an attempt to recover the Transvaal from recent British annexation, the Boers defeated a British force at Majuba Hill. The subsequent Convention of Pretoria restored the Transvaal to the Boers but tensions remained high nonetheless. The intensifying British exploitation of gold and diamonds and its accompanying political machinations led to a renewal of hostilities in 1899. Paul Kruger*, President of the Transvaal, and Joseph Chamberlain*, Colonial Secretary, provoked a three-year war over the issue of British paramountcy in South Africa. After a slow start, during which the Boers won a series of victories, the British employed harsh and sometimes controversial measures against Boer guerilla fighters who were known as 'commandos', including the establishment of concentration camps in which over 20,000 Boer men, women, and children died, mostly from disease. In 1902, the Treaty of Vereeniging* formally ended the war and proclaimed British rule – though now in a somewhat chastened form – over all of South Africa.

Further Reading

Denis Judd (2002). *The Boer War* (London, John Murray)

John Laband (2005). *The Transvaal Rebellion: The First Boer War, 1880–1881* (New York, Longman/Pearson)

Borden, Sir Robert L. (1854–1937). The eighth Prime Minister of Canada, Borden was in office from 1911 until 1920, and was a crucial figure in the transition of the Empire to the Commonwealth. Born in Nova Scotia, Borden became a teacher but left the classroom after a short time in order to pursue a career as a lawyer. Success in his new profession came quickly and after moving to Halifax he became a senior partner in a law firm with blue-chip Conservative Party credentials. He entered Parliament in 1896. Five years later he became leader of the Conservatives. From 1901 until 1911 he served as Leader of the Opposition, becoming Prime Minister in the latter year. The crucible of the war years convinced him that Canada was emerging as a nation in its own right, and that this fact needed to be reflected in how Canadian troops were deployed, and later how the country would be represented at the Paris Peace Conference. To British and US objections leading up to Paris, Borden replied that the Canadians had lost more men on the battlefield than had the Americans (60,000 to 48,000) and therefore Canada deserved to have separate representation at the conference table. His argument won the day and was instrumental in ensuring that each of the Dominions signed the Treaty of Versailles individually and that each of them received separate membership in the League of Nations.

Further Reading

Robert Craig Brown (1965). *Robert Laird Borden: A Biography* (Toronto, Canada Publishing Corporation)

Harold A. Wilson (1966). *The Imperial Policy of Sir Robert Borden* (Gainesville, FL, University Press of Florida)

Botha, Louis (1862–1919). First Prime Minister of the Union of South Africa*, Botha had been a Boer soldier and commander. He was the architect of the defeat of the controversial Jameson Raid* of 1895 and of victories early in the Second Boer War*, as well as the use of commandos. His was a moderate though persistent voice at the Vereeniging* peace negotiations and afterwards he argued for Anglo–Boer reconciliation. He became Prime Minister of the Transvaal in 1907, and three years later assumed the same post in a unified South Africa, a position he held until 1919. A staunch supporter of the British Empire throughout the First World War, he led a successful invasion of German South-West Africa (Namibia*) in 1915. He represented South Africa at the Paris Peace Conference in 1919 and died shortly thereafter.

Further Reading
F.V. Engelenburg (1929). *General Louis Botha* (London, Harrap)
Johannes Meintjes (1970). *General Louis Botha: A Biography* (London, Cassell)

Botswana. Known first as the Bechuanaland* Protectorate, this diverse territory in southern Africa, which contains both the Kalahari Desert and the Okavango Swamp, was claimed by the British in 1885. Ten years later its Protectorate status was affirmed by the Colonial Office. It is a vast territory teeming with game and is home to the world's largest population of elephants. In 1966, independence was gained under the new name of Botswana.

Further Reading
Fred Morton (2008). *Historical Dictionary of Botswana* (Lanham, MD, Scarecrow Press)
Olufemi Vaughan (2003). *Chiefs, Power, and Social Change: Chiefship and Modern Politics in Botswana, 1880s–1990s* (Trenton, NJ, Africa World Press)

Bourassa, J.-N.-Henri (1868–1952). A French-Canadian nationalist and anti-Imperialist, Bourassa was the most prominent journalistic and political voice in Quebec* in the late nineteenth and early twentieth centuries. Elected to the House of Commons in 1896, a few years later his opposition to the Second Boer War* was a key influence in Canada choosing to send a volunteer, rather than a conscripted, force to the conflict. His public career focused on denouncing European and British Imperialism. He formed the Nationalist League in an attempt to instill a sense of Canadian nationalism in his fellow Quebeckers over against the Imperial nationalism espoused by most contemporary English-speaking Canadians at the time. In 1910, a few years after founding the League, he established the newspaper *Le Devoir* and used it to further publicize his views. During the First World War* he denounced the Canadian government's plan to institute conscription, sparking a national crisis in 1917. He remained in Parliament with some interruptions until 1935, and during the Second World War* again took up the cause of anti-conscription, but this time with much less success.

Further Reading

Henri Bourassa (1970). *Henri Bourassa on Imperialism and Biculturalism, 1900–1918.* Joseph Levitt, ed. (Toronto, Copp Clark)

Casey Murrow (1968). *Henri Bourassa and French-Canadian Opposition to Empire* (Montreal, Harvest House)

British Antarctic Territory. A British Overseas Territory of approximately 1.7-million square kilometres, Britain's contact with Antarctica began with Captain Cook*, and its continuous presence there dates from 1833. In 1908, Britain declared sovereignty over what today constitutes the BAT. The Robert Falcon Scott and Ernest Shackleton* expeditions to Antarctica were among the biggest British explorations of the twentieth century. Three permanent research stations exist within the Territory, as well as other seasonal ones. Argentina and Chile, with claims of their own, do not recognize British sovereignty in Antarctica.

Further Reading

Stephanie L. Barczewski (2007). *Antarctic Destinies: Scott, Shackleton and the Changing Face of Heroism* (London, Hambledon Continuum)

Beau Riffenburgh (2004). *Nimrod: Edward Shackleton and the Extraordinary Story of the 1907–09 British Antarctic Expedition* (London, Bloomsbury)

British Borneo (see Sabah)

British Columbia. Joining the Canadian Confederation as the sixth province in 1871, after being promised a trans-continental link (road or rail) by the federal government in Ottawa, British Columbia gave Canada a long Pacific coastline and interrupted US expansionism in the Northwest. The BC coast was claimed by the Hudson's Bay Company* in 1821 and called 'New Caledonia.' Vancouver Island was made a Crown Colony in 1849, followed by the mainland in 1859 on the heels of a gold rush along the Thompson and Fraser Rivers. In 1866, the two colonies were united and over the next few years the HBC's land rights were surrendered. Confederation's promise of a land-link was realized in 1885 with the completion of the Canadian Pacific Railway*. In 1906, the Royal Navy departed Esquimalt on Vancouver Island, which had been its main Pacific base. BC's enormous timber, mineral, maritime, and hydro-electric resources have made it one of Canada's wealthiest provinces.

Further Reading

Jean Barman (2007). *The West Beyond the West: A History of British Columbia* 3rd edn (Toronto, University of Toronto Press)

Mark Forsythe (2007). *The Trail of 1858: British Columbia's Gold Rush Past* (Madeira Park, BC, Harbour Publishing)

British Commonwealth Air Training Plan. Known also as the Empire Air Training Scheme, this was a massive undertaking during the Second World War* to train aircrew for the various Empire-Commonwealth countries. Canada, with plenty of space and far from the reach of German or Japanese bombers, was chosen as the primary training ground, although Australia*, New Zealand*, Southern Rhodesia*, and Britain were also similarly used. Dating from December 1939, the Plan trained prospective pilots and aircrew from the Dominions, as well as from other allied countries. Graduates of the program served either in the Royal Air Force or in the air force of their home country. In Canada alone from 1940 until 1945 there were 231 training sites, the majority of which were in the Prairie provinces of Manitoba*, Saskatchewan*, and Alberta*, containing some 10,000 aircraft and almost 170,000 students. Called the 'Aerodrome of Democracy' by US President Franklin D. Roosevelt, Canada's integral role in the Plan was one of its key contributions to the war effort.

Further Reading

Ted Barris (2005). *Behind the Glory: The Plan that Won the Allied Air War* (Markham, ON, Thomas Allen & Son)

Spencer Dunmore (1994). *Wings for Victory* (Toronto, McClelland & Stewart)

British East Africa (see Kenya)

British Empire Economic Conference. Held in Ottawa during the summer of 1932 as the Great Depression deepened, the Conference was attended by representatives of the British and Dominion governments, as well as many of the Empire's dependent colonies. Furthering the Empire's economic integration through Imperial Preference was the main item under discussion, an idea that was championed by Canadian Prime Minister, Richard B. Bennett. An agreement to this end was achieved, which struck a controversial blow against Free Trade but guaranteed preferential mutual market access between the Dominions (later to include the colonies) and Britain.

Further Reading
P.J. Cain and A.G. Hopkins (1993). *British Imperialism: Crisis and Deconstruction, 1914–1990* (London, Longman)
Ian M. Drummond (1974). *Imperial Economic Policy, 1917–1939* (Toronto, University of Toronto Press)

British Guiana (see Guyana)

British Honduras (see Belize)

British Somaliland. In 1884, the British extended Protectorate status to this small territory in the Horn of Africa, largely to secure the nearby port of Aden*. From 1905 until 1960 British Somaliland was governed by the Colonial Office. It had a colourful history, including that of the so-called 'Mad Mullah'*, Mohammed Abdullah Hassan, who controlled and terrorized the desert interior of the country from 1899 until 1920, and against whom the British had little success. Upon gaining independence in 1960, British Somaliland quickly joined with Italian Somaliland to create the new Somali Republic, which since then has endured a sad and violent history.

Further Reading
Angus Hamilton (1970). *Somaliland* (Westport, CT, Negro Universities Press)

Margery Perham (1970). *Major Dane's Garden* (Chicago, Holmes & Meier)

British South Africa Company. Founded in 1889 by Cecil Rhodes* and headquartered in the Transvaal* diamond town of Kimberley, the BSAC spearheaded British settlement in the territories that came to be known as Southern Rhodesia (Zimbabwe)* and Northern Rhodesia (Zambia)*. Rhodes was the company's director-general for most of the years from its founding until his death in 1902. The BSAC was Rhodes's attempt to outflank Afrikaner expansion and was never less than controversial. The company remained in existence until 1924.

Further Reading
Robert Cary (1970). *Charter Royal* (Cape Town, H. Timmins)
John S. Galbraith (1974). *Crown and Charter: The Early Years of the British South Africa Company* (Berkeley, University of California Press)

British Virgin Islands. Located in the northern Caribbean, the BVI has been British-held since 1766. A remaining outpost of Empire, its governor is appointed from London and works through an executive council and elected legislature located in Road Town on Tortola, the largest island in the BVI chain.

Further Reading
Bill Maurer (1997). *Recharting the Caribbean: Land, Law, and Citizenship in the British Virgin Islands* (Ann Arbor, University of Michigan Press)
V.P. Moll (1999). *Virgin Islands* (Oxford, Clio)

British West Indies Federation. A short-lived federation of eight British Caribbean islands that lasted from 1958 until 1962. Its capital was located in Port-of-Spain in Trinidad and Tobago, and its first Prime Minister was Sir Grantley Adams of Barbados. The BWIF had a rocky history from the beginning as its larger and richer members – especially Jamaica and Trinidad and Tobago – believed themselves to be subsidizing the smaller members. Jamaica seceded from the Federation in 1961 and the next year it was dissolved.

Further Reading

F.R. Augier (1964). *The Making of the West Indies* (Kingston, Longman Caribbean)

Sir John Mordecai (1968). *The West Indies: The Federal Negotiations* (London, Allen and Unwin)

Brooke, Sir James (1803–68). The intrepid founder of the so-called White Rajahs of Sarawak, and a startling example of 'freelance Imperialism', Brooke was born to an East India Company* official in Bengal*, later joining the Bengal Infantry. He first visited the Sarawak region of Borneo in 1838, returning two years later to assist in the stamping out of a rebellion. As a reward he was given control of Sarawak by its overlord, the Sultan of Brunei*, a position agreed to by the British government and perpetuated by his heir, Sir Charles Brooke (1829–1917).

Further Reading

Nigel Barley (2002). *White Rajah* (London, Little, Brown)

Cassandra Pybus (1997). *The White Rajahs of Sarawak: Dynastic Intrigue and the Forgotten Canadian Heir* (Toronto and Vancouver, Douglas & McIntyre)

Brunei. A British Protectorate from 1888 until becoming independent in 1983, the Sultanate of Brunei occupies a coastal strip of Borneo. It is well endowed with oil and natural gas, and is also a significant producer of timber. Brunei's per capita income is among the highest in the world.

Further Reading

Harun Abdul Majid (2007). *Rebellion in Brunei: The 1962 Revolt, Imperialism, Confrontation and Oil* (London and New York, I.B.Tauris)

Graham E. Saunders (1994). *A History of Brunei* (Oxford, Oxford University Press)

Buganda (see Uganda)

Burma. The East India Company* established a factory in Burma in 1612, just a year after its first one at Surat, India*. The British fought two wars in the nineteenth century (1824–6 and 1852) against the old Burmese Empire, and later, in 1885, deposed King Thebaw (1858–1916) in order to maintain control of their local commercial and geo-strategic interests. Burma was ruled as part of British India* until 1937, when it was granted a modicum of self-government. The Second World War* brought Japanese occupation from 1942 to 1945, when they were expelled by the British under the command of Lord Mountbatten*. In 1947, independence was achieved, the culmination of a nationalist movement that had begun in the 1930s under Aung San (1915–47) and was completed after his assassination by U Nu (1907–95).

Further Reading

Thant Myint U (2001). *The Making of Modern Burma* (New York, Oxford University Press)

Philip Ziegler (1985) *Mountbatten: The Official Biography* (London, Collins)

Burton, Sir Richard (1821–90). One of the great personalities of Empire, Burton was a master linguist, intrepid explorer, and social iconoclast who became one of the best-known figures in Victorian Britain. Born in Devon, Burton's family went abroad in 1826, travelling through Italy and France, and he was brought up in a cosmopolitan atmosphere. In 1840, he matriculated at Trinity College, Oxford, but persistent misconduct led to his expulsion two years later. He then went to India and served seven years in the army of the East India Company*. He travelled unrelentingly during these years, followed by a harrowing journey to Mecca disguised as an Arab. This exploit brought him to the attention of the Royal Geographical Society*, which commissioned him to undertake an exploration of the African interior. Ultimately, in 1858, this meant becoming the first European to see Lake Tanganyika, part of a wider attempt to discover the source of the Nile. Accompanied by John Hanning Speke*, the two men spent an arduous two years together, only to have a falling-out shortly thereafter over the location of the Nile's source. Burton's fame grew in the 1880s with his translation into English of *The Arabian Nights*, and his notoriety with that of the *Kama Sutra*. Always controversial and seen to be socially suspect, he was nonetheless brilliant and in later life he was honoured with a KCMG and was successively British Consul to Fernando Po, Damascus, and Trieste, where he died.

Further Reading

Fawn M. Brodie (1967). *The Devil Drives: A Life of Sir Richard Burton* (New York, Norton)

Frank McLynn (1993). *Snow on the Desert: The Life of Sir Richard Burton* (London, John Murray)

Bustamante, Sir W. Alexander (1884–1977). Jamaica's* first Prime Minister, Bustamante was the legally adopted name of W.A. Clarke. In the 1930s he became a trade union leader, later founding the Jamaica Labour Party and sitting in the colonial legislature. Knighted in 1955, he held the independent Jamaica's Prime Ministership from 1962 until 1967.

Further Reading

George E. Eaton (1975). *Alexander Bustamante and Modern Jamaica* (Kingston, Kingston Publishers)

Trevor Munroe (1972). *The Politics of Constitutional Decolonization: Jamaica, 1944–62* (Mona, University of the West Indies)

C

Cairo Conference. Held in 1921, and presided over by Winston Churchill*, Colonial Secretary, the conference was an attempt by the British to honour the spirit of their First World War* promises to the nationalist Arabs. The two major decisions of the Conference, whose membership was comprised of a large number of Middle East specialists such as Gertrude Bell* and T.E. Lawrence*, were the creation of Iraq out of the British mandate of Mesopotamia*, and of Transjordan (Jordan*). The brothers Faisal and Abdullah from the Hashemite dynasty were selected to lead each country respectively. The Cairo Conference was responsible for creating the map of the modern Middle East. At the time, its provisions were mostly uncontroversial, but as the years passed, and as objections grew to the configurations it had established, the Cairo Conference was seen by many as an attempt to subjugate regional Arab interests to Western ones.

Further Reading

Christopher Catherwood (2004). *Churchill's Folly: How Winston Churchill Created Modern Iraq* (London, Carroll & Graf)

Aaron S. Klieman (1970). *Foundations of British Policy in the Arab World: The Cairo Conference of 1921* (Baltimore, Johns Hopkins Press)

Cameron, Sir Donald (1872–1948). A leading colonial governor, especially in Nigeria*, Cameron was born the son of a sugar planter in British Guiana*. His mother was Irish and he was sent to Dublin to be educated. But rare for someone who rose high in the Colonial Service*, he did not obtain a university education; rather, he returned to Guiana in 1890 and commenced his career as a clerk in the Inland Revenue. His ability was soon recognized and after marrying in 1903 and the subsequent birth of a son, Cameron went the next year with the former governor of Guiana to Mauritius* as assistant colonial secretary. There he remained until 1908, when he took up the same position in the Protectorate of Southern Nigeria. Thus began sixteen years in Nigeria*, culminating in a knighthood and appointment as chief secretary in 1923. These initial years in Africa brought him into close contact with Lord Lugard*, whom he admired greatly and sought to emulate, particularly when he was appointed governor of Tanganyika* in 1924. Cameron spent the next seven years as governor, involving himself closely in economic development and the extension of infrastructure such as harbours and railways. He, like most other disciples of Lugard, was a constitutional gradualist when it came to the participation of Africans in government, slowly creating opportunities for Africans to enter the civil service. In 1931, he was appointed governor of Nigeria*, a position he held until retiring to England four years later on account of his wife's failing health. His gubernatorial years in Nigeria were busy and complex, including successful attempts to maintain the export of staple products such as groundnuts and palm oil. In retirement, he was used as a sometime consultant by the Colonial Office* and spent time writing his memoirs. Very much a man of his time, Cameron's commitment to Indirect Rule* was unwavering as both the best possible method of colonial rule, and of preparing Africans to rule themselves.

Further Reading

Sir Donald Cameron (1982). *My Tanganyika service and some Nigeria* 2nd edn, Robert Heussler, ed. (Washington, DC, University Press of America)

Harry A. Gailey (1974). *Sir Donald Cameron, Colonial Governor* (Stanford, CA, Hoover Institution Press)

Canada. The territory that the local Iroquoian-speaking people called 'ka-na-ta' (place of the small huts, or meeting place) was first visited by a European when Jacques Cartier sailed up the St Lawrence River* in 1535. Further French exploration followed with Samuel de Champlain establishing an encampment named Quebec* in 1608, which became a base for the ensuing fur trade. By that date and further to the east, the English had begun their seasonal whaling and fishing cycle based at St John's, Newfoundland*. The colony of New France developed throughout the seventeenth and eighteenth centuries, while to the east and south a number of English colonies grew apace also. English-French territorial competition in North America climaxed in 1759 when under the command of General James Wolfe* a British force defeated the French at the Plains of Abraham* just outside the walled city of Quebec. The Royal Proclamation of 1763 established the British colony of Quebec. In 1791, the Constitution Act created Upper and Lower Canada out of the old province of Quebec. The nineteenth century saw modern Canada develop through great economic expansion, rebellion in 1837, the Act of Union uniting the two Canadas in 1841, and Confederation in 1867, which joined the Atlantic colonies of Nova Scotia* and New Brunswick* with Canada West (Ontario*) and Canada East (Quebec) to create the Dominion of Canada. At the behest of the British government, and with one eye on the expansion-minded United States and the other on rebellion in the Northwest in 1870, the Canadians enlarged their federation steadily: Manitoba* (1870); British Columbia* (1871); Prince Edward Island* (1873); Alberta* and Saskatchewan* (1905); and Newfoundland (1949). Canada became a model for constitutional development within the British Empire. The Balfour Report (1926) and the Statute of Westminster* (1931) styled Canada and the other major settler colonies as 'autonomous communities' within the Empire. In 1982, Canada patriated the British North America Act (1867), its foundational constitutional document, symbolizing its independence, which, in practical terms, had been gained long before.

Further Reading

Robert Bothwell (2006). *The Penguin History of Canada* (Toronto, Penguin)
Phillip Buckner, ed. (2008). *Canada and the British Empire* (Oxford, Oxford University Press)

Canadian Pacific Railway. One of the great Imperial railways of the nineteenth century and a marvel of contemporary engineering, the CPR was completed in 1885. The new railway joined the far-flung provinces and territories of the young Canadian Confederation, giving it an east-west economic logic that built on that provided historically by the St Lawrence River*. The CPR was constructed over fourteen years and was marked by enormous capital outlays, the importation of thousands of Chinese labourers, and political scandal. Sir John A. Macdonald*, Canada's Scottish-born first Prime Minister, was its leading spirit, along with William Cornelius Van Horne, a hard-driving American-born railway magnate. The 'Last Spike' was driven in November 1885 high in British Columbia's Rocky Mountains, and by the next summer transcontinental trains were running across the vast country.

Further Reading

Pierre Berton (2006). *The Last Spike: The Great Railway* (Toronto, Random House)

Clarence B. Davis and Kenneth E. Wilburn, Jr, with Ronald E. Robinson, eds (1991). *Railway Imperialism* (Westport, CT, Greenwood)

Canning, Charles John, 1st Earl Canning (1812–62). The first Viceroy of India*, Canning arrived in the sub-continent in 1856 as Governor-General. Educated at Eton and Christ Church, Oxford*, Canning was the son of a former Prime Minister, George Canning. His tenure in India coincided with increased tensions between the British and their Hindu and Muslim subjects over a range of issues, which boiled over in 1857 in the Indian Mutiny*. In its aftermath he advocated for the end of East India Company* rule and assumed the Viceroyalty in the autumn of 1858, holding it until not long before his death four years later. He took a relatively moderate position on the nature and extent of the punishments meted out to the mutineers and for his perceived leniency received the (pejorative) nickname of 'Clemency Canning'.

Further Reading

H.S. Cunningham (1891). *Earl Canning* (Oxford, Clarendon Press)

Michael Maclagan (1962). *'Clemency Canning': Charles John, 1st Earl Canning, Governor-General and Viceroy of India, 1856–1862* (London, Macmillan)

Cape Colony. The key British colony in South Africa*, first settled in 1652 by the Dutchman Jan van Riebeeck. Within a decade of van Riebeeck's arrival, the Dutch East India Company had founded a settlement. It grew into a colony, only to fall to the British in 1795, who saw it as a strategic requirement during the French Revolutionary and Napoleonic Wars. The Cape changed hands twice more before becoming permanently British in 1814. Many years of territorial expansion and warfare against the native African population and the Dutch 'Boer'* colonists ensued, leading to a mass Boer exodus northward in 1835 known as the Great Trek*. Later in the century the discovery of diamonds led to the annexation of the Anglo-Boer disputed territory of Griqualand and ultimately more warfare with the Zulu* and the Boers. The Union of South Africa in 1910 was led by the Cape, and in the twentieth century it became the anvil upon which race relations were hammered out in the country, while at the same time being dominant economically.

Further Reading

Peter B. Boyden, ed. (2001). *The British Army in Cape Colony: Soldiers' Letters and Diaries, 1806–58* (London, The Society for Army Historical Research)

Leonard Thompson (1991). *A History of South Africa* (New Haven, CT, Yale University Press)

Carey, William (1761–1834). In the history of modern Christian missions few names are better known than that of William Carey. To many he is the 'father' of the missionary movement, a religious and social hallmark of the nineteenth century. Born in 1761 in Northamptonshire, Carey received an education locally and then, at the age of sixteen, he was apprenticed to a shoemaker in the nearby village of Paddington. Over the course of the next ten years Carey continued as a shoemaker, and deepened his commitment to dissenting Christianity, to which he had been introduced by a friend. To this end, in 1783 he joined the Baptist denomination and of particular importance in stirring his mind in this direction were the published accounts of the voyages of Captain Cook*. In 1792, Carey published *An Enquiry into the Obligations of Christians to Use Means for the Conversion of the Heathens*. In this pamphlet Carey gave full voice to the Calvinist injunction requiring that prayer be accompanied by action. In May 1792, Carey preached a momentous sermon at Nottingham before the assembled Baptists of the Northampton Association. In it, he expounded his view that incumbent upon them as Christians was the responsibility of taking the Gospel of Jesus Christ to all those who had never heard it. The implication of Carey's impassioned message was that the tentacles of the increasingly far-reaching British Empire were making it possible to go forward successfully with the Great Commission. 'Expect great things,' exclaimed Carey. 'Attempt great things.' A few months later, in October, Carey's insistence paid off with the founding of what became the Baptist Missionary Society (BMS), history's first evangelical missionary society and the stimulus for the formation of a number of similar societies in the near future. By January 1793 funds were starting to come in and Carey volunteered to go to Bengal* as the Society's first missionary. Apart from the chaplaincy offered to those in the East India Company's* service in the Bengal Presidency, missionary activity was illegal in the Company's territory and would remain so until 1813. Nonetheless, three days after his arrival Carey preached in the Calcutta bazaar and very quickly began to learn the Bengali and Hindi languages. Once achieved, he then set about translating the Bible into Bengali. Carey's vision for the work of the Society was to establish a string of mission stations across Bengal and beyond, which would be islands of Christian community life in the midst of the surrounding Hindu population. Carey himself continued to gain expertise in indigenous languages, so much so that in 1801 the Company invited him to take up an appointment as professor of Bengali at its new Fort William College in Calcutta. His appointment yielded some extraordinarily productive years as he produced grammars of a number of Indian languages, including Bengali, Marathi, and Punjabi, as well as dictionaries and works in translation. His role as an important agent in the development of literature in Bengali, and in the wider renaissance of Bengali culture, has long been recognized, as has his campaign against sati* and infanticide, a practice that targeted baby girls as being economically liable.

Further Reading

E. Daniel Potts (1967). *British Baptist Missionaries in India: the History of Serampore and its Missions* (Cambridge, Cambridge University Press)

George Smith (1885). *The Life of William Carey, D.D.* (London, John Murray)

Cary, Joyce (1888–1957). A writer whose three novels set in colonial Africa eventually found a large readership and proved an important influence on later African writers such as Chinua Achebe*, Cary was born in Ireland* and educated at Clifton College, Edinburgh, and at Trinity College, Oxford*. In 1912, he went to Montenegro where he served as an orderly with the Red Cross. His sense of adventure whetted, he joined the Northern Nigeria Political Service in 1914 and soon found himself fighting the Germans in Cameroon. Wounded in 1915, he returned to England, got married, and then resumed his colonial service in Nigeria*, where he remained until 1920, all the while writing short stories and novels. In that year, hopeful that he could live the life of a fulltime writer, he settled in England for good. From then until his death, Oxford* became home. Among the many novels written during these years were three based on his experiences serving the Empire in Nigeria. *Aissa Saved* came out in 1932, followed by *The African Witch* four years later, and then in 1939 the best known of his African works was published, *Mister Johnson*. Though none of them sold well or were critically acclaimed at the time of their publication, their reputation eventually grew, especially that of *Mister Johnson*, which tells the tragic-comic story of a district officer, Rudbeck, and his clerk, Johnson, in the years just after Nigerian colonial unification in 1914. Cary's depiction of the life of an upcountry district officer in colonial Africa is unmatched by any other novelist of the period.

Further Reading

Joyce Cary (1995). *Mister Johnson* (London, J.M. Dent)

Malcolm Foster (1969). *Joyce Cary: A Biography* (London, Michael Joseph)

Casement, Roger (1864–1916). British diplomat and Irish nationalist, Casement was among the first to report on the horrific exploitation and abuse of Congolese Africans under King Leopold of the Belgians. Born in Dublin, Casement was raised and educated in Ulster. His first job was in a shipping company. In 1884, he went to Africa, where he would spend much of the next twenty years. During the 1890s he became British Consul in successive locations, and in 1903 was serving in this capacity at Boma in the Congo Free State when asked by the British government to conduct an eyewitness investigation into the abuse of native Congolese by their Belgian overlords. The Casement Report, issued in 1904, built on his own examination of the situation and on a decade's worth of accounts by others of the scandalous ill-treatment of Africans. Its impact was immediate and the Belgian Parliament acted to force Leopold to establish a commission of inquiry into conditions in the Congo. Casement's observations were essentially confirmed by the inquiry and in light of sustained international pressure the Belgian Parliament forced Leopold to relinquish his personal hold over the Congo Free State. In its place was formed the Belgian Congo under Parliamentary control. Casement went on to write a similar report about the abuses of Peruvian natives. His experiences with the worst face of Imperialism made him its foe, wherever it was found. In 1911, he was made Companion of the Order of St Michael and St George but the next year he resigned from the consular service and soon was swept along by the tide of Irish nationalism. In Germany in the midst of the First World War*, he assisted in the planning for the Irish Rising. He was caught shortly after his arrival in Ireland in April 1916. Four months later, convicted of treason, he was executed.

Further Reading

Adam Hochschild (1998). *King Leopold's Ghost: A Story of Greed, Terror, and Heroism in Colonial Africa* (Boston, Houghton Mifflin)

Seamas O Siochain (2008). *Roger Casement: Imperialist, Rebel, Revolutionary* (Dublin, Lilliput Press)

Cavendish Bentinck, Lord William (1774–1839). The first Governor-General of India, Cavendish Bentinck began a long military career in the 1790s. His first Indian service was as Governor of Madras from 1803 to 1807. In 1827, he was appointed Governor-General of Bengal*, the richest and most important of the East India Company's* territories in the subcontinent. This led to his subsequent appointment as Governor-General of India in 1833, which he held until retiring to England in 1835. His last years in India* were marked by a largely successful campaign to eliminate the practice of sati*, a Hindu ritual whereby wives would commit suicide by climbing onto the funeral pyres of their dead husbands.

Further Reading

Isaiah Azariah (1978). *Lord Bentinck and Indian Education, Crime, and Status of Women* (Washington, DC, University Press of America)

John Rosselli (1974). *Lord William Bentinck: The Making of a Liberal Imperialist, 1774–1839* (London, Chatto & Windus)

Cayman Islands. Located in the Caribbean near Jamaica*, the Caymans are comprised of three islands and were first sighted by a European when Columbus arrived in 1503. The islands became formally British in 1670 and settlement began in the 1730s. Crown Colony status was granted in 1859. Since 1972 the Caymans have been designated a British Overseas Territory.

Further Reading

J.A. Roy Bodden (2007). *The Cayman Islands in Transition: The Politics, History and Sociology of a Changing Society* (Miami, Ian Randle Publications)

Roger C. Smith (2000). *The Maritime Heritage of the Cayman Islands* (Gainesville, FL, University Press of Florida)

Central African Federation. In 1953, as African nationalism began to emerge in earnest, the white minority political leaders in the Rhodesias* and Nyasaland* attempted to secure their increasingly embattled position by uniting the three colonies in a federation governed from Salisbury (Harare). Its leading advocate was Sir Roy Welensky* (1907–91), who became federal premier in 1956. The Federation was marked by extreme racial tension and political strife, however, and came to an end in 1963. The next year two-thirds of the former CAF, Northern Rhodesia and Nyasaland, became independent as, respectively, Zambia* and Malawi*.

Further Reading

Henry Franklin (1963). *Unholy Wedlock: The Failure of the Central African Federation* (London, Allen & Unwin)

Robin Short (1973). *African Sunset* (London, Johnson)

Cetshwayo (1826–84). Gaining fame as a Zulu* king in the 1870s, Cetshwayo was an imposing physical presence and a defiant ruler who resisted both

Boer and British imprecations upon Zulu authority and land in South Africa*. In 1879, in the midst of an attempt by the Cape Colony* to sponsor north-ward expansion, a British column under General Chelmsford was attacked and annihilated at Isandlwana* by 4,000 Zulu warriors acting under Cetshwayo's command. Later that year, however, the British gained their revenge and defeated the Zulu at Ulundi*. Cetshwayo was imprisoned and then, ultimately, taken to London, where he was presented to Queen Victoria*. In 1883, he was restored to his former position as King of the Zulu, but Britain's gesture in this regard failed when Cetshwayo's kingship was chal-lenged successfully by a rival. Deposed, he spent the last year of his life languishing in Eshowe, the capital of Zululand. Despite political machina-tions upon Cetshwayo's death, his son, Dinizulu, nevertheless became his successor.

Further Reading

C.T. Binns (1963). *The Last Zulu King: The Life and Death of Cetshwayo* (London, Longman)

Jeff Guy (1979). *The destruction of the Zulu Kingdom: The Civil War in Zululand, 1879–1884* (London, Longman)

Ceylon (see Sri Lanka)

Chamberlain, Joseph (1836–1914). One of the best known of British colo-nial secretaries, Chamberlain's political power base was in Birmingham, where he served as mayor from 1873 to 1875. He entered national politics as a Liberal MP in 1876, and in 1880, at the beginning of Gladstone's* second ministry, he was named to the Cabinet as President of the Board of Trade. Chamberlain later fell out with Gladstone over the divisive issue of Irish Home Rule, however, and gradually reconstituted himself politi-cally as a Conservative. To that end, in 1895, Lord Salisbury made him Colonial Secretary, a post he would hold for over eight years. Chamberlain took a significant part in all of the major Imperial events of the period, particularly the Jameson Raid*, the Second Boer War*, and British territo-rial expansion in Africa. He keenly supported the idea of closer ties between Britain and the colonies, including preferential trade as espoused by the

Imperial Federation* movement. His colonial record remains controversial, particularly as it pertains to political and military machinations in South Africa* leading up to and during the Second Boer War*.

Further Reading

Peter T. Marsh (1994). *Joseph Chamberlain: Entrepreneur in Politics* (New Haven, CT, Yale University Press)

Neil Parsons (1998). *King Khama, Emperor Joe, and the Great White Queen: Victorian Britain through African Eyes* (Chicago, University of Chicago Press)

Chanak Crisis. A turning point in how the Dominions conducted their external and military relations with the mother country. In September 1922, nationalist Turks under the command of Mustapha Kemal triggered a crisis over the terms of the Treaty of Sèvres, one of the five treaties negotiated at the Paris Peace Conference three years earlier. In violation of the Treaty's terms, Kemal's troops expelled the resident Greeks of Smyrna, declaiming that the city's majority Turks would decide its future. Kemal's provocative action was felt throughout the de-militarized Dardanelles region, especially in 'Chanak', where a small British regulatory force was garrisoned. Assuming that war with Turkey was imminent, British Prime Minister Lloyd George – through the Colonial Secretary, Winston Churchill* – requested military assistance from the Dominions. The request was refused, first by Canada*, and then by Australia* and South Africa*, but was acceded to reluctantly by New Zealand* and Newfoundland*. At all events the crisis passed, but Chanak demonstrated a new willingness for the senior members of the Empire to take a more autonomous line in international affairs, something recognized by the creation in 1925 of a Cabinet post called the 'Secretary of State for Dominion Affairs'.

Further Reading

John A. Gallagher (1982). *The Decline, Revival and Fall of the British Empire: The Ford Lectures and Other Essays*, Anil Seal, ed. (Cambridge, Cambridge University Press)

Philip G. Wigley (1977). *Canada and the Transition to Commonwealth: British–Canadian Relations, 1917–26* (Cambridge, Cambridge University Press)

Churchill, Sir Winston L.S. (1874–1965). British Prime Minister, vigorous exponent of the Empire, and considered by many to be the greatest Englishman of the twentieth century, Churchill was born into a titled family and educated at Harrow and Sandhurst. Military service in India* and the Sudan* followed. As a journalist he went to South Africa* to cover the Second Boer War*. Taken prisoner, he escaped and later returned to Britain a hero. A long Parliamentary career began in 1900 with his election as a Conservative MP. In 1904, however, he left and joined the Liberals and two years later was elected for them. Various Cabinet appointments ensued, including First Lord of the Admiralty, 1911–15, and Colonial Secretary, 1921–2. In the latter position he presided over the Cairo Conference* (1921), which created the political map of the modern Middle East. He was defeated in the 1922 General Election and resigned from the Liberals. He sat briefly as an independent and then in 1925 he rejoined the Conservatives, where he would remain for the rest of his political life. Throughout the 1930s he campaigned for the centrality of India* to the Empire, and his dislike of Gandhi – 'a half-naked *fakir*' – and Indian constitutional concessions helped keep him out of office, as did his criticism of the government's policy of appeasement toward Nazi Germany. Upon Britain's entry into the Second World War* on 3 September 1939, he was appointed to his old post as First Lord of the Admiralty, and then in May 1940 he became Prime Minister when the embattled Neville Chamberlain resigned. In 1945, after the defeat of Germany, Churchill himself was defeated at the polls and until 1951 served as Leader of the Opposition. He strongly opposed Indian independence in 1947 and the gradual dissolution of the Empire. Prime Minister again, 1951–5, he remained convinced of the necessity of the Empire to Britain's position in the world, denouncing nationalist demands and condemning colonial violence such as the outbreak of Kenya's Mau Mau* movement in 1952.

Further Reading

Martin Gilbert (1991). *Churchill: A Life* (London, Heinemann)

Roy Jenkins (2002). *Churchill: A Biography* (New York, Plume)

Church (of England) Missionary Society (see Missionaries)

Clifford, Sir Hugh C. (1866–1941). A colonial governor of considerable reputation and skill, Clifford was born in London and educated locally. He was destined for the military and was admitted to Sandhurst, but the early death of his father forced him to make his own way in the world and he did so as a junior government official in Malaya*, arriving there in 1883, barely seventeen. He spent most of the next eighteen years in the region, rising to resident of Pahang and then, briefly, governor of North Borneo. Ill-health was a constant nemesis for Clifford and in 1901 he returned home to convalesce. Two years later he began the mature phase of his career by being appointed colonial secretary in Trinidad*. In 1907, he moved on in the same capacity to Ceylon*, before spending five years as governor of the Gold Coast* and then a further six governing Nigeria*. The latter was an exhausting assignment, as he sought to bring administrative harmony to the recently amalgamated Northern and Southern Nigeria. A brief return to Ceylon, this time as governor, commenced in 1925, followed by a final two years, 1927–9, governing his beloved Malaya. Clifford was almost proto-typically proconsular; tall and commanding, he had vast amounts of energy, but long service overseas compromised his health and his last years were ones of diminishment and confinement.

Further Reading

Sir Hugh Clifford (1929). *Bushwhacking and other Asiatic tales and memories* (New York, Harper & Brothers)

Harry A. Gailey (1982). *Clifford: imperial proconsul* (London, Collins)

Clive, Robert, 1st Baron Clive (1725–74). Considered to be the founder of British India, Clive arrived in Madras in the employ of the East India Company* in 1744. A natural affinity for warfare and the leading of troops in battle led to promotion within the EIC, and in 1755, now a colonel, he was stationed at Bombay. The next year his martial expertise was used to defeat the Nawab of Bengal, Suraj-ud-Dowlah, at the Battle of Plassey* near Calcutta, and in so doing consolidate the EIC's ascendant position in the province. After three years as the de facto ruler of Bengal*, he returned to England using his lately won wealth to secure a peerage. In 1764, Clive returned to Bengal as governor and was successful in reforming the EIC's operations, which had come under heavy public criticism for the excessive accrued wealth of its senior officeholders. He left India in 1766 after ensuring the EIC's formal control of Bengal, but the Parliamentary attacks on both the EIC and Clive continued. These attacks proved debilitating psychologically and he died a broken man, likely committing suicide aged forty-nine.

Further Reading

Mark Bence-Jones (1974). *Clive of India* (London, Constable)

James Philip Lawford (1976). *Clive: Proconsul of India* (London, Allen & Unwin)

Cohen, Sir Andrew (1909–68). A colonial administrator, Cohen was born into a prominent Anglo-Jewish family. A scholarship to Malvern College was followed by the same to Trinity College, Cambridge, where he took a double first in the classical tripos in 1931. The next year he entered the Civil Service but remained there only briefly before transferring to the Colonial Office*. During the Second World War* he was seconded to Malta* but otherwise continued to concentrate on African affairs, his understanding of which gave him considerable sympathy for the black populations living under colonial rule. In 1947, Cohen was appointed assistant under-secretary of state for the Colonial Office's African division. He was in the vanguard of those who saw decolonization on the horizon, and thought hard about how best to undertake it. He saw African nationalists, then just beginning to become choate, as the means by which both to bring Empire to an end and to build independent civil societies. Accordingly, he cultivated them in both West and Central Africa. In the latter especially, he was deeply concerned about the impact that apartheid – spreading northward from South Africa – might have on the Rhodesias and Nyasaland*. He thus proposed their confederation, which, in a modified form, was later carried out, though unsuccessfully. In the meantime, in 1952, he was appointed governor of Uganda*, serving until 1957. On the whole his term in office was successful: Africans were advanced in central government; he expanded Makerere University; local political parties grew. But his controversial decision to deport the Kabaka of Buganda in 1953, whose people, the Baganda, wished for independence from the rest of Uganda, elicited a strong traditionalist and nationalist backlash to which he eventually bowed. Nonetheless, in a number of ways, he laid the groundwork for Uganda's independence, which would come in 1962. His later career took him to the United Nations as Britain's permanent representative on the Trusteeship Council and then as permanent secretary of the Ministry of Overseas Development. He died unexpectedly from a heart attack in London, aged just fifty-eight.

Further Reading

David Apter (1967). *The Political Kingdom in Uganda* 2nd edn (Princeton, NJ, Princeton University Press)

Sir Andrew Cohen (1959). *British Policy in changing Africa* (London, Routledge & Kegan Paul)

Colenso, John W. (1814–83). A colonial Anglican churchman who gained both fame and notoriety through his championing of South Africa's native Zulu* people, Colenso arrived in Natal* in 1853 as its first Anglican bishop. The ensuing thirty years in South Africa* were marked by his flouting of conventional missionary norms and contemporary Anglican theological orthodoxy. In 1863, Colenso's adoption of a position on the atonement contrary to that held by the Church of England, led to his deposition. On appeal, Colenso was restored to the bishopric of Natal. But in 1866, his original accuser, Archbishop Robert Gray* of Cape Town, excommunicated him. A protracted ecclesiastical and civil court battle ensued, but during it Colenso maintained his traditional defence of Zulu social and cultural practices and was especially outraged in 1879, not long before his death, when the British took up arms against the Zulu.

Further Reading

Jonathan A. Draper, ed. (2003). *The Eye of the Storm: Bishop John William Colenso and the Crisis of Biblical Inspiration* (London, T&T Clark International)

Peter B. Hinchliff (1964). *John William Colenso: Bishop of Natal* (London, Nelson)

Collins, Michael (1890–1922). A leading Irish nationalist who became Chairman of the Provisional Government and Commander-in-Chief of the Armed Forces following the Anglo-Irish Treaty of December 1921, Collins was assassinated by anti-Treaty republicans the following summer. Born in County Cork, as a fifteen-year-old he moved to London to take a job with the Post Office. Already a jejeune nationalist, during his years in London he joined the Irish Republican Brotherhood and became dedicated to the cause of Irish independence. Returning to Ireland during the First World War*, he participated in the Easter Rising 1916 and was arrested by the British and sent to a prison camp in North Wales. Released the next year, Collins returned to Ireland and as a member of the new nationalist political party, Sinn Fein, was elected to Parliament as MP for Cork South in 1918. Collins, along with other nationalist MPs, refused to take up their seats at Westminster, however, choosing instead to establish a new Irish Parliament, the Dail Eireann. Its first sitting occurred in 1919 and marked the beginning of the Irish War of Independence. Collins became the Director of Intelligence of the Irish Republican Army and Minister of Finance, organizing a highly successful National Loan scheme to finance the war. By 1920, Collins had become one of the main targets of the Royal Irish Constabulary and of the British agents working out of Dublin Castle. Remarkably adept at undercover operations – which included anonymously riding around Dublin on a bicycle – and able to keep out of the hands of those sent to capture or assassinate him, Collins directed an increasingly successful guerilla war against the British. Ultimately, with casualties rising and political costs mounting, the Lloyd George government authorized a truce and negotiations ensued. The Anglo-Irish Treaty* of 1921 was the result, establishing the Irish Free State but with the possibility of partition in the Protestant north. Republican purists found the arrangement unacceptable and began a campaign against it. As the Treaty's chief defender, Collins found himself in a struggle with his erstwhile colleagues, and the anti-Treaty faction led by Eamon de Valera* targeted him. Civil War ensued in June 1922 and in August, while visiting Cork, Collins was ambushed and killed by a small group of anti-Treaty IRA members. He died a hero to all those who endorsed the Treaty, and in the years that followed the legend of the 'man who won the war' and gave Ireland its independence grew apace. He remains a heroic but controversial figure in modern Irish history.

Further Reading
Tim Pat Coogan (1990). *Michael Collins* (London, Hutchinson)
Peter Hart (2005). *Mick: The Real Michael Collins* (New York, Viking Penguin)

Colonial Office. In its modern form the Colonial Office was established by William Pitt the Younger's government in 1801, and soon thereafter its functions were divided into five departments: North America; Australia; West Indies; Africa and Mediterranean; and General. (The India Office handled Indian and Far Eastern Affairs.) For most of the nineteenth century the Colonial Office was located at 14 Downing Street, afterwards moving twice before ceasing traditional operations in 1966.

Further Reading
Brian L. Blakeley (1972). *The Colonial Office, 1868–1892* (Durham, NC, Duke University Press)
J.M. Lee (1982). *The Colonial Office, War, and Development Policy: Organisation and the Planning of a Metropolitan Initiative, 1939–1945* (London, M.T. Smith)

Colonial Service. Under the authority of the Secretary of State for the Colonies and the Colonial Office*, the Colonial Service (CS) was responsible for administering the colonies and Protectorates of the Dependent Empire (exclusive of the Dominions and India*). In 1837, the first Colonial Regulations were issued, which started a half-century's development of the CS into a full-fledged Crown service. By the beginning of the twentieth century the CS comprised some 1,500 officers, but in precise terms they were officers of a number of different territorial services rather than of the CS *per se*. Only in 1930 were all of these services united to form a single, unified CS, of which the Colonial Administrative Service (CAS) was the first of twenty constituent services that came under the umbrella of the CS. Arguably the most prestigious of the CS services, fully three-quarters of CAS officers served in Africa. The organization and operation of the unified CS were mainly the work of its first director, Sir Ralph Furse*. He remained in the post until 1948, just six years before the abolition of the CS as a career service in 1954. In that year the CS was replaced by Her Majesty's Overseas Civil Service.

Further Reading
A.H.M. Kirk-Greene (1999). *On Crown Service: A History of HM Colonial and Overseas Civil Services, 1837–1997* (London and New York, I.B.Tauris)
_____ (2006). *Symbol of Authority: The British District Officer in Africa* (London and New York, I.B.Tauris)

Committee of Imperial Defence. Formally established in 1902, not long before the treaty was signed that ended the Second Boer War*, the CID was the considered response of the Balfour government to many years of discussion about the need for coordinated Imperial defence policies. Naval and land inter-service cooperation ensued, with a view to the Empire's global strategic concerns and epitomized by the first Imperial Conference held in 1911 and attended by the Dominion Prime Ministers.

Further Reading
Franklyn A. Johnson (1960). *Defence by Committee: The British Committee of Imperial Defence, 1885–1959* (London, Oxford University Press)
William J. McDermott (1970). *British Strategic Planning and the Committee of Imperial Defence, 1871 to 1907* (Toronto, Department of History, University of Toronto)

Commonwealth. Coming into common usage in the twentieth century to denote the organic successor of the British Empire, 'Commonwealth' was used first in 1884 to describe the essence of the Empire by Lord Rosebery, then a member of Gladstone's* Cabinet. In 1916, Lionel Curtis* used it in the title of his book (see below), and it soon began to appear in places of official importance, including the Imperial Conference of 1926, when it was employed to describe the 'British Commonwealth of Nations.' Long-time defenders of the traditional understanding of the British Empire, such as Winston Churchill*, refused to use the term, but in the years after the Second World War* its use became normative.

Further Reading
Lionel Curtis (1916). *The Commonwealth of Nations: An Inquiry into the*

Nature of Citizenship in the British Empire, and into the Mutual relations of the Several Communities thereof (London, Macmillan)

Nicholas Mansergh (1982). *The Commonwealth Experience* (Toronto, University of Toronto Press)

Cook, James (1728–79). The most famous mariner of the First British Empire, and someone who set the geographic parameters for the Second, Cook was the first Briton to see New Zealand* and Australia*. Born into humble circumstances in Yorkshire, he began a lifetime of seafaring at Whitby in 1746. Eventually joining the Royal Navy, Cook proved himself an exceptional navigator. In the late 1750s he began a survey of Newfoundland* and the St Lawrence River*. His charts of the latter were important to the British conquest of New France, beginning in 1759. Later, in 1768, Cook departed on the first of what would be three voyages to explore the vast reaches of the Pacific Ocean. For much of the next eleven years until his death at the hands of native Hawaiians, Cook sailed the waters off Australia, New Zealand, Antarctica, and the North American west coast. Long accorded heroic status in the antipodes, his reputation began to suffer in the post-colonial era of the 1960s. Still, Cook – man and myth – remains strong, especially in those areas of the South Pacific where he is considered the founder of European society.

Further Reading

J.C. Beaglehole (1974). *The Life of Captain James Cook* (Stanford, CA, Stanford University Press)

Brian Richardson (2005). *Longitude and Empire: How Captain Cook's Voyages Changed the World* (Vancouver, University of British Columbia Press)

Cook Islands. Named for their British discoverer, James Cook*, and located in the mid-Pacific, the Cook Islands saw the arrival of English missionaries in 1821. In 1888, it became a British Protectorate. Control of the fifteen-island archipelago was transferred to New Zealand* in 1901, where it has remained.

Further Reading

Richard P. Gilson (1980). *The Cook Islands, 1820–1950* (Wellington, Victoria University Press)

Mel Kernahan (1995). *White Savages in the South Seas* (London, Verso)

Cox, Sir Percy (1864–1937). A colonial administrator in Africa and the Middle East, Cox was born in Essex and educated at Harrow School and at the Royal Military College, Sandhurst. Commissioned in 1884, he was sent to India*. Later posted to British Somaliland*, he was transferred to Berbera in 1894. Promoted Captain the next year, he was appointed Political Agent and Consul at Muscat in 1899. Promoted Major in 1902, in 1904 he was appointed Acting Political Resident in the Persian Gulf, becoming Resident in 1909 and remaining so for the next five years. During the First World War* he spent considerable time in the Persian Gulf as Chief Political Officer in the British campaign against the Ottoman Empire. At the conclusion of the war in November 1918, he was appointed Acting Minister for Tehran and was an instrumental figure along with Gertrude Bell* in negotiating the Anglo-Persian Agreement, which was the basis for the modern state of Iraq*. He served as High Commissioner for Iraq until 1923, at which time he retired to England. Praised by some and criticized by others for his work in the founding of Iraq, he died unexpectedly of a heart attack in 1937.

Further Reading

Georgina Howell (2006). *Daughter of the Desert: The Remarkable Life of Gertrude Bell* (London, Macmillan)

Karl E. Meyer and Shareen Blair Brysac (2008). *Kingmakers: the Invention of the Modern Middle East* (New York, W.W. Norton)

Cricket. 'The Battle of Waterloo was won on the playing fields of Eton,' the Duke of Wellington was reputed to have said. If so, one of those games played was cricket and perhaps it is the English pastime most associated with the spread of Empire. A modern form of cricket began to be played in England around 1598, but the formation of the Hambledon Club in London in the 1760s and a short time later the Marylebone Cricket Club are key to its growth. Lord's Ground opened in 1787 and since then has been the centre of the English game. The first record of cricket being played in the Empire is a match in Virginia in 1709. In 1844, Canada played the United States in the first international match, but international cricket owes its most important origins to the English touring side of 1859, and to the first Test Match against Australia in 1877. All of the world's great cricketing countries – the UK, Australia*, New Zealand*, India*, Pakistan*, Sri Lanka*, Zimbabwe*, and Barbados* (West Indies) – are former members of the Empire.

Further Reading

Derek Birley (1999). *A Social History of English Cricket* (London, Aurum)
_____ (1993). *Sport and the Making of Britain* (Manchester, Manchester University Press)

Cripps Mission. In March 1942, Prime Minister Winston Churchill* sent Sir Stafford Cripps, Lord Privy Seal and former British ambassador to the Soviet Union, to India* in order to win the support of the Indian National Congress Party* in the ongoing war against Japan. Gandhi*, by then totally committed to immediate Indian independence, rejected Cripps's offer of post-war independence, however, and Cripps returned to London with nothing to show for his efforts.

Further Reading

Prashanto K. Chatterji (2004). *The Cripps Mission, 22 March–11 April 1942: An In-depth Study* (Kolkata, Minerva Associates)
P.F. Clarke (2002). *The Cripps Version: The Life of Stafford Cripps, 1889–1952* (London, Allen Lane)

Cromer, Earl of (1841–1917). Evelyn Baring, Imperial pro-consul and long-time governor of Egypt*, was born into wealth and privilege. He began his career in the military but moved quickly into administration, first in the Ionian Islands*, then in Malta*, Jamaica*, India*, and Egypt. Appointed British Agent and Consul-General in Egypt in 1883, he remained in office until 1907. During the intervening twenty-four years he exercised great authority in the country, as well as in contiguous Sudan*, over which Egypt had suzerainty. He was closely involved in all of the important events of the period: Gordon's* defeat at Khartoum in 1885; the Sudan's re-conquest under Kitchener* in 1898; and the establishment of the Anglo-Egyptian condominium that came afterwards and lasted until Sudanese independence in 1956; the modernization of the Egyptian economy and society. He was well rewarded for his Imperial service, the pinnacle of which was an earldom in 1901. Nicknamed 'Over-Baring' by many of those who worked for him, his reputation in post-colonial Egypt is controversial.

Further Reading

Roger Owen (2004). *Lord Cromer: Victorian Imperialist, Edwardian Pro-Consul* (Oxford, Oxford University Press)

Lawrence J. Zetland (1932). *Lord Cromer: Being the Authorized Life of Evelyn Baring, First Earl of Cromer* (London, Hodder & Stoughton)

Curtis, Lionel (1872–1955). One of the best-known publicists of the Empire-Commonwealth, Curtis was educated at Haileybury* and Oxford* before qualifying as a barrister. He went to South Africa* on the eve of the Second Boer War* in 1899, fought in it, and then stayed for ten years, during which time he was a strong advocate of South African union. His time there brought him into close contact with Lord Milner* and his 'kindergarten' of Imperial thinkers, and upon his return to England he devoted himself to the promotion of the transition of Empire to Commonwealth* through the *Round Table* journal he founded in 1910, his appointment as Beit Lecturer in Colonial History at Oxford, extensive travel to Imperial capitals, and, in 1916, the publication of a manifesto, *The Problem of the Commonwealth*. In later years his work on constitutional reform in India* and on international affairs (he helped organize the Royal Institute of International Affairs) convinced him that the United States must re-join the Commonwealth and that its logical conclusion was a federal world government.

Further Reading

John E. Kendle (1975). *The Round Table Movement and Imperial Union* (Toronto, University of Toronto Press)

Deborah Lavin (1995). *From Empire to International Commonwealth: A Biography of Lionel Curtis* (Oxford, Oxford University Press)

Curzon, George N., Lord Curzon of Kedleston (1859–1925). Perhaps the most famous Viceroy in the history of British India*, Curzon was born into a prominent aristocratic family and received an Eton and Balliol College, Oxford* education before entering Parliament as a Conservative in 1886. During the 1880s and '90s he travelled widely in Asia and gained a detailed knowledge of Afghanistan, Persia, India, and parts of Russia. His knowledge and expertise as an 'Oriental' specialist were rewarded in 1895 when he was made Parliamentary Under-Secretary for Foreign Affairs, and three years later he was appointed Viceroy, aged just thirty-nine, and took up his duties at the beginning of 1899. He plunged into life in India, taking a particular interest in Indian history and architecture, ensuring, for example, the restoration of the Red Fort in Delhi and Agra's Taj Mahal. He was involved in all manner of agricultural, economic, and communication projects. But a protracted confrontation with the Commander-in-Chief, of the Indian Army, Lord Kitchener, over military re-organization beginning in 1903 weakened his authority, and in 1905 he resigned, vexed too by the illness of his wife who died the next year. Earlier in life, most of his contemporaries thought that Curzon – socially superior, well-connected, handsome, and championed by Benjamin Jowett, Master of Balliol and the 'maker of statesmen' – was destined to become Prime Minister. But after his return from India such high promise faded and the Conservative Party chose others to lead it instead of Curzon. Eventually, he became Foreign Secretary from 1919 until 1924, but he died the next year, not quite fulfilling the potential that had inspired envious Oxford undergraduates to rhyme off: 'My name is George Nathaniel Curzon, I am a most superior person, my cheeks are pink, my hair is sleek, I dine at Blenheim once a week.'

Further Reading

G.H. Bennett (1995). *British Foreign Policy During the Curzon Period, 1919–1924* (New York, St Martin's Press)

David Gilmour (2003). *Curzon: Imperial Statesman* (New York, Farrar, Straus & Giroux)

Cyprus. Prime Minister Benjamin Disraeli* saw to it that the Berlin Congress made Cyprus, located in the eastern Mediterranean, a British Protectorate in 1878, although it remained under Turkish Ottoman overrule until it was annexed by the British in 1914, shortly after the start of the First World War*. Crown Colony status was granted in 1925. The heavily Greek population, long dissatisfied with their national and constitutional situation, demanded union with Greece, which desired it too, but the resident Turks and the British government were resistant. Protests and riots marked Cypriot history until the 1950s, leading to independence as a republic within the Commonwealth in 1960. Animus between the Greek and Turkish communities remained strong, however, and in 1975 the Turks established a separate Turkish Cypriot Federated State in the northern part of the island. In 1983, the Turkish Republic of Northern Cyprus was proclaimed. And that is how things remain. Despite the protracted efforts of the international community to enable a reunion, Cyprus remains divided.

Further Reading

Hubert Faustmann and Nicos Peristianis, eds (2006). *Britain in Cyprus: Colonialism and Post-Colonialism 1878–2006* (Mannheim, Bibliopolis)

William Mallinson (2005). *Cyprus: A Modern History* (London and New York, I.B.Tauris)

D

Dalhousie, 1st Marquess (James Broun-Ramsay) (1812–60). A key British administrator in mid-nineteenth-century India*, Dalhousie left a record that is controversial to this day. Born in Dalhousie Castle, Scotland, he spent part of his childhood in Canada*, where his father was sometime Governor-General. Educated at Harrow and Christ Church, Oxford*, Dalhousie entered Parliament in 1837 and rose quickly among the Peelite Conservatives. In 1845, he was appointed President of the Board of Trade, and two years later was offered the position of Governor-General of India. He arrived in Calcutta and took up his duties in January 1848. For the next eight years he presided over the roil of British India, including the Second Anglo-Sikh and Second Burmese Wars, the extensive building of railways and telegraph lines, the creation of a postal system, the expansion of state education, and the implementation of the Doctrine of Lapse. Dalhousie was convinced that all of India should be brought under British rule. Accordingly, whenever an Indian Princely State* was found to be lacking a proper male lineal heir, the Doctrine of Lapse would apply and the British duly expanded their territory to include the erstwhile Princely State. Altogether, Dalhousie's reforms were far-reaching, but for many Indians provocative and potentially culturally threatening. In 1853, his wife died and two years later his own health broke down. He resigned in 1856 and returned to England. The next year the Indian Mutiny* erupted. In the view of some, he had stirred up Indian opinion to the breaking point. Dalhousie's reforming rule would mark the end of the East India Company's* existence and betoken the arrival of the Raj. Meanwhile, his health did not improve and he died at the relatively young age of forty-eight.

Further Reading

K.N. Chauduri, ed. (1971). *The Economic Development of India, 1814–58: A Selection of Contemporary Writings* (Cambridge, Cambridge University Press)

William Lee-Warner (1904). *The Life of the Marquis of Dalhousie* (London, Macmillan)

Deakin, Alfred (1856–1919). Three-time Prime Minister of Australia*, Deakin championed both Australian federation and Imperial unity, describing himself as an 'independent Australian Briton.' The son of English immigrants, Deakin graduated from the University of Melbourne in 1877 and became a barrister. Elected to the Victoria* legislature in 1879, he sat for the next twenty-one years until the achievement of Australian federation in 1900, at which time he became a member of the House of Representatives. Liberal- and reformist-minded, he became Australia's second Prime Minister in 1903. His three ministries were spread throughout the next seven years until 1910. The Imperial Federation movement coincided with his time as Prime Minister, and he endorsed it strongly along with the idea of a preference for goods traded within the Empire. Deakin was a key figure in the twentieth-century move from Empire to Commonwealth.

Further Reading

Al Gabay (1992). *The Mystic Life of Alfred Deakin* (Cambridge, Cambridge University Press)

John A. La Nauze (1965). *Alfred Deakin: A Biography* (Melbourne, Melbourne University Press)

De Beers Consolidated Mines Ltd. The De Beer brothers' (Diederik and Johannes) farm at Vooruitzigt in the northern part of Cape Colony* is perhaps the most noteworthy farm in the history of the British Empire, for it was here in the summer of 1871 that diamonds were found. Not much interested in mining, however, the De Beers' sold their rights to diamond speculators who in turn sold them to the Cape Colony* government. By that time, 1875, Cecil Rhodes* had arrived in what was now called Kimberley (after the Colonial Secretary at the time) and over the next few years he steadily increased his share of the diamond mining industry and in 1880 formed De Beers Mining Company. By the end of the decade De Beers had achieved a stranglehold on the industry by buying out its rivals, such as the companies run by Barnato* and Beit,* and De Beers Consolidated Mines Ltd exercised a monopoly over the diamond trade, something which in one way or another continues to this day.

Further Reading

Peter Carstens (2001). *In the Company of Diamonds: De Beers, Kleinzee, and the Control of a Town* (Athens, Ohio University Press)

Stefan Kanfer (1993). *The Last Empire: De Beers, Diamonds, and the World* (New York, Farrar, Straus & Giroux)

Delamere, 3rd Baron (Hugh Cholmondeley) (1870–1931). Colonial settler and advocate in Kenya* (British East Africa). Born into a titled family, Hugh Cholmondeley succeeded his father to become 3rd Baron Delamere when he was just seventeen. Educated at Eton, he was a restless youth who travelled extensively, including coastal Africa in the early 1890s. His greatest adventure began in late 1896, when he set out south-westwards on a trekking expedition that would take him some 1,000 miles into what is today central Kenya. So taken with the country was Delamere, and so sure of its prospects for white settlement, that he decided to make it his home, and did so beginning in 1903. He acquired a 100,000 acre ranch – Soysambu – in the upcountry area around Njoro, on which he raised cattle and sheep and from which he advocated relentlessly for settler interests in Kenya. He was President of the Colonialists' Association and later served on the legislative council. He believed strongly in a racially divided colony and spoke out strongly against the British government's policy (beginning in 1925) of African racial paramountcy in Kenya's future. He was a colourful, hard-working, and highly influential leader of Kenyan pioneer life, but held apartheid-style racial views that became increasingly untenable in colonial Kenya.

Further Reading

Elspeth Huxley (1969). *White Man's Country: Lord Delamere and the Making of Kenya* (New York, Praeger)

Errol Trzebinski (1985). *The Kenya Pioneers* (London, Heinemann)

De Valera, Eamon (1882–1975). First President of the Irish Republic and long-time nationalist and political leader, De Valera was the main strategist behind winning Irish independence from Britain. Born in New York City to an Irish mother and a Spanish-speaking father, he moved to Ireland as a child and was raised in County Limerick. Graduating from the Royal University of Ireland and becoming a schoolteacher, his nationalism was shaped by the revival of Irish Gaelic and he took up arms in the Easter Rising of 1916. His great physical height and authoritative presence as a commandant during the failed revolt propelled him into a leading position with Sinn Fein following his release from prison in 1917. Arrested again by the British in 1918, he was imprisoned in Lincoln, from which he escaped the following year. Taking up the presidency of the new Dail Eireann in 1919, he led the war against the British until the truce of 1921, but then controversially absented himself from the treaty negotiations because, it was believed by some, he assumed that clear independence would not be the result. Consequently, he opposed the Anglo-Irish Treaty*, leading the struggle against Michael Collins and the Provisional Government. As President in the 1930s, he abolished the oath to the Crown and in 1937 the Irish Republic was established, a move declared constitutionally binding in 1948.

Further Reading

Tim Pat Coogan (1993). *De Valera: Long Fellow, Long Shadow* (London, Hutchinson)

Owen D. Edwards (1987). *Eamon de Valera* (Washington, DC, Catholic University of America Press)

Dilke, Sir Charles W. (1843–1911). An Imperial publicist, Dilke was educated in law at Cambridge, where he was also President of the Cambridge University Society, and then proceeded to travel the world. He developed his ideas about the British Empire while touring, and having returned to England published them in 1868 in a book entitled *Greater Britain*, a disquisition on the nature of Imperial power and how best to exercise it. He was, however, a 'Radical Imperialist,' arguing that British overseas rule was essentially benevolent but that it needed the constant hand of reform. That same year he was elected MP, eventually rising in the Liberal Party and becoming Under-Secretary at the Foreign Office in 1880 and gaining a place in Gladstone's* Cabinet as President of the Local Government Board from 1882 until 1885. A protracted divorce and seduction scandal, of which he was likely innocent, almost ruined him politically after 1886 (scuttling realistic hopes of becoming Prime Minister) and so he continued his inveterate travelling, including a tour of India*. In 1890, Dilke published a two-volume sequel to his first book, *Problems of Greater Britain*. Re-elected in 1892, but never again holding office, Dilke continued to focus on Imperial issues for the rest of his Parliamentary career.

Further Reading

Roy Jenkins (1996). *Dilke: A Victorian Tragedy* (London, Macmillan)
A.N. Wilson (2002). *The Victorians* (London, Hutchinson)

Dinesen, Isak (Karen Blixen) (1885–1962). A Danish writer who penned one of the best-known evocations of life in early colonial Kenya*, Dinesen was the pseudonym of Karen Blixen who arrived in British East Africa* with her Swedish husband, Bror Blixen, in 1914 and established a coffee farm near Nairobi in what is now the suburb of Karen, later named for her. Initially excluded by British colonial society there (although when her younger brother, Thomas Dinesen, won the Victoria Cross fighting for the Canadian Army during the First World War* her status was transformed), and never successful as a farmer, she finally sold her land and left the colony in 1931, never to return. In 1937, she published *Out of Africa*, a memoir of her years in Kenya, which included much contact with early British colonizers and administrators, including Lord Delamere* and the aristocratic hunter Denys Finch Hatton, with whom she fell in love but who was killed in a flying accident just before she left Africa to return to her home in Denmark. Not long before Dinesen's death she published *Shadows on the Grass* (1960), a final memoir of her life in colonial Kenya.

Further Reading

Isak Dinesen (1981). *Letters from Africa*. Frans Lasson, ed. (Chicago, University of Chicago Press)
Judith Thurman (1983). *Isak Dinesen: The Life of Karen Blixen* (New York, Viking Penguin)

Disraeli, Benjamin, Earl of Beaconsfield (1804–81). Two-time British Prime Minister and champion of Empire, Disraeli was born into a Jewish literary family in London. His education did not include any of the great public schools or Oxbridge, but combined with being baptized in the Church of England as a youth, he set his sights on high social and political position anyhow. Initially, in the 1820s, he sought to establish himself as a writer like his father, Isaac D'Israeli. But he failed to do so, and after running up enormous gambling debts he left England for an extensive tour of the Near East, spending considerable time in Turkey. Beginning in the 1830s, he sought election as a Tory to the House of Commons, succeeding finally in 1837. For the next thirty years he rode the vicissitudes of Parliamentary and personal life, breaking with Peel in 1846 over Free Trade, endorsing reform, and continuing to write novels, especially his commercially and artistically successful 'Political Trilogy.' Briefly Prime Minister in 1868 before losing to his archnemesis Gladstone,* Disraeli won election in 1874 and served as Prime Minister until 1880. Earlier, in 1872, he had spoken strongly of Britain's Imperial duty and destiny at the Crystal Palace, and during his second ministry enlarged the Empire's territory, as well as purchasing almost half the shares of the Suez Canal Company for the British government in 1875. The next year he buttressed his warm relationship with Queen Victoria through introducing the Royal Titles Bill, which named her Empress of India. In the run-up to the 1880 General Election, Gladstone attacked Disraeli and the Tories for their 'earth hunger,' as he chose to call their brand of Imperialism. Such denunciation struck a chord with the electorate and Gladstone went on to victory. Disraeli, while really no more 'Imperial' than Gladstone would be in policy, nonetheless made the Conservatives the Party of Empire for a least a generation, a mantle assumed easily by his successor Lord Salisbury* in the 1890s.

Further Reading
Robert Blake (1967). *Disraeli* (New York, St Martin's Press)
C.C. Eldridge (1996). *Disraeli and the Rise of a New Imperialism* (Cardiff, University of Wales Press)

Dominica. Located in the Caribbean, Columbus landed on Dominica in 1493, but fierce resistance by its Carib inhabitants precluded settlement. The

English made an attempt to settle in 1627 and failed, followed by the French in 1635. The fall of New France in 1763 saw the reversion of the island to the British and it gained colony status in 1805. Undisputed British control over Dominica came in 1815 with the defeat of Napoleon and the signing of the Treaty of Paris. A volcanic, mountainous island, Dominica depended on agriculture, especially bananas, as the basis of its marginal economy. In 1838, in the aftermath of the emancipation of the slaves, Dominica became the first British Caribbean colony to have a black-controlled legislature. Later, in the twentieth century, Dominica became part of the short-lived British West Indies Federation* and afterwards, in 1967, achieved self-government. Independence as a republic within the Commonwealth came in 1978.

Further Reading

Lennox Honeychurch (1995). *The Dominica Story: A History of the Island* (London, Macmillan)

Michel-Rolph Trouillot (1988) *Peasants and Capital: Dominica in the World Economy* (Baltimore, Johns Hopkins University Press)

Dominion. First used in 1867 to describe the status of the new Canadian Confederation and drawn from a Biblical (Psalms 72:8) allusion, Dominion came to be used to designate those colonies that had achieved self-government, even though some, like the 'Commonwealth of Australia,' styled themselves otherwise. The 1907 Colonial Conference determined that all self-governing Imperial territories would henceforth hold the status of 'British Dominion,' and the Statute of Westminster* passed in 1931 enshrined the concept.

Further Reading

Stephen Constantine (1990). *Emigrants and Empire: British Settlement in the Dominions between the Wars* (Manchester, Manchester University Press)

John Darwin, 'A Third British Empire? The Dominion Idea in Imperial Politics.' In *The Oxford History of the British Empire: The Twentieth Century* (1999). Judith M. Brown and Wm. Roger Louis, eds (Oxford, Oxford University Press), 64–87

Durbar. A Hindi word meaning royal court celebration, durbars were held in Delhi three times in the history of the Raj*. In 1877, the first durbar was held in order to proclaim and celebrate Victoria's* elevation to Queen-Empress. The coronation durbar of her son and successor, Edward VII*, was held in 1903, although the King-Emperor himself and Alexandra, the Queen-Empress, were not in attendance. A spectacular event located outside the city and given minute planning by Curzon*, the durbar lasted for two weeks and required its own railway, electrical system, and postal service. The last of the three durbars took place in 1911, when for the first time a reigning British monarch visited India. George V* and Queen Mary landed at Bombay, where a grand ceremonial arch, the Gateway of India, was constructed. They proceeded to go on a royal progress through the country that lasted several weeks and included visiting historic ruins, holding audiences of maharajas, and tiger-shooting. No other British monarch visited India while it was part of the Empire.

Further Reading

David Gilmour (2003). *Curzon: Imperial Statesman* (New York, Farrar, Straus & Giroux)

Denis Judd (2004). *The Lion and the Tiger: The Rise and Fall of the British Raj, 1600–1947* (Oxford, Oxford University Press)

Durham Report. One of the most influential examinations of governance in the history of the Empire, the *Report on the Affairs of British North America* (1839) fundamentally re-organized the way in which nineteenth-century colonials related to the mother-country. In 1838, the Whig government of Lord Melbourne appointed the Earl of Durham (John Lambton) Governor-General and sent him to Upper and Lower Canada in order to investigate the causes of the rebellions that had occurred in each colony the year before and to make recommendations for their constitutional future. Durham was a reformer and already had spent considerable time examining the way in which Britain governed its colonial subjects. Arriving in May 1838, he spent just four months in British North America, enough time, however, to observe that there were 'two nations warring in the bosom of a single state.' He recommended that the two provinces be unified in order to produce a common sense of citizenship, and that responsible government – the idea that the executive needed to be directly accountable to the legislature – be implemented. In 1840, the Canada Act was duly passed, bringing about the union of the two colonies and creating the Province of Canada. Responsible government took additional time to enact, but by 1849 it too was in place. The Canadian example, whereby power would flow from the Imperial centre to the colonial periphery, would prove to be greatly influential within the Empire in the years to come.

Further Reading

Janet Ajzenstat (1988). *The Political Thought of Lord Durham* (Kingston, ON, McGill-Queen's University Press)

Phillip A. Buckner (1985). *The Transition to Responsible Government: British Policy in British North America, 1815–1850* (Westport, CT, Greenwood)

E

East Africa Company (see Imperial British East Africa Company)

East Africa Protectorate (see Kenya)

East India Company. Established by Queen Elizabeth I in 1600 near the end of her reign, 'The Company of Merchants of London Trading into the East Indies' became the main commercial instrument whereby trade and rule led to a British Indian Empire. Throughout the seventeenth century the EIC secured footholds in Mughal India, ultimately establishing three trading 'Presidencies' at Calcutta, Bombay, and Madras. Cotton, silk, indigo, dye, saltpetre, and tea were the EIC's mainstays, and in effect it maintained a monopoly over all Anglo-Indian trade. Dutch, Portuguese, and French trading interests were all present on the Indian sub-continent too, but beginning in the 1740s the EIC – backed by its own army – busily began to eliminate its rivals from the lucrative Indian market. The symbolic turning point came in 1757 when Clive* defeated the Nawab of Bengal*, a client of the French, at Plassey*, ensuring that Bengal*, then the richest region in India, fell under exclusive EIC control. For the next century, the Company dominated Indian life. It pushed its way into the emergent and highly lucrative opium trade with China, while many of its highest-ranking officers became extraordinarily wealthy. They used such wealth to rise in British society, many of them entering Parliament. The British government, increasingly concerned that the EIC was becoming too independently powerful, passed a pair of East India Company Acts (1773 and 1784) to regulate its operations, especially to impress upon the Company that sovereignty over British affairs in India lay with the Crown alone. Still, despite much resentment at home and the celebrated impeachment trial of Warren Hastings*, first Governor-General of Bengal*, in the 1780s, the Company grew apace as its sturdy ships, the East Indiamen, plied the world's oceans. Its (India) trade monopoly was overturned by Parliament in 1813, but by the middle of the nineteenth century the EIC's rule held perhaps 20 per cent of the world's people in its commercial thrall, and extended over most of India*, Burma*, Malaya*, Singapore*, and Hong Kong*. The iron fist behind the Company's trading pre-eminence in India was the 100,000-strong sepoy army, officered by graduates of the EIC's military academy in Surrey, later known as Haileybury College*. But many of those same sepoys would prove to be the Company's ultimate downfall when they, increasingly agitated by Dalhousie's* reforms, rebelled in 1857, sparking the Indian Mutiny*. As a result, the following year the Company was dissolved and the passage of the Government of India Act transferred all of its assets, its army, and complete control of British India to the Crown. The era of the Raj had begun.

Further Reading

John Keay (1991). *The Honourable East India Company: A History of the English East India Company* (London, HarperCollins)

Sudipta Sen (1998). *Empire of Free Trade: The East India Company and the making of the Colonial Marketplace* (Philadelphia, University of Pennsylvania Press)

Eden, Anthony, 1st Earl of Avon (1897–1977). British Prime Minister and known best for presiding over the Suez Crisis*, symbolizing for most the final decline of the British Empire, Eden was born in County Durham and educated at Eton and Christ Church, Oxford*. He served with distinction in the British Army during the First World War* and entered Parliament for the Conservatives in 1923. He achieved Cabinet rank in 1931 as Under-Secretary of State for Foreign Affairs and in 1935 became Foreign Secretary, holding office until resigning in 1938 over Neville Chamberlain's policy of appeasement. Churchill* made him Foreign Secretary in 1940, and again during his last administration from 1951 until 1955, during which he was also Deputy Prime Minister and was knighted. Churchill's natural successor, he became Prime Minister upon his chief's retirement in 1955 and led the Conservatives to an election victory later that year. In Egypt*, about which Eden knew much, the increasing nationalism embodied by President Gamal Abdel Nasser led to the country's takeover of the Suez Canal*, a move opposed strenuously by both Britain and France. Negotiations failed to solve the crisis and in October 1956 an Anglo-French-Israeli force invaded Egypt and occupied the Canal Zone. Eden expected the endorsement and help of the United States. However, when it did not come, Britain's weakened position as a great power in the Middle East was exposed and British troops ultimately were withdrawn. The Suez débâcle broke Eden's already tenuous health and in January 1957, after intense pressure from leading Cabinet ministers, he resigned. His reputation destroyed (although recently partially rehabilitated), he lived in retirement for twenty years until his death.

Further Reading

Sidney Aster (1976). *Anthony Eden* (London, Weidenfeld & Nicolson)

D.R. Thorpe (2003). *Eden: The Life and Times of Anthony Eden, First Earl of Avon, 1897–1977* (London, Chatto & Windus)

Edward VII (1841–1910). Becoming King-Emperor in 1901 upon the death of Queen Victoria*, Edward VII had been heir to the throne for longer than anyone else in British history. As a young man he travelled extensively within the Empire, including a celebrated progress through pre-Confederation Canada* in 1860. His eventual coronation in 1902 was celebrated throughout the Empire, in no place more grandly than in Delhi at the durbar* organized by the Viceroy, Lord Curzon*. Edward reigned over the Empire at a time when it was nearing its maximum territorial size. He was highly concerned with German naval expansion and arms competition, and feared that war between the two countries was likely. He took an active hand in pushing for an increase in the size of the Royal Navy but his death in 1910 cut short his long-term impact on Imperial affairs.

Further Reading

Roy Hattersley (2004). *The Edwardians* (London, Little, Brown)

Philip Magnus (1964). *King Edward VII: A Biography* (London, John Murray)

Egypt. Occupied by the British from 1882 until 1922, although apart from the final eight of those years not formally a member of the Empire. The period of the Napoleonic Wars had first brought Britain to the ancient land of the Pharaohs. France's short-lived control of Egypt lasted just three years, 1798–1801. Nelson's* victory at the Battle of the Nile* hastened their departure and with it came a brief six-year British suzerainty before Egypt reverted to Ottoman control in 1807. By the late 1870s, however, Egypt was in the midst of a financial crisis as the foreign controllers of its economy began to lose faith in the regime of the Khedive Ismail* as it struggled with the cost of the recently completed Suez Canal* and with the increasingly strident demands of Egyptian nationalists who were intent on expelling the foreigners, especially the British and the French. In the summer of 1882 the British under Gladstone* chose to bombard and invade the country following a revolt by the nationalist Colonel Urabi Pasha*. In short order, the British succeeded in their military operations and by mid-September a British Controller-General was in place. In 1883, Sir Evelyn Baring (later Earl of Cromer*) was appointed Consul-General, a position he would maintain until 1907 and in the process do much to shape Egypt's sustained encounter with the modern world. Many see the British occupation of Egypt as initiating the Partition of Africa*. In any event, together the British and the Egyptians maintained joint sovereignty over the Sudan*, the vast desert territory located to Egypt's immediate south. Anglo-Egyptian Sudan existed as a condominium from 1899 until 1956. For Egypt itself, Britain's promise of eventual independence made during the First World War* led to the establishment of the sovereign Kingdom of Egypt in 1922.

Further Reading

Peter Mansfield (1971). *The British in Egypt* (London, Weidenfeld & Nicolson)

Robert L. Tignor (1966). *Modernization and British Colonial Rule in Egypt, 1882–1914* (Princeton, Princeton University Press)

Elgar, Sir Edward (1857–1934). Elgar was the most important composer in creating a musical mythology of Empire. Born in 1857 in Worcestershire, he was educated locally, which included piano lessons. By the time he was ten he had gained a local reputation as something of a musical prodigy and later, in 1879, he became music director of the County Lunatic Asylum in nearby Powick, whose progressive doctors endorsed the therapeutic effects of music. In 1889, Elgar married Alice Walker and moved immediately to London, inspired by Alice's insistence that he give up teaching and any other pursuits that would distract him from the main task of forging a career as a composer of real worth. Significant works followed, the most important of these – because it introduced his name to the wider British public – being *Imperial March*, composed for the Queen's 1897 diamond jubilee. Over the next ten years Elgar would reach the zenith of his popularity, becoming the musical embodiment of the British nation at the peak of its world position. The first such representative work was *Caractacus* (1898). To Elgar, the Empire was a high and noble calling, a spreader of justice and peace and expressed a British world-view that had near-complete contemporary currency. In 1901, he wrote the first of what would become the five *Pomp and Circumstance* marches. The No. 1 march assured Elgar's popularity and it reinforced a style that was fast making him the clear musical expositor of Empire. Just the year before *Pomp and Circumstance* was written, Elgar had attended the premiere of *The Dream of Gerontius*, in which he had set to music the poem of the same name by John Henry Newman. The piece may not have been an expressly Imperial work, but its genesis in Elgar's mind had come from that greatest of Imperial heroes, General Charles Gordon*. During Gordon's last stand in the Sudan* he had had Newman's poem with him and in its margins had scribbled various words of endorsement and interpretation. Gordon's copy of the poem, brought back from the destroyed Governor's residence in Khartoum by the ill-fated relief mission in 1885, made the rounds of late-Victorian society in a set-piece example of contemporary memorialization. In this way Elgar, who had received a copy of it as a gift at his wedding in 1889, apotheosized the poem and in 1898 began a sketch of a Gordon symphony. In the end, the proposed Gordon symphony morphed largely into *The Dream of Gerontius*. For Elgar, his Imperial compositions continued apace. In 1902, he wrote the *Coronation Ode* for the new King-

Emperor, Edward VII*, and was recognized formally two years later with a knighthood. Even more explicitly Imperial, however, was Elgar's composition *The Crown of India*, for the 1911 Delhi Durbar*. That year he was rewarded with the Order of Merit. In 1924, Elgar conducted mass choirs in the singing of *Land of Hope and Glory* at the British Empire Exhibition*. Later during the exhibition his new eight-song *Pageant of Empire* and the *Empire March* were performed. But the musician of Empire was nearing the end. In 1931, he was created a baronet. He died three years later as the musical tribune of the Imperial British people.

Further Reading
Robert Anderson (1993). *Elgar* (London, J.M. Dent)
Jeffrey Richards (2001). *Imperialism and Music: Britain 1876–1953* (Manchester, Manchester University Press)

Elizabeth II (1926–). Born when the Empire was at its largest, Queen Elizabeth II presided over the period of its eclipse some forty years later. Upon the death of her father, King George VI, in 1952, Elizabeth acceded to the throne. She did so while on a royal visit to Kenya*, en route to Australia* and New Zealand*. The first years of her reign saw a colonial crisis in Kenya* (Mau Mau*), followed by the sustained rise of African nationalism elsewhere. The second decade of the so-called 'new Elizabethan age' saw the decolonization of most of British Africa, while the British Caribbean did likewise. As Head of the Commonwealth, the Queen maintains a tangible link to her great-grandmother Victoria's era of the Queen-Empress, and as Head of State in countries such as Canada* and Australia* she continues to exercise a strong constitutional and symbolic role. The early to middle years of her reign were marked by the struggle over Southern Rhodesia's* 1965 Unilateral Declaration of Independence* and the consequent drive to Zimbabwe's* independence in 1980. In 1997, the sun finally set on the British Empire in the Far East when Hong Kong* was turned over to the People's Republic of China. Queen Elizabeth continues to travel extensively, especially in the countries of the former Empire, and in so doing has fulfilled her 1947 pledge to dedicate her life to 'the service of our great Imperial Commonwealth.'

Further Reading

Robert Lacey (2002). *Monarch: The Life and Reign of Elizabeth II* (New York, Free Press)

Ben Pimlott (2007). *The Queen: Elizabeth II and the Monarchy* (New York, HarperCollins)

Emin Pasha (1840–92). The adopted name of Eduard Schnitzer, a Silesian of German-Jewish heritage, Emin Pasha became the focus of a relief expedition headed by Henry Morton Stanley* which succeeded in rescuing him from entrapment in Mahdist Sudan in 1888. Years earlier he had qualified as a medical doctor in Berlin, but not being allowed to practice in Germany, he left for Constantinople and for some years lived a peripatetic life, changing his name and perfecting his ability in a number of languages, including Turkish and Greek. In 1876, Emin joined the staff of General Gordon* at Khartoum, who sent him into the vast southern reaches of Equatoria and beyond as a personal envoy. In 1878, he was appointed Governor of the province. However, he became cut off once the Mahdist revolt began a few years later, which culminated with Gordon's death at Khartoum in January 1885. Emin's imperilled position evoked considerable interest and sympathy in Europe, the result of which was Stanley's rescue mission. Emin was unconvinced of his own peril, however, and was reluctant to leave for the East African coast with Stanley, only finally doing so in 1889 and arriving in Bagamoyo to great acclaim. But from there he refused to budge and Stanley returned to Britain without him. He later entered the service of the German East Africa Company and shortly thereafter was killed by Arab slave traders.

Further Reading

Daniel Liebowitz (2005). *The Last Expedition: Stanley's Mad Journey through the Congo* (New York, W.W. Norton)

Olivia Manning (1985). *The Remarkable Expedition: The Story of Stanley's Rescue of Emin Pasha from Equatorial Africa* (New York, Atheneum)

Empire Day. In 1899, in Hamilton, Ontario*, the first Empire Day was held. Celebrated by schoolchildren, it coincided with the marking of Queen Victoria's birthday, 24 May, which had been a holiday in Ontario* (Upper

Canada/Canada West) since 1845 and would become a Canadian national holiday in 1901. Near the outset of his reign in 1902, and at the conclusion of the Second Boer War*, King Edward VII* took up the Canadian example, proposing that Empire Day be celebrated as a mark of thanks to those colonies who had supported Britain in its war against the Boers*. Thereafter, throughout the Empire, schoolchildren would salute the Union Jack and sing *God Save the Queen* and *Jerusalem*. In 1958, as the Empire dissolved, British Commonwealth Day became its new name, and in 1966 the appellation British was dropped and its date changed to the second Monday in March. It has since faded away almost completely, although Queen Elizabeth* continues to mark it with a service at Westminster Abbey and through a message sent to the youth of the Commonwealth*. In Canada *, alone among the colonies of the former Empire, the original day, 24 May, continues to be celebrated as Victoria Day. It marks the traditional start of the Canadian summer.

Further Reading

Carl Berger (1970). *The Sense of Power: Studies in the Ideas of Canadian Imperialism, 1867–1914* (Toronto, University of Toronto Press)

Stephen Heathorn (2000). *For Home, Country, and Race: Constructing Gender, Class, and Englishness in the Elementary School, 1880–1914* (Toronto, University of Toronto Press)

Empire Games. In 1911, a Festival of Empire was held at the Crystal Palace, long since removed from its original Hyde Park site and re-located in suburban London. The event included a number of athletic challenges competed in by teams from Britain, Australia*, New Zealand*, South Africa*, and Canada*. The First World War* intervened but in 1930, and building on the example of the 1911 event, the first 'British Empire Games' was held in Hamilton, Ontario*. By 1954, the word Commonwealth had been added to the title and in 1970 the word Empire was dropped. In 1978, the British designation was removed from the name and ever since they have been simply the Commonwealth Games. Results are dominated by the largest and wealthiest members of the Commonwealth such as Britain (England, Scotland, Wales and Northern Ireland), Australia, and Canada, but the inclusive nature of the event, competitions in sports played principally in Commonwealth countries such as lawn bowls and netball, and to some extent the shared history of Crown rule, make it a unique occasion on the world sporting calendar every four years.

Further Reading

Cleve Dheensaw (1994). *The Commonwealth Games: The First 60 Years, 1930–1990* (Victoria, BC, Orca Book Publishers)

Bob Phillips (2000). *Honour of Empire, Glory of Sport: The History of Athletics at the Commonwealth Games* (Manchester, Parrs Wood)

Empire Marketing Board. In 1926, the Baldwin Conservative government formed the EMB under the chairmanship of Leo Amery*, Colonial and Dominions Secretary. The intention was to promote intra-Empire trade and its slogan was 'Buy Empire.' The Board focussed its efforts on supporting scientific research and undertaking economic analysis by which to promote trade within the Empire. Its publicity arm was especially active, organizing poster campaigns, lectures, radio talks, and exhibitions. It even sponsored 'Empire Shopping Weeks' and developed its own film unit, directed by John Grierson, who would go on to become a legendary documentary filmmaker. The advent of the Great Depression reinforced colonial protectionism, however, and the 1932 Imperial Conference* in Ottawa, which introduced a system of Imperial Preference in trade, spelled the EMB's demise in 1933.

Further Reading

Stephen Constantine (1986). *Buy & Build: The Advertising Posters of the Empire Marketing Board* (London, HMSO)

Chandrika Kaul, ed. (2006). *Media and the British Empire* (London, Palgrave Macmillan)

Equiano, Olaudah (*c.*1745–97). Equiano became a prominent voice – and the only African one – in the debate over the abolition of slavery in Britain during the late eighteenth century. Born in modern-day Nigeria, he was enslaved domestically as a child and then later sold abroad, arriving in Barbados* in the late 1750s, from where he was sent to Virginia. He then became the personal servant of a Royal Navy captain, who saw to it that he became literate and was baptized in the Church of England. Subsequently, Equiano was acquired by an American trader, from whom he eventually purchased his freedom. In the mid-1770s it is believed that he settled in England, where he began to support the abolitionist cause. In 1789, his autobiography was published: *The Interesting Narrative of the Life of Olaudah Equiano or Gustavus Vassa the African*. The book recounted the horrors of the slave trade, especially the Middle Passage across the Atlantic. It sold briskly, making him well known and ultimately financially secure, and helped to popularize the abolitionist cause. Both his writing and his public speaking made him an important ally of William Wilberforce*, but he died before seeing the abolitionist cause succeed with the outlawing of the slave trade within the Empire in 1807.

Further Reading

Vincent Carretta (2005). *Equiano, the African: Biography of a Self-Made Man* (Athens, University of Georgia Press)

James Walvin (2007). *The Trader, the Owner, the Slave: Parallel Lives in the Age of Slavery* (London, Jonathan Cape)

F

Fabian Colonial Bureau. Created in 1940 as a department of the Fabian Society, the Fabian Colonial Bureau effectively functioned as the Labour Party's research wing on colonial affairs. Co-founded by Arthur Creech Jones* and Rita Hinden, a South African economist, the Bureau's socialist analysis of colonial issues thrust it into Parliamentary and popular debates over decolonization, especially after the Labour Party came to power in 1945. Its influence on government policy, particularly when Jones served as Colonial Secretary from 1946 until 1950, was strong. The Bureau's journal, ultimately known as *Venture*, developed a wide readership in the post-war years. In 1958, the Bureau was re-named the Commonwealth Bureau. A few years later, in the aftermath of the rapid decolonization of the African Empire in the early 1960s, it was dissolved.

Further Reading
Ronald Hyam, ed. (1992). *The Labour Government and the End of Empire, 1945–51*, 4 vols (London, British Documents on the End of Empire Project)
Daniel R. Smith (1985). *The Influence of the Fabian Colonial Bureau on the Independence Movement in Tanganyika* (Athens, OH, Ohio University, Center for International Studies)

Falkland Islands. A self-governing British Overseas Territory located in the South Atlantic Ocean near the Argentine coast, the Falkland Islands have been in British hands in an almost unbroken fashion since 1771. Settlement, based on fishing and limited farming, was difficult, however, and three years later the Falklands were abandoned, only to be firmly reclaimed in 1832 when Argentina attempted to declare the islands part of its territory. In that year Britain made the Falklands a Crown Colony and throughout the nineteenth and twentieth centuries resisted regular Argentine overtures to claim the 'Malvinas' Islands, as they were called in Spanish. So rancorous was this claim that in 1982, in a reprise of a Victorian-style colonial war, the Argentinians invaded and wrested control of the Falklands from the British. In response, the Conservative government of Margaret Thatcher* sent a force of 6,000 troops, fighter aircraft, and warships to challenge Argentina's occupation. Within weeks the Falklands had been re-captured in an exercise that at least one London tabloid described as the 'Empire Strikes Back!'

Further Reading

Mary Cawkell (2001). *The History of the Falkland Islands* (Shropshire, Anthony Nelson)

Lawrence Freedman (2005). *The Official History of the Falklands Campaign* (London, Routledge, Taylor & Francis Group)

Famine. In British India* and colonial Africa, famine occurred with devastating regularity. Beginning in 1860, Bengal* was struck by five periods of famine, the worst two being 1896–7 and 1900. It is estimated that close to six million people perished in these latter famines alone. At nearly the same time in South-Central Africa, famine ravaged the Maasai* and Kikuyu* peoples. The causes of these famines vary, but drought combined with the re-orientation of farmers away from the production of staple foods toward cash crops is prominent. Maladministration was also a factor in exacerbating the effects of famine, such as in India during the Second World War*. Famine within the Empire aroused considerable sympathy in Britain, reaching a peak during Curzon's* Indian Viceroyalty.

Further Reading

David Hall-Matthews (2005). *Peasants, Famine and the State in Colonial Western India* (New York, Palgrave Macmillan)

John Iliffe (1987). *The African Poor: A History* (Cambridge, Cambridge University Press)

83

Farrell, J.G. (1935–79). A British novelist known best for his 'Empire Trilogy' of *Troubles* (1970), *The Siege of Krishnapur* (1973), and *The Singapore Grip* (1978), Farrell became one of the most important practitioners of post-colonial fiction. The three books revolve thematically around the collapse of Imperial power while set in three distinct times and places in the history of the Empire: Ireland around 1920; India during the 1857 Mutiny; and Southeast Asia between the First and Second World Wars*. Recognized both during his lifetime and since his tragic early death as a master novelist, *The Siege of Krishnapur* won Farrell the 1973 Booker Prize.

Further Reading

J.G. Farrell (2004). *The Siege of Krishnapur* (New York, New York Review Books)

Lavinia Greacen (1999). *J.G. Farrell: The Making of a Writer* (London, Bloomsbury)

Fashoda. Located in the Sudan*, Fashoda was the site of the capstone event in Britain's re-capturing of the country in 1898 and a defining episode in the Partition of Africa*. In that year, Lord Kitchener* led a British force to Khartoum that overthrew the Mahdiya*, which had been ruling Sudan* since the defeat of the Anglo-Egyptian garrison and the death of General Gordon* in 1885. The decisive battle was fought just outside the capital city at Omdurman*. Once having restored British suzerainty, Kitchener continued up the Nile, arriving at Fashoda only to discover the presence of Major Jean-Baptiste Marchand, who had trekked from Brazzaville in the Congo in order to claim a French Protectorate over Fashoda and the surrounding region. Kitchener immediately disputed Marchand's claim, and indeed asserted a British counter-claim to all of the Sudan based on right of conquest. For a few weeks, war between Britain and France seemed likely as the British Prime Minister, Lord Salisbury*, demanded that the French renounce their claim and withdraw. The Royal Navy was put on a war alert and doing so had the desired effect: the French reluctantly complied with Salisbury's demand and withdrew. In 1899, France formally renounced all claims to the Nile Valley, yielding a singular, bloodless victory for the British Empire in North and Central Africa.

Further Reading

David Levering Lewis (1987). *The Race to Fashoda: European Colonialism and African Resistance in the Scramble for Africa* (New York, Weidenfeld & Nicolson)

Patricia Wright (1972). *Conflict on the Nile: The Fashoda Incident of 1898* (London, Heinemann)

Fiji. An archipelago in the south-west Pacific of some three hundred islands, one-third of which are permanently inhabited. Captain James Cook* landed at Fiji in 1774. It was not until a century later, however, in 1874 that the British made Fiji a Crown Colony. Sugar was the mainstay of the economy, worked by native Fijians and imported Indian contract labourers. Fiji achieved independence in 1970, choosing to remain in the Commonwealth* as the Dominion of Fiji. In 1987, however, Fiji proclaimed itself a republic and eventually left the Commonwealth*, only to re-join it a decade later. As recognized by the Great Council of Chiefs, Queen Elizabeth* remains the Great Chief of Fiji.

Further Reading

Brij V. Lal (1992). *Broken Waves: A History of Fiji in the Twentieth Century* (Honolulu, University of Hawaii Press)

Deryck Scarr (1984). *Fiji: A Short History* (Sydney, Allen & Unwin)

First Fleet. The essential founding event in the history of Australia*, the First Fleet sailed from Portsmouth in the spring of 1787, landing at Botany Bay in January 1788. The journey had lasted 252 days and had covered approximately 15,000 miles (24,000 kilometres), remarkably without the loss of a single one of the nine ships, two of which were converted slavers. The First Fleet delivered almost 1,400 British immigrants, just over half of which were convicts punished with the sentence of transport-ation, to Australia. They formed the kernel of the new Australian popu-lation and the colony of New South Wales*, and their number was added to quickly by a Second Fleet from Britain in 1790 and another the year after that.

Further Reading

Geoffrey Bolton (1988). *Spoils and Spoilers: Australians Make Their Environment, 1788–1980* (Sydney, University of Sydney Press)

Robert Hughes (1987). *The Fatal Shore: A History of the Transportation of Convicts to Australia, 1787–1868* (London, Pan)

First World War (1914–18). When the long-predicted war in Europe broke out in August 1914, the Empires of the various great states of Europe were immediately ranged against one another in different parts of the globe. At the same time, the British Empire called into action men and materiel from its far-flung colonies, especially Canada*, Australia*, New Zealand*, South Africa*, and India*. Constitutionally, Britain's declaration of war against Germany on 4 August 1914 bound the members of the Empire to fight, and so they did. About 250,000 troops from around the Empire died in the war, approximately half their number coming from Canada and Australia. Meanwhile, on the frontiers of Empire, especially in Africa where British and German colonies sometimes shared borders, fighting broke out quickly and was sustained throughout the war – in East Africa even lasting beyond the Armistice in November 1918 as some did not receive word of the war's end in Europe until two weeks after it was over. The British Empire's territorial size was added to by the war through the creation of the League of Nations mandates system, which notably transferred German East Africa (Tanganyika*) to British control, as well as other territories.

Further Reading

Martin Gilbert (2004). *The First World War: A Complete History* (New York, Henry Holt)

Hew Strachan (2004). *The First World War in Africa* (Oxford, Oxford University Press)

Football (Association and Rugby). Exceeding even cricket in popularity as a sporting export of Empire were the two kinds of football developed in the British Isles, Association and Rugby (both Union and League). The Football Association, with its 'Laws of the Game', was established in London in 1863, reflecting the rapid development of the domestic game, especially in the north of England. Football was taken abroad by immigrants within a generation and grew in popularity, especially in British Africa. Known as 'soccer' in most parts of the Empire, it was slower to catch on in Australia* and New Zealand*, and slower still in Canada*, where ice hockey dominated, followed by Canadian football, baseball, and basketball. Rugby football originated in the 1820s at Rugby School in Warwickshire and began to be played at other schools and then at Oxbridge by mid-century. The Rugby Football Union was established in London in 1871 and the Rugby League (with slightly different rules, such as fewer players per side) in 1895. By that time the game was being played in various colonies throughout the Empire, particularly in New Zealand where it enjoyed great popularity among the Maori*. It rapidly gained popularity in Australia and South Africa too. In Canada, the home-grown style of football was an amalgam of Rugby and American football and precluded Rugby's growth, but the first games played in the country date from the 1880s. In the early twentieth century, the British Lions touring side was challenged by the New Zealand 'All Blacks' and the 'Springboks' from South Africa, and by the waning days of Empire Rugby, like soccer before it, had become a world sport.

Further Reading

Adrian Harvey (2005). *Football: The First Hundred Years* (London, Routledge)
Huw Richards (2006). *A Game for Hooligans: The History of Rugby Union* (Edinburgh, Mainstream)

Franklin, Sir John (1786–1847). Explorer of the Canadian Arctic and a sometime colonial governor, Franklin was born in Lincolnshire and joined the Royal Navy as a fifteen-year old midshipman. He fought in the Battle of Trafalgar* aboard HMS *Bellerophon* – the ship that later would transport Napoleon to his South Atlantic exile on the island of St Helena. After the arrival of peace in Europe in 1815, Franklin became closely involved in exploration. Beginning in 1818, he led three expeditions to the Arctic, the sum of which was to see him knighted in 1829. Not long thereafter he became Lieutenant-Governor of Van Diemen's Land*, serving for nine years until 1843. But the event for which Franklin is best known is the search for the elusive Northwest Passage*, which had bedevilled British mariners since before the days of Cook*. Sponsored by the Admiralty, Captain Franklin set out in May 1845 with two small ships (HMS *Erebus* and HMS *Terror*), determined to crack the mystery of a northern route to Asia. He was never seen in England again. His route took him to Baffin Bay and Lancaster Sound, but after wintering on Beechey Island his ships got trapped in sea-ice off King William Island in September 1846. Pneumonia, perhaps tuberculosis, scurvy, starvation, and, as was discovered much later, lead poisoning from badly soldered metal cans containing provisions, contributed to the complete loss of life – 128 men. Franklin himself is thought to have lived until the summer of 1847, and many of his men – wild with hunger and resorting to cannibalism – until the next year. Attempted rescue missions at the time demanded by his wife, Lady John Franklin, and modern scientific expeditions much later, were able to piece together the fate of the expedition, most clearly in the 1980s when the bodies of three crew members were exhumed from their shallow graves on Beechey Island, their features almost perfectly intact because of the refrigeration effect of the year-round permafrost. Franklin's peregrinations made important contributions to Canadian Arctic geography, but the Northwest Passage itself continued to prove resistant until the successful expedition of the Norwegian Roald Amundsen in 1903.

Further Reading

Owen Beattie and John Geiger (2004). *Frozen in Time: The Fate of the Franklin Expedition* (Vancouver, Greystone Books)

Ann Savours (1999). *The Search for the Northwest Passage* (New York, St Martin's Press)

Frere, Sir Henry Bartle, 1st Baronet (1815–84). Imperial administrator in India and Africa, Frere was Welsh-born and educated at Haileybury*. In 1834, he went to Bombay as a writer in the Civil Service and most of his career was spent in India, including a decade as Commissioner of the Sindh*, during which time he created the modern Indian postal service. In 1877, after having been created a baronet, Frere was made Governor of the Cape Colony* and First High Commissioner of South Africa*. The next three years were a trial for Frere, however, as his idea of a British southern Africa federation was not yet broadly appealing and his aspirations to become Governor-General of such a union foundered on the rocks of the struggle with the Zulu* and with the First Boer War*, for which he was unjustly blamed. His career ended desultorily in 1880 upon the election of the Liberal (Gladstone) government.

Further Reading

John Martineau (1895). *The Life and Correspondence of the Right Hon. Sir Bartle Frere* (London, John Murray)

Rekha Ranade (1990). *Sir Bartle Frere and his Times: A Study of his Bombay Years* (New Delhi, Mittal)

Furse, Sir Ralph D. (1887–1973). The 'father of the modern Colonial Service,' Furse was an outstanding administrator and the leading spirit in forging a unified system of recruiting and training a cadre of Imperial civil servants. Born in London, he was educated at Eton and Oxford*, and shortly after taking his degree he accepted the position of assistant private secretary to the colonial secretary. The First World War* intervened, during which Furse saw active service and was wounded and decorated. In 1919, he returned to the Colonial Office*. For the next decade Furse was close to much of the reform that characterized the Colonial Service* at that time, particularly as it moved away from appointment to individual colonial governments and toward the unification of the entire Service. To that end, in 1931 he became director of recruitment in the new personnel division of the Colonial Office. In the meantime, he had already begun to recruit potential Colonial Service officers from the Dominions, and in 1926 he had gained the co-operation of Oxford and Cambridge to initiate training courses for Colonial Service cadets. By the time of his retirement in 1948, Furse had achieved what he had hoped for in 1931: a Colonial Service of first-rate officers who had, in the words of one historian, brought it to 'a peak of prestige.'

Furse, Sir Ralph D.

Further Reading

R.D. Furse (1962). *Aucuparias: Recollections of a Recruiting Officer* (London, John Murray)

A.H.M. Kirk-Greene (1999). *On Crown Service: A History of HM Colonial and Civil Services, 1837–1997* (London and New York, I.B.Tauris)

G

Gallipoli. The site of the most famous battle in the history of Australia*
and New Zealand*, Gallipoli is a peninsula in the Dardanelles, Turkey,
which in the First World War* was controlled by the Ottoman Empire. It
was heavily fortified, as befit the entrance to a strategic choke-point, and
from the Allied perspective was a key prize that, if taken, would lower
the pressure on the Western Front and create a direct link with the Russian
Crimea across the Black Sea. Winston Churchill*, at that time First Lord
of the Admiralty, devised a plan for its taking, which included a naval
assault in March 1915. The operation went badly (and cost Churchill his
cabinet post), but the landing at Suvla Bay proceeded despite this as planned
at the end of April. It fared badly, as did a later operation in August, and
the majority Australian and New Zealand (ANZAC) troops in action paid
a high price: approximately 12,000 killed and some 25,000 wounded. By
the end of the year it had become clear that the Gallipoli campaign was
a failure and the theatre was evacuated of Allied troops by early 1916.
For the Australians and New Zealanders, Gallipoli had been a terrible
baptism by fire in the horrors of the First World War – for which there
was much animus directed at the British high command – and by the
1920s 25 April, ANZAC Day, had become an annual moment of national
commemoration in both countries.

Further Reading
Jenny Macleod (2004). *Reconsidering Gallipoli* (Manchester, Manchester
    University Press)

Victor Rudenno (2008). *Gallipoli: Attack from the Sea* (New Haven, CT, Yale University Press)

Gambia, The. First encountered by English traders in the late sixteenth century, and then famously so by the Scottish explorer Mungo Park* beginning in the 1790s, The Gambia is located in coastal West Africa and is a long, narrow strip of territory that the British made a Crown Colony in 1843 in an attempt to keep at bay French and Portuguese interests in the surrounding area. Of some strategic but of little economic importance (its chief product was groundnuts), The Gambia languished. Nonetheless its borders were made secure in 1890 when the British and the French agreed on a treaty that set the boundaries of neighbouring Senegal. Independence was achieved in 1965.

Further Reading
Harry A. Gailey (1964). *A History of The Gambia* (London, Routledge & Kegan Paul)
Arnold Hughes (2006). *A Political History of The Gambia, 1816–1994* (Rochester, University of Rochester Press)

Gandhi, Mohandas K. (1869–1948). The Great Teacher or 'Mahatma' of the Indian people, and the guiding spirit behind Indian independence, Gandhi was born in Western India and as a young man went to London to train as a barrister. He was called to the Bar of the Inner Temple in 1891, by that time having become a westernized Indian. Two years later, he left for South Africa, after also having re-vivified his Hinduism through various religious influences, including then-fashionable theosophy. For over twenty years Gandhi lived in South Africa and it was here that his acute racial sense developed and his campaign to resist racism and segregation began. He led a number of campaigns, first against the British, and then after the Union of South Africa* was formed in 1910, against the ascendant Afrikaners. In the midst of the First World War*, and by then married with children, Gandhi sailed for home, settling in Bombay. He was immediately taken up by the Indian National Congress*, a movement begun in 1885 as little more than a polite society that sponsored formal socializing between Indians and the British, but which had gradually transformed itself into the main instrument of Indian nationalism. During the 1920s and 1930s, Gandhi fashioned a political platform that stressed Indian independence, socio-racial inclusiveness, and political non-violence. Imprisoned a number of times by the British for agitation, the last occasion saw him spend almost two years behind bars during the Second World War*. These years saw Gandhi push for independence using the anti-British slogan, 'Quit India'. But independence for Hindu-dominant British India was complicated by the persistent demands for a parallel independence for India's Muslims. Led by M.A. Jinnah*, the Muslim League campaigned for the creation of the new state of Pakistan*. Clement Attlee's* election in 1945 inaugurated a speedy drive to independence, which was achieved in August 1947. Gandhi conceded that the partition of British India into two states was required politically, but he regretted its necessity. Meanwhile, both Hindu and Muslim nationalists resented both Gandhi's moralism and his moderation and, in their view, his lack of *realpolitik*. One of the former acted on these beliefs by assassinating Gandhi in 1948, less than a year after independence.

Further Reading

James D. Hunt (1993). *Gandhi in London* (New Delhi, Promilla & Co.)
Kathryn Tidrick (2007). *Gandhi: A Political and Spiritual Life* (London and New York, I.B.Tauris)

George III (1738–1820). George III's sixty-year reign was marked by the loss of the American colonies and what is usually regarded as the consequent end of the First British Empire. Acceding to the throne in 1760 in the midst of the Seven Years' War*, George was sympathetic to the Tory cause. Beginning in 1770, when Lord North became Prime Minister, discontent in the American colonies became the focus of government policy and action abroad. Though some taxes were repealed in response to American complaints, the tea duty was left in place and ultimately it symbolized an intolerable tax burden in the eyes of some radical American colonists. Fighting broke out in 1775, followed by the American Declaration of Independence the next year. The King was named in the list of grievances enunciated by the Americans, which outraged him. Determined to hold the colonies, George insisted that the war be prosecuted. Eventually resigned to Britain's inevitable loss, he nonetheless wished to prolong the war in an effort to punish disloyal Americans. In 1781, the British were overcome at the Battle of Yorktown, which signalled the Americans' victory in the War of Independence. George resisted this defeat but in time authorized the negotiation of a peace, which became the Treaty of Paris in 1783. Over the balance of his reign, which included the nine-year Regency from 1811 until 1820 when he was incapacitated by disease, George presided over the long period of war with revolutionary and Napoleonic France, and the revival of the Empire.

Further Reading
Jeremy Black (2006). *George III: America's Last King* (New Haven, CT, Yale University Press)

C.A. Bayly (1989) *Imperial Meridian: The British Empire and the World 1780–1830* (London, Longman)

Ghana. Located in West Africa along the Gulf of Guinea, Ghana (essentially the pre-independence Gold Coast) began to come under direct British rule in 1821. Expansion inland proceeded apace, especially against the Ashanti* people. In 1874, Crown Colony status was declared. The Ashanti were gradually defeated and their land annexed in 1901. One of the first British colonies in Africa to engender African nationalism, in 1946 a new constitution was adopted in which the Gold Coast legislative assembly would contain a majority of African representatives. The road from there to independence was a short one, pushed forward by Kwame Nkrumah* and the Convention Peoples' Party. In March 1957, the Gold Coast – re-named Ghana in recognition of an ancient West African kingdom – became a black-majority Dominion, the first such in British Africa. Three years later Ghana declared its complete independence as a republic, although choosing to remain within the Commonwealth.

Further Reading
Roger Gocking (2005). *The History of Ghana* (Westport, CT, Greenwood Press)

David Kimble (1965). *A Political History of Ghana: The Rise of Gold Coast Nationalism, 1850–1928* (Oxford, Clarendon Press)

Gibraltar. A vital choke-point at the entrance to the Mediterranean, especially in the age of wood, wind, and sail, Gibraltar was first captured by the British in 1704. In 1713, through the provisions of the Treaty of Utrecht, the Spanish ceded their rights to Gibraltar in perpetuity, although they have long contested British sovereignty nonetheless. Throughout the years of the Royal Navy's dominance of the high seas, Gibraltar was its main base for the western Mediterranean, as well as for all sea routes south. Granted self-government in 1964, Gibraltar remains a British Overseas Territory.

Further Reading

Edward G. Archer (2006). *Gibraltar: Identity and Empire* (New York, Routledge)

Simon Winchester (2004). *Outposts: Journeys to the Surviving Relics of the British Empire* (New York, Harper Perennial)

Gilbert and Ellice Islands. A chain of tiny islands in the south-west Pacific including Tokelau* that spent sixty years, 1916–76, as a Crown Colony, the Gilbert and Ellice Islands were probably visited by Europeans as early as the mid-sixteenth century. In 1892, they were made a British Protectorate. In 1976, they became self-governing colonies and in 1978, the Ellice Islands became the independent nation of Tuvalu*. A year later, the Gilbert Islands became the predominant part of the new nation of Kiribati*.

Further Reading

Austin Coates (1970). *Western Pacific Islands* (London, HMSO)

Barrie Macdonald (2001). *Cinderellas of the Empire: Towards a History of Kiribati and Tuvalu* (Suva, Fiji, University of the South Pacific)

Girouard, Sir Percy (1867–1932). Railway engineer and colonial administrator, Girouard was also one of a small number of Canadians to rise high in Imperial service. Born in Montreal, he was educated there and later at the Royal Military College of Canada in Kingston, Ontario*. Employed briefly by the Canadian Pacific Railway*, he took up a commission in the Royal Engineers in 1888. Beginning in 1890, he spent five years as manager of railway traffic at the Royal Arsenal, Woolwich. In 1896, he went to Egypt*

95

in advance of the re-conquest of the Sudan* under Kitchener*, and there played an important role as director of Sudan railways. Awarded the DSO in 1898, Girouard was appointed President of the Egyptian Railway and Telegraph Administration. By now he was in Africa to stay and further service followed in the Second Boer War* and afterwards in the Transvaal* and the Orange River Colony.* Appointed KCMG in 1900, midway through his South African service, he returned to England briefly in 1904 before being appointed in 1907 to succeed Lord Lugard* as High Commissioner and then Governor of Northern Nigeria*. He remained in the colony until 1909, all the while planning and building a railway network as well as investigating the complex thicket that was local land tenure policy. He was transferred to the British East Africa Protectorate* in that year, serving as Governor until 1912. A company directorship and then appointment as Director-General of Munitions Supply during the First World War* rounded out Girouard's influential career. He spent his retirement in London and died there in 1932.

Further Reading

A.H.M. Kirk-Greene (1984). 'Canada in Africa: Sir Percy Girouard, Neglected Colonial Governor', *African Affairs*, vol. 83, no. 331, pp. 207–39

Roy MacLaren (1978). *Canadians on the Nile, 1882–1898: being the adventures of the voyageurs on the Khartoum relief expedition and other exploits* (Vancouver, University of British Columbia Press)

Gladstone, William E. (1809–98). The 'biggest beast in the forest,' according to one of his many biographers, William Gladstone was four times British Prime Minister, throughout which he had an uneasy relationship with the Empire. Born into wealth and rising respectability in Liverpool, he was educated at Eton and Christ Church, Oxford* and, after some serious contemplation and pronounced fatherly persuasion, entered politics rather than the Church. First elected MP in 1832, he served in Parliament for the next sixty-four years. His initial exposure to the Empire was through the family's sugar estates in Demerara. In the 1830s he served as undersecretary at the Colonial Office. Then later, beginning in 1868, came his protracted attempt to 'pacify Ireland.' But in the late 1870s Gladstone began to articulate precise views on Britain's place in the world and the nature of Imperial power. In his 1879 Midlothian Campaign, which helped to propel the Liberals back to power the following year, Gladstone criticized the ruling Disraeli* Tories over what he took to be their brand of rapacious Imperialism. Once back in power, however, Gladstone faced his own Imperial dilemma over a nationalist revolt in Egypt* and the government's ultimate decision to invade and occupy the country, which brought with it the additional problem of the Sudan*. Public belief that the death of General Charles Gordon* during the Mahdi's* Islamist uprising in Sudan was caused by Gladstone's inaction contributed to the government's defeat at the polls in 1885. Back in office briefly in 1886, and then finally from 1892 to 1894, Gladstone's last ministry foundered in part over his refusal to allow a British Protectorate to be extended over Uganda.

Further Reading

Robert T. Harrison (1995). *Gladstone's Imperialism in Egypt: Techniques of Domination* (Westport, CT, Greenwood Press)

H.C.G. Matthew (1998). *Gladstone: 1809–1898* (Oxford, Oxford University Press)

Gokhale, Gopal Krishna (1866–1915). A key Indian nationalist who was instrumental in moving the Indian National Congress* from social club to political force, Gokhale graduated from Elphinstone College in Bombay in 1888. He then embarked on a teaching career, most of which was spent at Fergusson College in Pune, which he helped found in 1895. A moderate but persistent reformer throughout his career, he championed Hindu-Muslim unity and was a mentor to both Gandhi* and Jinnah*.

Further Reading

B.R. Nanda (1998). *Gokhale: The Indian Moderates and the British Raj* (Oxford, Oxford University Press)

Stanley Wolpert (1962). *Tilak and Gokhale: Revolution and Reform in the Making of Modern India* (Berkeley, University of California Press)

Gold Coast (see Ghana)

Goldie, Sir George D. (1846–1925). A prominent trader and colonialist in Nigeria, Goldie was born on the Isle of Man, educated at the Royal Military Academy, Woolwich, and commissioned a Royal Engineer. In 1875, he entered the West African palm oil trade and a few years later established the United Africa Company. He used the UAC and its successors to push for a stronger British regional presence to offset that of the French and the Germans on the Niger River. A charter for the Royal Niger Company in 1886 was the result. The next year Goldie was knighted and for the next several years he used the RNC's trading strength, administrative mandate, and military power to create the new colony of Nigeria* in 1897. In 1900, the Colonial Office* decided to take over control of Nigeria directly and the RNC was bought out for the then-enormous sum of £865,000. Goldie remained a prominent presence during his London retirement, among other things serving as President of the Royal Geographical Society* from 1905 to 1908.

Further Reading

John E. Flint (1960). *Sir George Goldie and the Making of Nigeria* (London, Oxford University Press)

Dorothy Wellesley (1977). *Sir George Goldie: Founder of Nigeria* (New York, Arno Press)

Gordon, Charles G. (1833–85). In the annals of British Imperialism there is little that matches the Sudanese epic of General Charles Gordon. His death at Khartoum in January 1885 was seen by much of the Victorian public as the ultimate Imperial sacrifice, and was honoured by them as such. A graduate of the Royal Military Academy, Woolwich, Gordon served in the Crimea, where he was part of the great British siege of Sevastopol that had begun in the fall of 1854. After peace was declared in 1856, he was assigned to successive boundary commissions charged with delineating the new borders of the Ottoman and Russian Empires. Later, in 1860, he volunteered to go to China to fight against the Taiping insurgents, ultimately at the head of the Ever Victorious Army. In Britain, to which he returned early in 1865, Gordon's exploits in China had made him a celebrity, but reacting against it he took an out-of-the-way position as commander of the Royal Engineers at Gravesend where he would spend six years. By 1871, however, he was ready to go elsewhere. The Gladstone Liberal government duly tapped him to be its representative on the Danube Commission. 'Chinese' Gordon's reputation preceded him there and he was queried by the Prime Minister of Egypt about his interest in serving the Egyptian government in the Sudan. He agreed, and the main task that would occupy Gordon throughout the almost six-years of his Governor-Generalship – first of Equatoria, and then beginning in 1877 of all of the Sudan – was the attempt to eradicate the slave trade. Reasonably successful in this attempt, he later returned home to England a hero once again. Gordon's next few years were ones of restless activity. His Christian religiosity became more intense and his travels unscripted. Early in 1884, he consented to entering the service of King Leopold of the Belgians in the Congo. But instead of acting on Leopold's commission, Gordon returned to Khartoum in February 1884. In Egyptian-occupied Sudan, a revolt was brewing under the charismatic Islamic leadership of the forty-year-old Muhammad Ahmad, who had proclaimed himself the Mahdi*. For the next eleven months, Gordon would occupy the British Governor's palace at Khartoum. After a number of failed attempts at negotiating with the Mahdi, Gordon and what remained of the original 10,000-man Egyptian garrison came under siege. From May until his death on 26 January 1885, Gordon held out against the Mahdi. Earlier, in September 1884, under enormous pressure Gladstone became convinced that Gordon was trapped and a relief mission was sent from England. An expedition, the first part of which consisted of some 10,000 troops, arrived too late – the garrison had fallen two days earlier and Gordon was dead. From the moment that the news arrived in London, Gordon has been at the centre of any discussion that conjoins British Imperialism and heroism.

Further Reading

C. Brad Faught (2008). *Gordon: Victorian Hero* (Washington, DC, Potomac Books)

John Pollock (1993). *Gordon: The Man behind the Legend* (London, Constable)

Gore-Browne, Sir Stewart (1883–1967). In many respects the quintessential colonial Englishman in Africa, but substantially different in others, Gore-Brown was born in London and educated at Harrow and the Royal

Military Academy at Woolwich. He first went to Northern Rhodesia* in 1911 as part of a boundary survey team, and then following service in the First World War* acted on a long-standing dream to become a prominent landowner by purchasing a large property up-country in Northern Rhodesia on which he built an estate called Shiwa Ngandu. Beginning in 1914, he gradually built Shiwa at the same time that the British South Africa Company*, and then the British government, created a new colony. In the 1930s, he became politically active, gaining a seat on the legislative council. But his acceptance of the need for a shared political and economic destiny with the black population of the colony ultimately put him at odds with the white colonial government. Knighted in 1945, he fell out with the government in the 1950s over his opposition to Roy Welensky's* idea to unite the Rhodesias* with Nyasaland*. Increasingly he became an advisor to black political leaders within Northern Rhodesia, such as Kenneth Kaunda*, but his later years were spent mostly tending to Shiwa, which had grown into a remarkable, if incongruous, English-style estate. He became a firm supporter of African majority rule and celebrated Northern Rhodesia's independence as Zambia* in 1964. At the time of his death three years later, he received a state funeral from President Kaunda.

Further Reading

Christina Lamb (2004). *The Africa House: The True Story of an English Gentleman and his African Dream* (New York, HarperCollins)

Robert I. Rotberg (1977). *Black Heart: Gore-Browne and the Politics of Multiracial Zambia* (Berkeley, University of California Press)

Gorst, Sir J. Eldon (1861–1911). An Imperial proconsul in Egypt of considerable ability but little sympathy for the twentieth-century nationalist aspirations of Egyptians, Gorst was born in New Zealand* but raised in London and educated at Eton and Trinity College, Cambridge. In 1885, he qualified as a barrister, but rather than practice law he joined the British diplomatic corps and was sent to Egypt the next year. He spent the next twenty-one years there in various administrative roles until taking over from the Earl of Cromer* as British Agent and Consul-General in 1907. Appointed by the new Campbell-Bannerman Liberal government, he held the job until 1911, when opposition by Egyptian nationalists to his plan to extend the British concession over the Suez Canal* and his own ill-health forced him to resign and return to England. He died later that year, aged just fifty.

Further Reading

Sir Archie Hunter (2007). *Power and Passion in Egypt: A Life of Sir Eldon Gorst* (London and New York, I.B.Tauris)

Peter Mellini (1977). *Sir Eldon Gorst: The Overshadowed Proconsul* (Stanford, CA, Hoover Institution Press)

Grand Trunk Road. The great Imperial transportation, commercial, and military artery of India*, the Grand Trunk Road's modern construction became a half-century project beginning under the East India Company* in 1839. Eventually it ran some 2,000 miles from Calcutta to the North-West Frontier, passing through the principal cities of Allahabad, Delhi, and Lahore.

Further Reading

Rudyard Kipling (2000). *Kim* (Toronto, Penguin)

Raghubir Singh (1995). *The Grand Trunk Road: A Passage Through India* (New York, Aperture)

Great Game. The term used by the British to describe the mainly nineteenth-century Anglo-Russian rivalry in Central Asia. It was coined by Rudyard Kipling* in *Kim* (1901). Afghanistan was the fulcrum of the exploration, espionage, and diplomacy that dominated the relationship between the Russian and British Empires over a vast territory that was essentially unknown by and hostile to westerners. Though a direct war between the two powers never erupted, proxy wars were fought, especially the three Afghan Wars* engaged in by the British. As German militarism increased and the German Empire expanded around the turn of the twentieth century, relations between the two rivals warmed and in 1907 they signed the Anglo-Russian Convention, which formally brought the period of the Great Game to a close.

Further Reading

Peter Hopkirk (1996). *Quest for Kim: In Search of Kipling's Great Game* (London, J. Murray)

Robert Johnson (2006). *Spying for Empire: The Great Game in Central and South Asia* (London, Greenhill)

Great Trek. The formative and myth-making event of South Africa's* Afrikaners, the trek began in 1835 when several hundred *Voortrekkers* departed the Cape Colony* in protest over Britain's abolition of slavery throughout the Empire, which had taken effect the previous year. In short order, thousands of others took up the march northwards. The result was the establishment of two new Afrikaner homelands, the Orange River Colony (State)* and later the Transvaal*, once the *Voortrekkers* original settlement in Natal* was annexed by the British. The key event of the Great Trek was the defeat of the Zulu* king, Dingale, in 1838 at Blood River. This victory and the trek itself became foundational in the formation of Afrikaner national consciousness and to their understanding of themselves as a 'covenant' people requiring separation from others.

Further Reading

Donald H. Akenson (1992). *God's Peoples: Covenant and Land in South Africa, Israel, and Ulster* (Ithaca, NY, Cornell University Press)

Leonard M. Thompson (1985). *The Political Mythology of Apartheid* (New Haven, CT, Yale University Press)

Grenada. Located at the southern tip of the Caribbean chain of islands, Grenada became permanently British in 1763 under the terms of the Treaty of Paris. Its history is similar to that of the other British Caribbean islands in that sugar was central to its economy. But spices such as cinnamon, cloves, and ginger were also important. Crown Colony status was granted in 1877. Independence as a constitutional monarchy with Queen Elizabeth II as head of state came in 1974.

Further Reading

Beverley A. Steele (2003). *Grenada: A History of its People* (Kingston, Macmillan Caribbean)

Gordon K. Lewis (1968). *The Growth of the Modern West Indies* (London, MacGibbon & Kee)

Grogan, Ewart S. (1874–1967). An intrepid adventurer in Africa in his younger days and an influential and colourful colonist in Kenya* later on, Grogan became the first person to trek from Cape Town to Cairo, surveying as he went a possible route for Cecil Rhodes'* dream of a railway that would run the length of the continent. Between 1898 and 1900 Grogan succeeded in this passage, which produced a great deal of publicity and his own best-selling account, *From the Cape to Cairo: The First Traverse of Africa from South to North* (1900). Afterwards he spent some time in South Africa* attached to Lord Milner's* 'Kindergarten' of Imperial policymakers, before moving to Kenya where he settled and helped to build the colony, witnessing almost the entirety of the British colonial period there until independence in 1963.

Further Reading
Leda Farrant (1981). *The Legendary Grogan: The Only Man to Trek from Cape to Cairo: Kenya's Controversial Pioneer* (London, H. Hamilton)
Edward Paice (2001). *Lost Lion of Empire: The Life of 'Cape to Cairo' Grogan* (London, HarperCollins)

Guggisberg, Sir Gordon (1869–1930). Soldier and colonial administrator, Guggisberg embodied well the contemporary ethic of Imperial service. Born in Galt, Ontario*, with his family he left Canada* for England as a boy. Educated at the Royal Military Academy, Woolwich, he was commissioned in the Royal Engineers in 1889. Tall, handsome, and athletic, Guggisberg's service included Singapore* before, in 1902, being sent by the Colonial Office* to survey the Gold Coast* and Ashanti*. Appointed Director of Surveys there in 1905, he returned to England briefly prior to the same grade of appointment in Southern Nigeria in 1910. In 1913, he was appointed Surveyor-General of Nigeria* just before the union of Southern and Northern Nigeria. Afterwards, briefly Director of Public Works in the Gold Coast, the outbreak of the First World War* brought him back to England and to military service with the Royal Engineers. He served for the duration of the war and was awarded the DSO in 1918. Appointed Governor of the Gold Coast in 1919, he spent the rest of his career there and briefly, beginning in 1928, as Governor of British Guiana*. Animated always by a high sense of Christian and Imperial duty, he fell ill in 1929, forcing his resignation, and he returned to England, dying the next year.

Further Reading

H.B. Goodall (1998). *Beloved Imperialist: Sir Gordon Guggisberg, Governor of the Gold Coast* (Edinburgh, Pentland Press)

Ronald E. Wraith (1967). *Guggisberg* (London, Oxford University Press)

Gurkhas. One of the best-known fighting forces in British Imperial history, the Gurkhas originated in Rajput, India*, where they took the name of the ancient Hindu warrior-saint, Guru Gorakhnath, but came from Nepal where they defended the capital of Kathmandu from all foreign imprecations, including those of the British. Ultimately designated a 'Martial Race' by the British, they were willing to be recruited into the army of the East India Company*, where they proved fiercely loyal during the Indian Mutiny*. In the twentieth century, as the Brigade of Gurkhas in the British Army and in the Indian Army in the form of a number of Gurkha regiments, they fought with great valour for Britain in both World Wars, as well as serving in various far-flung areas of the Empire, especially Hong Kong. In Singapore, they formed the Gurkha Contingent within the police force.

Further Reading

Lionel Caplan (1995). *Warrior Gentlemen: 'Gurkhas' in the Western Imagination* (Providence, RI, Berghahn Books)

Tony Gould (1999). *Imperial Warriors: Britain and the Gurkhas* (London, Granta Books)

Guyana. Located along the northern coast of South America, the Dutch first settled the area early in the seventeenth century, but beginning in 1796 during the French Revolutionary and Napoleonic Wars, the British occupied what had become three colonies. In 1814, the Dutch ceded their claim to the colonies and in 1831 they were proclaimed British Guiana. Like elsewhere in the Caribbean, sugar was king, and after the implementation of abolition in the 1830s the plantations were worked increasingly by imported Indian labourers. Self-government was achieved in 1961, followed by independence as Guyana in 1966. In 1970, a republic was proclaimed, although Guyana remained within the Commonwealth.

Further Reading

D. Graham Burnett (2000). *Masters of all they Surveyed: Exploration, Geography and a British El Dorado* (Chicago, University of Chicago Press)

Brian L. Moore (1987). *Race, Power, and Social Segmentation in Colonial Society: Guyana after Slavery, 1838–1891* (New York, Gordon & Breach)

H

Haggard, Sir Henry Rider (1856–1925). Novelist and Imperial propagandist, Haggard was born in Norfolk and received a grammar school education before being sent to South Africa* in the summer of 1875 when he was nineteen. His father had secured him a position with the new Lieutenant-Governor of Natal*, Sir Henry Bulwer, a friend of the family, and the young Haggard took quickly to life in Africa. The adventure of being out on the land, and the struggle for superiority among Briton, Boer, and Zulu, fired his interest and imagination. He served briefly as a British government official in the Transvaal*, but love affairs, marriage, and the need to earn a regular living brought him back to England and to reading for the Bar, for which he qualified in 1885. By that time he had already begun to write, although with little success. But in that year, and inspired by Robert Louis Stevenson's *Treasure Island* and his own African adventures, he wrote *King Solomon's Mines*. The swashbuckling Imperial tale was an instant success and portended a writer's life for the erstwhile barrister. More books, including *She* (1887), followed quickly. His later years were spent in various pursuits in addition to writing. He failed in an attempt at election to Parliament. More successful was time spent as an advocate of British farming. In 1911, he served on the Royal Dominions Commission, which took him around the Empire. But none of these endeavours matched the excitement of his earlier life in Africa, nor of writing his two famous works, which, nonetheless, were followed by many other books. In 1912, he was knighted, and a few years later appointed KBE. He made out the Empire – especially in Africa – to be an adventurous, breathtaking place. His talent, especially compared to his contemporary and friend, Rudyard Kipling*, was limited, but his appeal broad and continuing.

Further Reading

Norman Etherington (1984). *Rider Haggard* (Boston, Twayne Publishers)

Wendy R. Katz (1987). *Rider Haggard and the Fiction of Empire* (Cambridge, Cambridge University Press)

Hailey, William Malcolm, 1st Baron Hailey (1872–1969). A leading colonial administrator and author of the most important survey of Africa written during the British colonial era, Hailey was educated at the Merchant Taylors' School and at Corpus Christi College, Oxford*. In 1894, he entered the Indian Civil Service*, thus beginning a long career in the Raj that saw him, among other things, become Governor of the Punjab in 1924 and four years later of the United Provinces. In 1930–1, he attended the Round Table Conference in London, during which he was a key participant and out of which emerged the Government of India Act of 1935. A year earlier he had more or less retired, returning to England after forty years in India*. In 1936, he was raised to the peerage as Baron Hailey of Shahpur and continued to advise the government on Indian affairs. In the meantime, however, he had undertaken a comprehensive study of Africa for the Royal Institute of International Affairs. Published in 1938 as *An African Survey*, Hailey had brought to bear on every aspect of African affairs his formidable intellect, nuanced observation, and synthetic powers to yield a weighty tome comprised of over a million words. In their composition he had travelled in excess of 20,000 miles, and for a generation after its publication the book was central to the British government's understanding of Africa. A second and significantly revised edition was published in 1957, although by then African nationalism was coming to the fore and was of much greater political importance than a written account of African affairs, no matter how comprehensive or authoritative. Possessed of an iron constitution, Hailey continued to advise and write on colonial issues into his nineties. He lived long enough to see almost the complete decolonization of British Africa, of which he greatly approved and to which he had contributed much. He died in London in 1969, aged ninety-seven.

Further Reading
John W. Cell (1992). *Hailey: A Study in British Imperialism* (Cambridge, Cambridge University Press)

Hailey, William Malcolm, Baron Hailey (1938). *An African Survey: A Study of Problems Arising in Africa, South of the Sahara* (London, Oxford University Press)

Haileybury College. Located near Hertford and founded by the East India Company* in 1805 as its training college, Haileybury was a key feature of British rule in India until the EIC was disbanded in 1858 following the Indian Mutiny*. Re-opening a few years later, Haileybury developed into a leading public school, a position that it continues to hold to this day. The school boasts a number of famous alumni, known as Old Haileyburians, connected to the Empire such as Rudyard Kipling* (who attended the United Services College, which amalgamated with Haileybury in 1942), Lord Allenby*, Lionel Curtis*, and Clement Attlee*, whose time as Prime Minister coincided with India's independence.

Further Reading
J. Mordaunt Crook (1964). *Haileybury and the Greek Revival: The Architecture of William Wilkins* (Hertford, Haileybury)

Andrew Hambling (2006). *The East India College at Haileybury, 1806–1857* (Hertford, Haileybury)

Harcourt, Lewis, 1st Viscount Harcourt (1868–1922). Colonial Secretary, he was born at Nuneham Courtenay, Oxfordshire and educated at Eton. A devoted Liberal who had been his father William's private secretary at the Home Office, 'Loulou' Harcourt was elected to Parliament in 1904 and the next year attained Cabinet rank as First Commissioner of Works under Sir Henry Campbell-Bannerman. In 1910, H.H. Asquith sent him to the Colonial Office*, where he would serve for the next five years. This was a period of relative quiescence throughout the Empire and Harcourt concentrated his efforts on railway building in Africa. He also presided over the amalgamation of Northern and Southern Nigeria* in 1914. Lord Lugard*, recently returned to Nigeria from his Governorship of Hong Kong*, honoured him with the naming of Port Harcourt, the terminus of the new Eastern railway. Harcourt opposed self-government for the white settlers of British East Africa*, which made him greatly disliked by the 'Kenya pioneers,' setting in train their two-generation struggle against the British government's decision to make African interests paramount there. He was made Viscount Harcourt in 1917. A troubled and occasionally scandalous private life was made worse by illness in his later years and in 1922 Harcourt committed suicide.

Further Reading
Roy Jenkins (1986). *Asquith* 3rd edn (London, Collins)

Patrick Jackson, ed. (2006). *Loulou: Selected Extracts from the Journals of Lewis Harcourt, 1880–1895* (Madison, NJ, Fairleigh Dickinson University Press)

Hastings, Warren (1732–1818). First Governor-General of India* and (in)famous for his impeachment trial, Hastings was born in Oxfordshire and went out to Calcutta in 1750 as a clerk with the East India Company*. He rose quickly in the EIC, returning to England in 1764 where he was a Company spokesperson, especially as it concerned Parliamentary affairs. In 1772, he became Governor of Bengal* and the next year Governor-General of India, a post he held until 1785. An exacting, prickly administrator, Hastings made enemies easily, one of which was Sir Philip Francis, a member of the Council of Bengal. Their disaffection resulted in a duel in 1781, during which Francis was wounded. In 1784, Hastings resigned as Governor of Bengal and returned to London. In time, and in light of continuous attacks made on the high-living 'Nabobs' of the EIC, Hastings was charged with corruption by the opposition Whigs in Parliament and underwent impeachment. His trial lasted seven years, at the end of which in 1795 he was acquitted. However, his reputation was in ruins, as were his personal finances. His retirement years were spent attempting to re-build his honour and, to some extent, his exhausted fortune. Hastings died having not fully achieved either objective, and he remains a disputed figure in the history of the British in India.

Further Reading
Jeremy Bernstein (2000). *Dawning of the Raj: The Life and Trials of Warren Hastings* (Chicago, Ivan R. Dee)

Colin Nicholson and Geoffrey Carnall, eds (1989). *The Impeachment of Warren Hastings: Papers from a Bicentenary Commemoration* (Edinburgh, Edinburgh University Press)

Hausa. Populous in northern Nigeria* and southern Niger, the Hausa are an ancient African people who had emerged as a major regional power by the twelfth century. Strongly Islamic since the fourteenth century, the British first encountered them in a sustained way near the end of the nineteenth century, by which time they had been invaded by the Fulani. In the form of the Sokoto Caliphate, the Hausa-Fulani posed strong opposition to British expansion in the area, and in order ultimately to administer Nigeria effectively, Indirect Rule* was here given its closest application.

Further Reading

I.F. Nicholson (1969). *The Administration of Nigeria, 1900–1960: Men, Methods, and Myths* (Oxford, Clarendon Press)

Paul Staudinger (1990). *In the Heart of the Hausa States* (Athens, OH, Ohio University Center for International Studies)

Havelock, Sir Henry (1795–1857). A British soldier famous in his time as a hero in the defence of Cawnpore and Lucknow during the Indian Mutiny*, Havelock was born in Sunderland. He chose not to pursue his early training as a lawyer, but instead, encouraged by a military brother, joined an infantry regiment at the conclusion of the Napoleonic Wars in 1815. In 1823, he went to India, studying Hindustani on the passage, and spent most of the rest of his career there. Deeply religious, he fought in the First Afghan War* and the Sikh campaigns of the intervening years, and by the 1850s he was a greatly respected soldier and commander. In 1857, now Adjutant-General to the British Army in India, and having been informed of the siege of Cawnpore by rebellious sepoys, Havelock undertook to march a column of men from Allahabad to Cawnpore, a distance of some 120 miles, in the searing summer heat of the Gangetic plain. He arrived in just over a week and set about successfully relieving the city. He then continued on to Lucknow, which he reached in September. Conditions there were dire. Havelock and his troops, with additional help, eventually relieved the town, but found themselves surrounded and under siege in the Residency. By November, the garrison's position was desperate and Havelock himself was deathly ill with dysentery. The siege was finally lifted near the end of the month, but shortly thereafter Havelock – having recently been appointed a baronet – died, saluted and mourned by Anglo-Indians and mid-Victorians alike.

Further Reading

Leonard Cooper (1957). *Havelock* (London, The Bodley Head)

John C. Pollock (1993). *Way to Glory: The Life of Havelock of Lucknow* (London, John Murray)

Herbert, H.H.M., Lord Carnarvon (1831–90). A long-time Tory Colonial Secretary, he became 4th Earl of Carnarvon aged eighteen, upon the death of his father. Educated at Eton and Oxford*, he served as Colonial Undersecretary in 1858-9. He held strong views on the desirability of Canadian Confederation, and in 1866-7 while Colonial Secretary he helped pilot the British North America Bill successfully through Parliament. His most notable period at the Colonial Office was from 1874 to 1878. During these years of Disraeli's second ministry, Carnarvon was an extraordinarily active Colonial Secretary, focussing much of his attention on South Africa*. Much like his earlier position regarding Canada, he advocated South African union, but he was in advance of his time in this regard. He resigned from Disraeli's Cabinet in 1878 after disagreeing with his chief over British policy towards Russia and the Eastern Question, and never held high office again.

Further Reading

Robert Blake (1967). *Disraeli* (New York, St Martin's Press).

P.B. Waite (2001). *The Life and Times of Confederation, 1864-1867: Politics, Newspapers and the Union of British North America* (Toronto, Robin Brass)

Hertzog, James B.M. (1866–1942). Prime Minister of South Africa* in its formative period, Hertzog gained influence as a Boer* general, which he used to pursue a political career. Born in Cape Colony*, Hertzog practiced law for a time in Pretoria and was appointed to the Orange Free State High

Court, but the outbreak of the Second Boer War* re-ordered his life. He was a staunchly anti-British republican and in 1912, just two years into the new Union of South Africa, he founded the Afrikaner-based National Party. He opposed South Africa's participation in the First World War*, and in its protracted aftermath Hertzog and his Party won enough seats in the 1924 election to form a government. He remained Prime Minister until 1939 and helped pave the way for the implementation of apartheid* and full racial segregation in South Africa in 1948.

Further Reading

C.M. van den Heever (1946). *General J.B.M. Hertzog* (Johannesburg, APB)
Shula Marks and Stanley Trapido, eds (1987). *The Politics of Race, Class and Nationalism in Twentieth-Century South Africa* (London, Longman)

Hill Station. The term applied in British India* especially to towns established at higher elevations as places of refuge from the intense summer heat of the plains. Altogether there may have been as many as eighty such stations operating during the Raj, the best known of which were Simla, Darjeeling, Mussoorie, and Ootacamund. At the advent of the summer season in May, much of the high administrative and some of the military and commercial population of British India would move to the Hill Stations for a few months until the intensity of the heat and humidity of the lower elevations had dissipated. Simla, located in the shadow of the Himalayas at an altitude of 7000 feet, became the most important of them, the 'Queen' of the Hill Stations, when the Viceroy, Sir John Lawrence*, made it his permanent off-season residence in 1864 by moving the seat of Indian government there. Later, between 1884 and 1888, Lord Dufferin built the Viceregal Lodge, confirming Simla as the government's summer capital. At the height of the Raj in the late nineteenth century, many Hill Stations became highly fashionable towns for the British, usually complete with club, mall, racecourse, polo ground, and church.

Further Reading

Vikram Bhatt (1998). *Resorts of the Raj: Hill Stations of India* (Middletown, NJ, Grantha)

Graeme D. Westlake (1993). *An Introduction to the Hill Stations of India* (New Delhi, Indus)

Hobson, John A. (1858–1940). One of the first and most influential critics of the British Empire, Hobson was an economist and social theorist. Born in Derby, he was educated locally and then at Oxford*, where he reluctantly read classics, or Greats, and did not distinguish himself academically. A desultory period of school-teaching followed in the early 1880s. He married in 1885 and then two years later decided that the life of a provincial classics master was unbearable. Consequently, he moved to London, began to teach in the newly formed university extension program offered by Oxford, and fell in with the metropolitan intelligentsia. As an undergraduate he had been exposed to considerable moral philosophizing about the economy and he pursued this direction, co-authoring a book, *The Physiology of Industry*, in 1889. Other publications followed, especially *The Evolution of Modern Capitalism* in 1894. Journalism soon became an avenue that the essentially non-academic Hobson followed, and in 1899 he was sent to South Africa* by the *Manchester Guardian* to report on the country and what most assumed was an inevitable war between the British and the Boers*. This assignment made Hobson's reputation and cemented his career as a radical. The next year he published *The War in South Africa: Its Causes and Effects*. Two years later he followed it up with *Imperialism: A Study*. Based mainly on his conclusion that the Second Boer War* was caused by a capitalist cabal with enormous economic power and with a similar capacity to influence public opinion through control of the press, Hobson made an immediate impact as a thinker who introduced anti-Imperialism as a sustained intellectual and political position. Using terms such as 'taproot' and 'sectional interests', Hobson created a new vocabulary to describe the workings of international capital which, in his view, had elicited a mad European rush for territory abroad in order to assuage the problem of under-consumption at home, especially in Britain. Later analyses would show that Hobson got many of his figures wrong, but the tone of his work caught the attention and approval of many, including V.I. Lenin, who used Hobson to fashion his anti-capitalist manifesto, *Imperialism, The Highest Stage of Capitalism* (1916). Hobson lived long enough to see the first obvious signs of the Empire's

decline, and went some distance in distinguishing the Empire of Canada*
and Australia* from that of Uganda* and Egypt*. His reputation as one of
the most important anti-Imperialist thinkers remains undiminished.

Further Reading

J.A. Hobson (1902). *Imperialism: A Study* (London, Constable)

Jules Townshend (1990). *J.A. Hobson* (Manchester, Manchester University
Press)

Hobson, William (1792–1842). First Governor of New Zealand*, Hobson
was born in Ireland and went to sea as a ten-year-old. In 1813, he was
promoted to lieutenant and was on station in various locations, principally
the West Indies. Eventually in command of HMS *Rattlesnake* in New South
Wales*, he was sent by the Admiralty to New Zealand as Governor in 1837,
in order to establish better treaty and land conditions for settlement. He
did so, negotiating the Treaty of Waitangi in 1840 with the indigenous
Maori* people. Later that year he declared New Zealand to be a colony
separate from New South Wales. He was deemed fair-minded by both settlers
and the Maori in the establishment of the colony, but a stroke suffered in
1840 led to his death two years later and his influence was sorely lacking
in the 'land wars' that followed.

Further Reading

Claudia Orange (1987). *The Treaty of Waitangi* (Wellington, Allen & Unwin)

G.H. Scholefield (1934). *Captain William Hobson, RN* (Auckland, Oxford
University Press)

Hong Kong. One of the last significant colonies to depart the Empire, Hong
Kong began to come under British control in 1841, when in the midst of
the Opium Wars* it was seized by the Royal Navy. In 1842, the Treaty of
Nanking* formalized its cession to Britain and the next year it was made
a Crown Colony. Its constitutional status remained unchanged until 1985,
when the legislative council was opened up to a small number of elected
members. In 1898, the New Territories had been added, through the
Convention for the Extension of Hong Kong Territory, on a ninety-nine-year

lease from Qing China. Throughout its long history as a British colony, Hong Kong was important economically, financially, and strategically. It also bore the Second World War* distinction of being the only British Crown Colony ever to fall to an invader, the Japanese in 1941. A century and a half of British rule over Hong Kong came to an end when its six million residents were handed over to the People's Republic of China in 1997, at the expiry of the 1898 lease, which was made to encompass both the original territory of Hong Kong Island, Kowloon, and Stonecutters Island, together with the New Territories.

Further Reading

Norman Miners (1987). *Hong Kong under Imperial Rule, 1912–1941* (Oxford, Oxford University Press)

Chris Patten (1998). *East and West: The Last Governor of Hong Kong on Power, Freedom and the Future* (London, Macmillan)

Hudson's Bay Company. Established in 1670 by King Charles II as 'the Governor and Company of Adventurers Trading into Hudson's Bay', the Hudson's Bay Company became the effective economic founder of Canada and today, though much changed, remains the last of the great Imperial chartered companies still in operation. The beaver fur used to create fashionable European hats was what much of eastern North America had in abundance, and the HBC eventually became unrivalled in its control of the land and waterways that yielded this and most other kinds of fur. Headed by the King's intrepid cousin, Prince Rupert of the Rhine, the HBC began to set up a series of trading posts in North America. Contested by the French and then by other trading companies, the HBC proved heartier and cannier than its rivals. Its chief competitor, the Montreal-based Northwest Company, was absorbed in 1821 and for the next half-century – especially under the Governorship of Sir George Simpson* – until Canadian Confederation in 1867, the HBC commanded a kind of economic kingdom over the upper half of North America. Three years later the Canadian government bought out the HBC's vast territories and its monopoly rights. But the HBC's economic position remained powerful nonetheless, and its place in Canada's national mythology is both deep and contested.

Further Reading

Michael Bliss (1987). *Northern Enterprise: Five Centuries of Canadian Business* (Toronto, McClelland & Stewart)

Peter C. Newman (1985). *The Company of Adventurers* (Toronto, Viking)

Huxley, Elspeth (1907–97). A prominent writer on the colonial history of Kenya*, having arrived there in 1912 with her English settler parents, Huxley was educated in Britain and the United States before returning to live in London and periodically in Kenya. Best known for her memoir of growing up on a hardscrabble farm near Nairobi, *The Flame Trees of Thika* (1959), and for her biography of early Kenya's most famous settler, entitled *White Man's Country: Lord Delamere and the Making of Kenya* (1935), Huxley became a controversial defender of the minority white population over the generation leading to Kenyan independence, conducting a long public debate with Margery Perham* over the issue. She later became an advocate of African independence and the creation of multi-racial states, but her writing usually displayed a nostalgic tone exemplified by one of her last books, *Out in the Midday Sun: My Kenya* (1985).

Further Reading

Phyllis Lassner (2004). *Colonial Strangers: Women Writing the End of the British Empire* (New Brunswick, NJ, Rutgers University Press)

C.S. Nicholls (2002). *Elspeth Huxley: A Biography* (London, HarperCollins)

I

Imperial British East Africa Company. A short-lived chartered company, the IBEAC was intended as a vehicle to open up about 250,000 square miles of territory – essentially constituting modern-day Kenya* – to commercial penetration and permanent settlement. Founded in 1887 by Sir William Mackinnon*, a Scottish shipping tycoon, the IBEAC was granted a royal charter the next year and established its first station upcountry at Machakos in 1889. One of its first operatives was Captain (later Lord) Frederick Lugard*, who would go on to much greater influence and fame as the theorist and leading practitioner of the style of colonial governance called Indirect Rule*. He established Fort Smith near present-day Nairobi in an attempt to give the Company a stronghold against any and all rivals, commercial and otherwise. But the Company was underfinanced and unsuccessful. At all events, Britain declared a Protectorate over East Africa in 1895, absorbing the IBEAC in the process.

Further Reading
John S. Galbraith (1972). *Mackinnon and East Africa 1878–1895: A Study in the 'New Imperialism'* (Cambridge, Cambridge University Press)
M.P.K. Sorrenson (1968). *Origins of European Settlement in Kenya* (Nairobi, Oxford University Press)

Imperial Conferences. The growth and development of the white-settler colonies spurred the creation of Imperial Conferences. Beginning in 1887 in London at the Golden Jubilee celebrations marking Victoria's fifty years on the throne, the colonial Prime Ministers met for discussion. Conferences were held again in 1894 in Ottawa and then in London during the 1897 Diamond Jubilee. After the latter meeting, they became routine and, notably beginning in 1911, the nomenclature was changed from 'Colonial' to 'Imperial.' The Imperial War Conference of 1917 and the Imperial War Cabinet were cognates of the Imperial Conferences, and after the First World War* subsequent Conferences focussed strongly on questions of constitutional development. They ceased in the 1930s, although they were taken up in a different form in the era of the Commonwealth.

Further Reading

John Kendle (1967). *The Colonial and Imperial Conferences, 1887–1911: A Study in Imperial Organization* (London, Longman)

Maurice Ollivier (1954). *The Colonial and Imperial Conferences from 1887 to 1937* (Ottawa, Queen's Printer)

Imperial Federation. Seen by its sponsors as a method to blunt colonial nationalism and thereby reconstitute the Empire, Imperial Federation became a prominent movement in the late nineteenth century. In 1884, the Imperial Federation League was formed and for the next thirty years or so found considerable support for the idea of a super-Parliament and a unified Imperial defence policy. Leading supporters included the journalist Richard Jebb, Alfred Deakin* of Australia, the Canadian George Parkin*, and Joseph Chamberlain*, Colonial Secretary. The movement petered out with the coming of the First World War* and the colonial autonomy it brought.

Further Reading

Duncan Bell (2007). *The Idea of Greater Britain: Empire and the Future of World Order, 1860–1900* (Princeton, NJ, Princeton University Press)

George R. Parkin (1892). *Imperial Federation: the Problem of National Unity* (London, Macmillan)

Imperialist, The. A novel published in 1904 and written by Sara Jeannette Duncan, a Canadian, in which she explores the attitudes of her fellow English-speaking Canadians to Britain at the height of the Empire. Using two romances as foils, and charting their progress through a comedy of manners, she examines Anglo-Canadian society in light of the strong external influence of both the mother country and, to a lesser extent, the United States.

Further Reading

Carl Berger (1970). *The Sense of Power: Studies in the Ideas of Canadian Imperialism* (Toronto, University of Toronto Press)

Sara Jeannette Duncan (1990). *The Imperialist* (Toronto, McClelland & Stewart)

India. The East India Company* established a factory at Surat on the subcontinent's east coast in 1611 and widespread trade grew from there. By the middle of the eighteenth century the Mughal Empire, in power since the early 1500s, had slipped into permanent decline. Both internal opponents – the Maratha Confederacy – and external ones – the British and the French – contributed to the decline, with the British proving incrementally victorious by the 1790s. Company rule continued apace. The Maratha Wars*, as well as wars against the Sikhs and the Afghans, gradually consolidated the EIC's rule over much of India. By the mid-nineteenth century, especially under the Governor-Generalship of Dalhousie*, India's transportation and economic infrastructure had begun to modernize. The Indian Mutiny* resulted in the British government choosing to replace the EIC, inaugurating what came to be called the Raj. It established the Indian Civil Service* in order to administer British India, and counted on the rest of the country – the nominally independent Princely States – to recognize British paramountcy by pledging loyalty to the Crown. Thereafter, Imperial rule deepened and expanded with Queen Victoria being proclaimed Empress of India in 1877. In 1885, the Indian National Congress* was founded, initially reflecting a polite nationalism, but it grew steadily and began to influence the British government's moves to reform its system of Indian governance in 1919 and 1935. The culmination of this process – much of it inspired and led by Gandhi* – resulted in the final drive for independence, which was reached in August 1947. The Indian Independence Act of that year created the new states of India and Pakistan*.

Further Reading

Judith M. Brown (1994). *Modern India: The Origins of an Asian Democracy* 2nd edn (Oxford, Oxford University Press)

Denis Judd (2004). *The Lion and the Tiger: The Rise and Fall of the British Raj, 1600–1947* (Oxford, Oxford University Press)

Indian Civil Service. Established in 1861, the ICS was a cadre of government officials – the so-called 'Heaven-born' – responsible for administering India until independence in 1947. Never numbering more than about 1,200 members, the ICS grew out of the old system of administration used by the East India Company*. The ICS was spread over a number of fields – finance, roads, forests, medicine, etc. – and though dominated by Oxbridge graduates successful in the required examination, some Indians gradually were successful in gaining places as well. Of the various Imperial services, the ICS cultivated the reputation of being supreme: supremely incorruptible and, to many, supremely insufferable.

Further Reading

Clive Dewey (1993). *Anglo-Indian Attitudes: The Mind of the Indian Civil Service* (London, Hambledon Press)

L.S.S. O'Malley (1965). *The Indian Civil Service, 1601–1930* 2nd edn (London, Frank Cass)

Indian Mutiny. In 1857, after a period of swift reform mainly under the Governor-Generalship of Lord Dalhousie*, part of the Indian Sepoy Army rebelled. The Mutiny began in Meerut north of Delhi in May. Precipitate causes included the use of both cow (offensive to Hindus) and pig (offensive to Muslims) fat to grease the cartridges issued for the Army's regulation Enfield rifles, and the belief that the flour sold at market had the bones and blood of cattle mixed into it. Deeper causes included the idea that the Hindu religion was being challenged by the Christianity of the British, and the controversial 'Doctrine of Lapse' whereby Princely States without an heir would 'lapse' and become part of British India. In any event, three sepoy regiments revolted and proclaimed the old Mughal emperor, Bahadur* Shah, the putative King of Delhi. The rebellion soon spread to other cantonments, especially in the north and west of India. The British responded immediately but it took some time to recapture Delhi and then to relieve the besieged garrisons of Cawnpore and Lucknow. By the summer of 1858 the violence was over, although considerable bitterness and mistrust remained. Very shortly thereafter the British government moved to abolish the East India Company and it gave way to Crown rule, the creation of the position of Viceroy, and the advent of the Raj.

Further Reading

David Saul (2002). *The Indian Mutiny: 1857* (London, Viking)

Julian Spilsbury (2007). *The Indian Mutiny* (London, Weidenfeld & Nicolson)

Indian National Congress. Formed in 1885 as a kind of social club to bridge 'east and west', the INC politicized itself gradually and by the period of the First World War* had become a nationalist body which, under Gandhi's* moral and tactical leadership, began to demand not simply reform of the Raj, but independence from British rule altogether. In the meantime, as a political instrument, the INC began to win seats in provincial elections after the India Act was implemented in 1935. The Second World War* effectively froze relations between Britain and India*. INC leaders, including Jawaharlal Nehru*, refused to support Britain's participation in the war and he, along with Gandhi, spent time in prison. After the war, the move to independence in 1947 continued under the dual auspices of the British government and the INC.

Further Reading

Deep Chand Bandhu (2003). *History of the Indian National Congress, 1885–2002* (Delhi, Kalpaz)

D.A. Low, ed. (2004). *Congress and the Raj: Facets of the Indian Struggle, 1917–47* (New York, Oxford University Press)

Indirect Rule. A form of Imperial rule stretching back to the Romans, its modern iteration in the British Empire is usually credited to Frederick, later Lord, Lugard* during his time as High Commissioner of the Protectorate of Northern Nigeria from 1900 to 1906. As he would argue in his summative work on the subject, *The Dual Mandate in British Tropical Africa* (1922), Indirect Rule was the best way to maintain British paramountcy while at the same time instructing the local native population in the development of modern society and government. The British practice of Indirect Rule, in which local elites and existing social structures were used, differed markedly from that form of colonial rule employed by the French, who chose mainly to govern their colonies directly as extensions of metropolitan power in Paris. For the British, 'IR' remained at the core of their colonial practice – especially in Africa – until the period of decolonization in the 1950s and '60s. Indirect Rule was both praised and criticized as the means by which the British exercised control over millions of dependent peoples, and today remains the subject of lively debate.

Further Reading

Lord Lugard (1970). *Political Memoranda* 3rd edn, A.H.M. Kirk-Greene, ed. (London, Frank Cass)

Margery Perham (1960). *Lugard: The Years of Authority 1898–1945* (London, Collins)

Ionian Islands. In 1815, Britain declared a Protectorate over this small group of Mediterranean islands centred on Corfu. Lasting until 1864, the 'United States of the Ionian Islands' had been formed at the conclusion of the Napoleonic Wars in order to preclude their domination by either Russia or the Ottomans. One of its more notable British High Commissioners was William Gladstone*. He arrived in 1858 as High Commissioner Extraordinary and then briefly in 1859 became Lord High Commissioner. At length he held the view that 'enosis' should take place and the islands be reunited with Greece as a gesture of support for its independence, which had been achieved in 1830. The British government chose not to do so at the time, but a few years later in 1864 that is exactly what happened and after forty-nine years of introducing Ionians to afternoon tea, cricket, contemporary harbour fortifications, and the protection of the Royal Navy, the British departed amicably.

Further Reading

Margarita Diaz-Andreu Garcia (2007). *A World History of Nineteenth-Century*

Archaeology: Nationalism, Colonialism and the Past (Oxford, Oxford University Press)

Robert Holland and Diana Markides (2006). *The British and the Hellenes 1850–1960* (Oxford, Oxford University Press)

Iraq. Known until 1921 as Mesopotamia, British interest in the country and region stemmed mainly from the holding of nearby India*. Archaeological, and especially oil, interests were developed in the period prior to the First World War*, which occasioned the opportunity to expel the Ottoman Empire from the Near and Middle East. Having done so in 1918, Mesopotamia became a British mandate at the Paris Peace Conference the next year, and then in 1921 as the semi-independent Kingdom of Iraq. Full independence was achieved in 1932, although Britain exerted a wartime occupation of the country from 1941 until 1947.

Further Reading

John Darwin (1981). *Britain, Egypt, and the Middle East: British Policy in the Aftermath of War, 1918–1922* (London, Macmillan)

Malcolm Yapp (1991). *The Near East since the First World War: A History to 1995* (New York, Longman)

Ireland. In popular lore known as England's 'oldest colony', Ireland always held an exceptional place in British Imperial history. The Act of Union in 1801 came in the aftermath of the Irish rebellion of three years earlier and folded Ireland constitutionally into the United Kingdom. Throughout the nineteenth century the main themes of contemporary Irish history were played out: Catholic Emancipation, the Famine, land reform, and Home Rule. By the beginning of the twentieth century the inability to achieve Home Rule through constitutional means had reinvigorated demands for Irish independence. The third Home Rule Bill was given royal assent in 1913, but its application was subsequently suspended for the duration of the First World War*. Meanwhile, and impatient for tangible progress, the Irish Volunteers had formed and began to push for an armed uprising against the British, which came in April 1916. The Rising, as it was known, was put down quickly and bluntly by the British, but it sparked a protracted period of Irish guerilla warfare and British reprisals that ended in 1921 when the Anglo-Irish Treaty was signed. The new and predominantly Roman Catholic Irish Free State was the result, which was accorded Dominion* status on a par with Canada* and Australia*. But its existence was contested by what was designated 'Northern Ireland.' The six predominantly Protestant counties that comprised it opted out of joining the larger Free State, choosing to remain under British sovereignty. The Irish Free State soon gave itself the name of Eire and in 1937 achieved independence from Britain. In 1949, the country was re-named the Republic of Ireland and left the Commonwealth.

Further Reading
John Kendle (1989). *Ireland and the Federal Solution: The Debate over the United Kingdom Constitution, 1870–1921* (Kingston, ON, McGill-Queen's University Press)

Deirdre McMahon (1984). *Republicans and Imperialists: Anglo-Irish Relations in the 1930s* (New Haven, CT, Yale University Press)

Irish Republican Army. Established in 1913 and growing out of the Irish Volunteers, the IRA's first major action was the failed Easter Rising of 1916. Three years later, the IRA was recognized by the Dail Eireann as the properly constituted army of the putative Irish Republic. For over two years it fought against the Royal Irish Constabulary, the Black and Tans, and the Auxiliaries under the direction of Cathal Brugha and then Michael Collins* in an intense and bloody guerilla war involving about 15,000 fighting men that resulted ulti-mately in the truce of July 1921 and the Anglo-Irish Treaty of later that year. Following the proclamation of the Irish Free State, the IRA split into pro- and anti-Treaty factions, which lasted until the end of the Irish Civil War in 1923.

Further Reading
Tom Barry (1981). *Guerrilla Days in Ireland* (Dublin, Anvil)

Peter Hart (2003). *The IRA at War, 1916–1923* (Oxford, Oxford University Press)

Isandlwana. Tension between the British and the Zulu* grew in the late 1870s as questions of South African regional paramountcy and territorial control abounded. In January 1879, such tensions boiled over, resulting in the stunning defeat of a British force under the command of Frederic Thesiger, 2nd Baron Chelmsford, at Isandlwana, a rocky outcrop about 200 feet high that dominated the surrounding *veld*. On 11 January, a British force of about 1,400 officers and men, along with perhaps 2,000 African troops, crossed into Zululand from the new British colony of Natal not far from Isandlwana. The reason for doing so was because Cetshwayo*, King of the Zulu, was seen as a threat to the colony. Already on the move, Chelmsford's force arrived in Zululand in order to impress upon Cetshwayo that British paramountcy would not be denied. But on 22 January, when as many as 25,000 Zulu *impis* descended on the British position at Isandlwana, British power and potential regional paramountcy lay briefly in tatters. After fierce fighting, just about every British officer and regular in the fray was dead: over fifty officers and some eight hundred soldiers. Hundreds of Africans fighting on the British side, as well as perhaps 1,000 Zulu, died in the battle too. Isandlwana became an immediate byword for British shock and humiliation: never before in British Imperial history had a force of regulars been put to the sword by native fighters with more devastating effect. Over-confidence, mistaken troop deployment, and the enemy's sheer numbers and fighting prowess proved the Redcoats' downfall. But revenge would be exacted shortly thereafter at the Battle of Ulundi*, where Chelmsford was victorious. Moreover, the victory at Isandlwana proved pyrrhic for Cetshwayo*, as he was soon deposed and marginalized.

Further Reading

Michael Barthorp (2002). *The Zulu War: From Isandhlwana to Ulundi* (London, Weidenfeld & Nicolson)

Adrian Greaves (2001). *Isandlwana* (London, Cassell)

J

Jamaica. The largest of Britain's Caribbean islands, Jamaica came into British hands in 1655 when it was taken from the Spanish. Sugar plantations were established soon thereafter by settlers from Barbados* and by the end of the eighteenth century the island had in excess of 1,000 plantations worked by tens of thousands of slaves. Planter-slave relations were especially acrimonious in Jamaica, with a significant revolt in 1831. In the post-emancipation years after 1833-4, constitutional development was slow. The Morant Bay rising of estate workers in 1865 dealt a serious blow to advancement in this regard, although a partially representative legislative council was implemented in 1884. In the twentieth century the assembly became more democratic, with significant reforms occurring during the Second World War*. After an unsuccessful experiment as part of the British West Indies Federation*, Jamaica became independent in 1962.

Further Reading

William A. Green (1976). *British Slave Emancipation: The Sugar Colonies and the Great Experiment, 1830–1865* (Oxford, Oxford University Press)

B.W. Higman (1976). *Slave Population and Economy in Jamaica, 1807–1834* (Cambridge, Cambridge University Press)

Jameson Raid. Dr Leander Starr Jameson, an associate of Cecil Rhodes* and a champion of British rights in South Africa*, led a raid in December 1894 attempting to cause an uprising against the Afrikaner government in the Transvaal*. The raiders consisted of some five hundred mounted horsemen who intended to rouse the politically debilitated *Uitlanders* (mainly British 'foreigners') to overthrow the Boer government of President Paul Kruger*. Riding towards Johannesburg from Bechuanaland*, Jameson's men arrived completely without the element of surprise, however, and were apprehended within a matter of days. The Raid's tentacles reached to the highest levels of government. In London, a Parliamentary committee deliberated over the Raid, eventually clearing Joseph Chamberlain*, the Colonial Secretary, of complicity in it, although his involvement was later shown to be true. Meanwhile, Rhodes was properly implicated, which cost him the premiership of Cape Colony* and the chairmanship of the British South Africa Company.* Jameson himself was sent briefly to prison. The Raid poisoned Anglo-Boer relations further and was one of the precipitate actions that contributed to the Second Boer War* which broke out in 1899.

Further Reading

Jeffrey Butler (1968). *The Liberal Party and the Jameson Raid* (Oxford, Clarendon Press)

No author (1996). *The Jameson Raid: A Centennial Retrospective* (Houghton, South Africa, Brenthurst Press)

Jardine, Matheson & Co. A legendary trading house founded in Canton in 1832 by two eponymous Scotsmen, Jardine, Matheson exported Chinese tea and silk and imported British manufactured goods and, over the strong objections of the ruling dynasty, Indian opium. As a rival trading agency, it was intrinsic to ending the East India Company's* monopoly over the China trade and soon thereafter helped push the British government into the Opium War* of 1839. The war led to the consolidation of the Treaty Ports* system in China and resulted in Jardine, Matheson moving operations to the newly acquired colony of Hong Kong*, where it still remains prosperously headquartered today.

Further Reading

W.E. Cheong (1979). *Mandarins and Merchants: Jardine Matheson & Co., a China Agency of the Early Nineteenth Century* (London, Curzon Press)

Edward Le Fevour (1968). *Western Enterprise in Late Ch'ing China: A Selective*

Survey of Jardine, Matheson and Company's Operations, 1842–1895 (Cambridge, MA, Harvard University Press)

Jinnah, Muhammad Ali (1876–1948). Regarded as the father of Pakistan*, Jinnah was born in Karachi, which was then part of Sindh* province in British India. His father was a prosperous merchant and Jinnah received a good education, part of which came at a Christian high school in Bombay, and culminated in him passing the matriculation examination for the University of Bombay in 1892. But instead of attending university he accepted a position with a London trading firm, only to leave it to pursue law at Lincoln's Inn. When called to the Bar in 1895, he became the youngest Indian ever to have done so. He soon returned to India, establishing a law practice in Bombay and entering politics. In 1896, he joined the Indian National Congress* and became one of its leading Muslim members. Initially sure that the Congress was the right way forward in pressing for constitutional change in India's subordinate position to Britain, he was slow to participate in the All India Muslim League*, joining only in 1913. Three years later he became its President, however, and during this period Gandhi*, recently returned from South Africa, began to make plain his method of non-violence and passive resistance as the ultimate means to achieve Indian independence. Jinnah disagreed strongly with Gandhi over this issue, arguing that only steady constitutional change gained through political and possibly violent means would lead to independence. He resigned from Congress in 1920, although he continued to hold out hope that Gandhi's methods and overwhelming Hindu support would not alienate India's Muslims. By the early 1930s, however, Jinnah had concluded that Gandhi's India would be narrowly Hindu, despite his protestations to the contrary, and therefore he began to take the Muslim League in the direction of becoming a fully fledged political instrument. He did just that, and with it came a call in 1940 for a partitioning of India upon Britain's withdrawal so as to create the new Muslim state of Pakistan*. Muslim-Hindu cleavages were exacerbated in the aftermath of this call for partition, and Jinnah adopted the controversial position of 'direct action' in order to ensure that the Muslim areas of India would become part of the projected new state of Pakistan. In the face of increasing Hindu-Muslim violence, the British disagreed strongly with Jinnah's position and in the negotiations leading up to Indian independence in 1947 worked much more closely with Gandhi and Nehru* than with him. In steadily declining health from tuberculosis and cancer, Jinnah lived long enough to see the creation of Pakistan as a Dominion* and himself made the first Governor-General, but he died the next year.

Further Reading

Akbar S. Ahmed (1997). *Jinnah, Pakistan, and Islamic Identity: The Search for Saladin* (London, Routledge)

Stanley Wolpert (2002). *Jinnah of Pakistan* (Oxford, Oxford University Press)

Johnston, Sir Henry (Harry) H. (1858–1927). An intrepid explorer and colonial administrator, Johnston was born in London and eventually spent four years at the Royal Academy studying painting. He first visited Africa largely in that regard in 1879, when he travelled to Tunisia. His interest in the continent sparked, he returned in 1882 as part of an expedition to Angola and the next year visited the Congo. By then he had gained a reputation as an explorer and in 1884 the Royal Geographical Society* appointed him to lead an expedition to East Africa and Mount Kilimanjaro. Already an area of contested European interest, Johnston began to push hard for those of Britain against Germany. His voice was heard in London, especially once Lord Salisbury* began his second ministry in 1886. That year Johnston was appointed British Vice-Consul in Cameroon and the Niger River delta and soon thereafter he was dispatched to negotiate with the Portuguese over their competing interests with the British in south-east Africa. In 1890, he worked at pulling the copper-rich Katanga region, then administered by the Belgians as part of King Leopold's Congo, into Britain's orbit. He failed, but not before ensuring that an enormous swath of territory that today comprises north-eastern Zambia* was put under the British flag. Made a KCB in 1896, he undertook subsequent government assignments but never achieved membership in the front rank of Imperial proconsuls. For his time, he was reasonably progressive and disagreed with Rhodes over the nature of colonial governance and the place of native peoples in it.

Further Reading

Alexander Johnston (1929). *The Life and Letters of Sir Harry Johnston* (London, Jonathan Cape)

Roland A. Oliver (1964). *Sir Harry Johnston & the Scramble for Africa* (London, Chatto & Windus)

Jones, Arthur Creech (1891–1964). Colonial Secretary following the Second World War*, Jones was born in Bristol and worked in a solicitor's office until entering the Civil Service in 1907. Later becoming a socialist, he opposed conscription during the First World War* and was imprisoned because of it for almost three years. Released in 1919, he worked for the trade-union movement and in 1922 was made one of the national secretaries of the Transport and General Workers' Union. During the 1920s and 1930s, he became interested in colonial issues, as well as in the prospect of a Parliamentary seat. Standing for the Labour Party, he entered Parliament for a Yorkshire constituency in 1935. In 1940, he became co-founder of the Fabian Colonial Bureau* and then, upon Clement Attlee's* election in 1945, Parliamentary Under-Secretary of State at the Colonial Office*. The next year he was appointed Colonial Secretary, holding the position until defeated at the polls in 1950. During these years he was committed to preparing for the dependent Empire's decolonization, which began in a significant way with Ceylon* in 1948. Though the bane of those who wished to perpetuate the old Empire, Jones was respected by all and worked up until his death in 1964 for Commonwealth development and understanding.

Further Reading

Ronald Hyam, ed. (1992). *The Labour Government and the End of Empire, 1945–1951*, 4 vols (London, British Documents on the End of Empire Project)

Arthur Creech Jones (1959). *New Fabian Colonial Essays* (London, Hogarth Press)

Jordan, Kingdom of (see Palestine)

Jubaland. In 1890, Jubaland, a small slice of territory located north-east of British East Africa*, became British when its former overlord, the Sultanate of Zanzibar, came under London's control. Five years later, when the Protectorate of British East Africa* was proclaimed, Jubaland was added to its territory. In 1925, Jubaland was ceded to Italy in an arrangement based upon Italy's participation on the Allied side in the First World War* and for a year it was known as Trans-Juba. In 1926, it formally became part of the much larger Italian Somaliland, where it remained until merging with British Somaliland* to form the independent Republic of Somalia in 1960.

Further Reading

I.M. Lewis (1980). *A Modern History of Somalia: Nation and State in the Horn of Africa* (London, Longman)

C.W.I. Wightwick Haywood (1927). *To the Mysterious Lorian Swamp: An Adventurous & Arduous Journey of Exploration through the Vast Waterless Tracts of Unknown Jubaland* (London, Seeley & Service)

Judicial Committee of the Privy Council. Established in 1833 and developed in part as the court of final appeal for the Empire, the JCPC continues to exist, although its powers abroad were gradually usurped by the establishment and constitutional development of supreme or high courts in most of the former colonies – such as Canada* and Australia* – where the JCPC's rulings traditionally had been final. British Overseas Territories and some Commonwealth countries retain the right of appeal to Westminster and therefore continue to avail themselves of the JCPC.

Further Reading

Peter C. Oliver (2005). *The Constitution of Independence: The Development of Constitutional Theory in Australia, Canada, and New Zealand* (Oxford, Oxford University Press)

D.B. Swinfen (1987). *Imperial Appeal: The Debate on the Appeal to the Privy Council, 1833–1986* (Manchester, Manchester University Press)

K

Kaunda, Kenneth D. (1924–). First President of Zambia*, Kaunda was born to Church of Scotland missionary parents in the Northern Province of Northern Rhodesia*. He grew up at Lubwa Mission in Chinsali, eventually becoming a teacher there and, from 1943 to 1945, its headmaster. A varied career of army instructor, state schoolteacher, mineworker, and choirmaster followed. By the early 1950s he had become politicized and in 1953 he was named Secretary General of the African National Congress* in Northern Rhodesia. As nationalist demands became more acute, so too did the state's response, and Kaunda tasted his first experience of imprisonment in 1955. Gradually, Kaunda moved to create his own nationalist party, forming the Zambian African National Congress (ZANC) in 1958. The next year it was banned and he was sent to prison for nine months. Meanwhile, in the volatile political atmosphere of the day, a plainly independence-seeking party was formed, the United National Independence Party (UNIP), and in 1960, upon Kaunda's release from prison, he was elected its president. He used this party as a vehicle to press for independence from Britain through civil disobedience, which, known as the 'Cha-Cha-Cha' campaign in a nod to emergent 1960s culture, occasionally turned violent. UNIP won the General Election of January 1964 and Kaunda became Prime Minister. Later that year he became independent Zambia's first President, remaining in power until 1991. In that year he stepped down and called for multi-party elections. The Movement for Multiparty Democracy won the ensuing election and Kaunda retired, one of the very few post-colonial African heads of state to leave office voluntarily.

Further Reading

Stephen Chan (2000). *Zambia and the Decline of Kaunda, 1984–1998* (Lewiston, NY, Edwin Mellen Press)

Stephen N. Esomba (1996). *Zambia under Kaunda's Presidency: The Conditions, Experiments with Socialism, and the Final Lap to Democracy* (Hamburg, Lit)

Keith, Arthur Berriedale (1879–1944). Brilliant and prolific, Keith became the leading historian and commentator on Commonwealth* affairs in the early part of the twentieth century. Born in Edinburgh, he was educated locally, and then at Balliol College, Oxford* where he was awarded a first-class degree in classics in 1901. He then took the civil service exam and upon receiving top marks entered into a long period of service at the Colonial Office*. Keith was instrumental in setting up the Dominions Department in 1907 and in organizing the 1911 Imperial Conference*. By the time he left the Colonial Office in 1914, he was private secretary to the Permanent Under-Secretary. His subsequent career was spent as Professor of Sanskrit, later Regius Professor, at Edinburgh University. All the while, however, he wrote extensively on Imperial and Commonwealth issues, ultimately becoming a decisive voice in the debate over Imperial Federation* versus his favoured position, Commonwealth autonomy. In all, he published twenty-one books on Imperial and Commonwealth history.

Further Reading

W. David McIntyre (2009). *The Britannic Vision: Historians and the Making of the British Commonwealth of Nations, 1907–48* (London, Palgrave Macmillan)

R.F. Shinn (1990). *Arthur Berriedale Keith: The Chief Ornament of Scottish Learning* (Aberdeen, University Press)

Kenya. Sustained British contact with the region that became a key African colony began with the arrival of the Imperial British East Africa Company* in 1888. Settlement began slowly, but increased after Protectorate status was extended to British East Africa in 1895. The enthusiasm of early settlers such as Lord Delamere* convinced the British government that the highlands of East Africa might become a breadbasket in the manner of the Canadian Prairies, and in 1896 the building of the Mombasa to Lake Victoria railway began. Completed in 1901, the so-called 'Lunatic Line' never paid for itself, but it did much to bind BEA together both economically and politically. A few years later in 1907, the Protectorate was granted its first legislative council, but already there were tensions among the white settlers, imported Asian (Indian) merchants and workers, and the vast Black African majority, much of whose land (especially the Kikuyu*) had been appropriated by whites for development as coffee and tea plantations and for farms and ranches. Following the First World War*, which saw considerable action along the border between BEA and German East Africa (Tanganyika*), a large influx of de-mobbed soldiers on a land grant scheme exacerbated the land crisis. A few years later, however, the relatively small (population 5,000) group of white settlers were outraged when the British government declared that African interests would be 'paramount' in the future of 'Kenya colony', a status received in 1920. Thus ensued a protracted forty-year struggle over the future of Kenyan society and politics, punctuated by the multi-faceted Mau Mau* uprising in the early to mid-1950s. Kenyan, Kikuyu-led, nationalism had become a powerful force by this point and under the direction of Jomo Kenyatta* the drive to independence culminated in 1963. The next year Kenya became a republic, although choosing to remain within the Commonwealth.

Further Reading

Bruce Berman and John Lonsdale (1992). *Unhappy Valley: Conflict in Kenya and Africa* (London, J. Currey)

Errol Trzebinski (1985). *The Kenya Pioneers* (London, Heinemann)

Kenyatta, Jomo (c.1895–1978). Kenya's first President was born Kamau wa Ngengi in a Kikuyu* village in the shadow of Mount Kenya and educated at a local Church of Scotland mission station, converting to Christianity as a young man. In the 1920s, Kenyatta worked as a municipal clerk in Nairobi, got married, and became interested in politics. He joined the Kikuyu Central Association (KCA), which was developing a keen interest in questions of land tenure and control since a large amount of Kikuyu land had been appropriated by white settlers. He showed immediate promise as a writer, speaker, and organizer, and was sent to London in 1929 to represent the KCA's interests. For most of the next seventeen years he lived in London, although he spent brief periods in Moscow – on what proved to be a short-lived flirtation with Communism – and then during the Second World War* as a farm labourer in Sussex. By this time he had changed his name, first to Johnstone Kamau and then to Jomo Kenyatta, taken an English wife, and earned a diploma in social anthropology from University College London. His thesis was published in 1938 as *Facing Mount Kenya*, which would prove to be an iconic tract for Kenyan nationalists. In 1946, he returned home, married again, and became the principal of Kenya Teachers College. He was now wholly politicized and the next year he was made president of the Kenya Africa Union. Like elsewhere in Africa, these were yeasty years in the history of colonial nationalism and in Kenya the 1950s saw the emergence of Mau Mau*, a violent land and freedom movement with anti-Christian overtones mixed with Kenyan nationalism. By this time Kenyatta was the acknowledged leader of the Kikuyu, who were at the centre of Mau Mau, although his role in it was marginal. He was imprisoned by the state anyway for much of the decade until his release in 1959. In the early 1960s, he became leader of the Kenya African National Union (KANU), the successor to the KAU, and used it as a vehicle to push for independence. In December 1963, Kenya gained its independence from Britain with Kenyatta as Prime Minister. Exactly one year later the country became a republic and Kenyatta assumed the Presidency, which he held for the next fourteen years until his death. His legacy is mixed. On the one hand he successfully promoted national unity and persuaded most white Kenyans to remain in the country after independence, promising reconciliation and security of land tenure; on the other hand, he moved quickly to bury the still-unresolved grievances exposed by Mau Mau, consolidated the position of his fellow Kikuyu as Kenya's ruling elite against all other competing tribal groups, eliminated the political opposition, and instituted one-party rule.

Further Reading

Jomo Kenyatta (1938). *Facing Mount Kenya* (London, Secker & Warburg)
Jeremy Murray-Brown (1972). *Kenyatta* (London, George Allen & Unwin)

Khama, Sir Seretse (1921–80). First President of Botswana*, Khama was heir to the throne of the Bamangwato people of the Bechuanaland* Protectorate, becoming king at the age of four. Later, in 1944, he graduated from Fort Hare University College before proceeding to Oxford for a stint of study and then to London where he became a barrister. In 1948, Khama married an Englishwoman, Ruth Williams, sparking a furore, especially in South Africa where he had spent much of his youth, over inter-racial marriage. The marriage was criticized too in Bechuanaland. Under pressure from South Africa, whose mineral exports were vital to Britain's post-war economic recovery, the British government exiled Khama and his wife in 1951. Five years later, they returned to Bechuanaland as private citizens and five years after that, in 1961, Khama re-entered politics by establishing the Bechuanaland Democratic Party. In 1965, running on a nationalist platform, the BDP won the national election and with Khama as Prime Minister the push for immediate independence ensued. Independence was declared in 1966 and Khama became the new state of Botswana's first President. Knighted that same year, Khama remained in office until his death fourteen years later.

Further Reading

Michael Dutfield (1990). *A Marriage of Inconvenience: The Persecution of Ruth and Seretse Khama* (London, Unwin Hyman)

Susan A. Williams (2006). *Colour Bar: The Triumph of Seretse Khama and his Nation* (London, Allen Lane)

Khyber Pass. One of the most storied of Imperial sites, the Khyber Pass is located in the Hindu Kush mountain range, running for about 53 kilometres along the border between Pakistan and Afghanistan and narrowing, at one point, to just three metres. Beginning with Alexander the Great in 326 BC, it has been used for centuries as a strategic gateway; in the period of the British Raj the Khyber marked the point at which the Northwest Frontier became Afghanistan, and as such was a key feature of the three Afghan Wars*. After the Second Afghan War in 1879, the British built a road through the Pass, and then later in the 1920s constructed a railway. To Victorian contemporaries, the Khyber Pass became a byword for violence and banditry and, according to Kipling, was 'a sword cut through the mountains.'

Further Reading
Paddy Docherty (2007). *The Khyber Pass: A History of Empire and Invasion* (London, Faber)
John H. Waller (1990). *Beyond the Khyber Pass: The Road to British Disaster in the First Afghan War* (New York, Random House)

Kikuyu. A prominent and populous Kenyan ethnic group, the Kikuyu became the most thoroughly politicized Africans within colonial Kenya*, emerging as leaders in nationalism and the move toward independence. Sustained contact with the British began in the 1890s, when the building of the Uganda Railway* and the arrival of white settlers made for incursions into historic Kikuyuland. The rich agricultural prospects of the Kikuyu highlands promised prosperity for the early settlers. Though never coming to pass in quite the way the settlers had hoped, the confiscation of much of what was Kikuyu ancestral territory produced great resentment, which issued in their political organization as early as the 1920s. From then until Kenyan independence in 1963, the Kikuyu took a leading role in pushing for a restoration of control over their lives, culminating in demands for an end to British rule. Spiked by the Mau Mau* uprising in the 1950s, the Kikuyu – led largely by Jomo Kenyatta* – were later successful in agitating for a peaceful transfer of power. Since independence the Kikuyu have remained the country's largest and most influential minority, the fact of which continues to spark protest – sometimes violent – by those tribal groups deemed to have been left out politically or discriminated against by the usually ascendant Kikuyu.

Further Reading
John Lonsdale and Bruce Berman (1992). *Unhappy Valley: Conflict in Kenya and Africa* (London, J. Currey)
Godfrey Muriuki (1974). *History of the Kikuyu, 1500–1900* (London, Oxford University Press)

King, W.L. Mackenzie (1874–1950). The longest-serving Prime Minister in the history of the Empire-Commonwealth, King led Canada for a total of almost twenty-two years, beginning in 1921 and ending in 1948. First elected to Parliament in 1908, King was a lifelong member of the Liberal Party, leading it for almost thirty years. Highly educated – like his near-contemporary, US President Woodrow Wilson, one of the few political leaders anywhere to possess a PhD – King developed strong views on the Empire and the rightful place of Canada in it. He advocated Canadian autonomy, made clear at the time of the Chanak Crisis* in 1922 when his government refused to send troops to Turkey, as requested by Colonial Secretary Winston Churchill. He was a prominent figure at the 1926 Imperial Conference* when the Balfour Definition of Dominion status was agreed upon, and increasingly saw Canada's main international relationship to be with the United States.

Further Reading

J.L. Granatstein (2002). *W.L. Mackenzie King* rev. edn (Markham, ON, Fitzhenry & Whiteside)

H. Blair Neatby (1963, 1976). *W.L. Mackenzie King 1923–32, 1932–9*, 2 vols (Toronto, University of Toronto Press)

King's African Rifles. A well-known colonial African regiment, the KAR was raised in 1902 upon the amalgamation of a number of smaller local regiments. Originally stationed in the form of one or two battalions in each of Nyasaland*, Kenya*, Uganda*, and British Somaliland*, the KAR saw service in a number of campaigns and wars, including the search for and defeat of Mohammed Abdullah Hassan, the so-called 'Mad Mullah'*, in British Somaliland* in 1920, the First and Second World Wars*, and the Mau Mau* uprising in Kenya in the 1950s. In 1957, the KAR was given a new name, the East African Land Forces, and in the period of African independence many of the traditions of the KAR lived on to influence the formation of new national armies.

Further Reading

John Nunneley (1998). *Tales of the King's African Rifles: A Last Flourish of Empire* (Petersham, Askari Books)

Malcolm Page (1998). *A History of the King's African Rifles and East African Forces* (London, Leo Cooper)

Kingsley, Mary H. (1862–1900). Mary Kingsley became synonymous in late-Victorian Britain with African travel and the British Empire. Her reputation as an inveterate and hardy traveller, an astute observer of African culture and society, and both a critic of and informal advisor to government, was made during these years. For Kingsley, the British Empire began and ended in Africa, which was a place wholly unlikely to bulk so large in the life of a respectable, though unmarried, Victorian woman. Born in Islington in 1862, her childhood and youth were quiet and secluded. She received, as was the custom of the time, no formal education, but in its absence became an autodidact and read voluminously. In 1886, with a brother on the verge of entering Cambridge to read for a degree in law, the Kingsleys moved to the university city itself. She read widely, as usual, but also met a number of dons, attended lectures, made friends, and, in 1888, enjoyed her first trip abroad. Later, a Cambridge friend, Hatty Johnson, who had a contact in the Canary Islands, suggested Kingsley visit and she went in June 1892 to this chain of islands just a hundred miles west of Africa. The trip seems to have awakened Mary's latent sense of adventure and confirmed her future course. She would go to Africa, she determined. Accordingly, in August 1893, she sailed for the West African coast. By December 1893 she was home again, strolling the streets of Liverpool with the exotic complement of a monkey perched on her shoulder. As it turned out, Kingsley's first trip to Africa was a mere prelude to her second and main voyage out, which lasted for almost a year, from December 1894 to November 1895. On her return to West Africa – this time to Calabar in Britain's Oil Rivers Protectorate (part of today's Nigeria*) – she came equipped with extensive collection materials supplied by the British Museum, as well as a London publisher's commission for a book on the region. These next months would be the most important in the establishment of Kingsley as a famous Victorian traveller, explorer, and naturalist, and bring her to the attention of the British government, especially the Colonial Secretary, Joseph Chamberlain*, whom she would later advise on colonial policy in Sierra Leone. Exhausted but exhilarated, Kingsley sailed for England. She brought with her a large collection of plants, insects, reptiles and fish, to go along with her copious notes and journal entries. Arriving home, she was met by immediate public interest in her feats. Invitations to give lectures and talks inevitably followed.

Publication of a book came early in 1897. *Travels in West Africa, Congo Français, Corisco and Cameroons* was well received and put Kingsley's name in front of an even wider audience. Part of this audience included businessmen and academics, and part too would soon include politicians such as Chamberlain. Her opinions ranged widely, from endorsing British trading interests – including the liquor trade, which immediately raised the ire of the missionary lobby – to criticizing the British government's implementation of what in her view was a punitive hut tax in Sierra Leone. Throughout this period of high visibility and sustained controversy, Kingsley maintained a steadfast desire to return to West Africa. But her return did not, alas, come where or when she anticipated. In the spring of 1900, as the Boer War* raged and while her own demands to speak and write seemed overwhelming, she decided to go to South Africa* and volunteer as a wartime nurse. Once the war was over she planned to return to West Africa. But in June, after a short bout of typhoid, which was endemic in the hospital in which she worked, she died. She was just thirty-seven years old.

Further Reading
Dea Birkett (1992). *Mary Kingsley: Imperial Adventuress* (London, Macmillan)
Katherine Frank (1986). *A Voyager Out: The Life of Mary Kingsley* (Boston, Houghton Mifflin)

Kipling, Rudyard (1865–1936). Famous as an Imperialist of the pen, Kipling was born in Bombay where his father, the artist John Lockwood Kipling, had gone to take up a teaching post in the mid-1860s. Kipling spent his first six years amid the 'light and colour and golden and purple fruits' of India before being sent to England to be educated. After years of only intermittent happiness there, he was glad to return to India*, doing so in 1882 to begin life as a journalist in Lahore, and quickly made his name as a chronicler of Raj military and social life. For the next seven years, first in Lahore and then later in Allahabad, Kipling observed and wrote. Not much of what constituted British life in India in those days escaped his keen eye and usually gently satirical pen. These years gave him a lifetime's material for his journalistic pieces, essays, poems, short stories, and novels, and upon the publication of *Plain Tales from the Hills* in 1888 his fame in both India and England was confirmed. The next year he re-located to London and embarked upon a literary career of unparalleled success. Wealth, social position, and public acclaim all came thick and fast, capped in 1907 with his winning of the Nobel Prize in Literature. His output was steady: *The Light that Failed* (1890); *The Jungle Book* (1894); *The Second Jungle Book* (1895); *Captains Courageous* (1897); and *Kim* (1901), among others. Together with his poetry, especially *Recessional*, written for Queen Victoria's Diamond Jubilee in 1897 and for which *The Times* hailed him as 'Laureate of the Empire,' Kipling emerged as the best-known literary figure in the English-speaking world. His admiration for the Empire was made plain, but it was no mere jingoism. In *Recessional* he had warned of Imperial hubris, and advocated that the 'Law,' above all else, was the foundation of a just Empire. Though he visited India only once after leaving in 1889, Kipling travelled often to South Africa*, to Australia*, and in 1907 to Canada* – 'Our Lady of the Snows,' he wrote admiringly – traversing its vast expanse by train in the only long-range speaking tour of his life. The death of a young daughter, and then later that of his only son in the First World War*, together with the obscene wastefulness of that conflict, altered him greatly, however. His later years were marked by both wistfulness and anger as he saw the end of Empire at hand and his place as its 'watchman' rendered anachronistic. In his time, Kipling captured the essence of what it meant to be British, and at his death it was clear that the Empire's lead 'trumpeter' had passed.

Further Reading

David Gilmour (2002). *The Long Recessional: The Imperial Life of Rudyard Kipling* (New York, Farrar, Straus & Giroux)

Angus Wilson (1994). *The Strange Ride of Rudyard Kipling: His Life and Works* (London, Pimlico)

Kiribati (see Gilbert and Ellice Islands)

Kirk, Sir John (1832–92). Explorer, physician, and colonial administrator, Kirk made his name as part of David Livingstone's* Zambezi Expedition from 1858 to 1864. Scottish-born and educated in medicine at the University of Edinburgh, he fell out with Livingstone on their shared arduous expedition.

Afterwards he became British Consul at Zanzibar*, where he was a key figure negotiating with the Sultan to bring an end to the Omani Arab slave trade.

Further Reading

Reginald Foskett, ed. (1965). *The Zambesi Journal and Letters of Dr John Kirk, 1858–63* (Edinburgh, Oliver & Boyd)

Daniel Liebowitz (1999). *The Physician and the Slave Trade: John Kirk, the Livingstone Expeditions, and the Crusade against Slavery in East Africa* (New York, W.H. Freeman & Company)

Kitchener, Horatio Herbert, Earl Kitchener of Khartoum (1850–1916). The iconic soldier of Empire, Kitchener was born in Ireland to English parents, lived briefly in Switzerland, and then entered the Royal Military Academy, Woolwich in 1868. He was commissioned into the Royal Engineers in 1871, then spent a few years at the School of Engineering at Chatham before being seconded to the Palestine Exploration Fund in 1874. Thus began a lifetime's connection with the Middle East and North Africa. A spell in Cyprus was followed by his unofficial attachment to the British force that bombarded Alexandria in the summer of 1882 in order to put down the Egyptian nationalist uprising led by Colonel Arabi Pasha*. Shortly thereafter he made a name for himself in the role of intelligence officer as part of the General Gordon* relief expedition and in the summer of 1885 he was promoted brevet lieutenant-colonel. Time spent afterwards in Zanzibar as part of the Boundary Commission bored him and so on his way home to England in the summer of 1886 he was happy to break course and take up an appointment as Governor-General of the eastern Sudan in an attempt to overturn Mahdist rule, which had proved triumphant the year before with the fall of Khartoum and Gordon's death. Though unsuccessful in the short term, his star continued to rise, and in 1892 Kitchener was appointed *Sirdar*, or Commander-in-Chief, of the Egyptian army. In this position, he launched the campaign that would re-take the Sudan from the Mahdists in 1898. The Battle of Omdurman* that year which sealed the victory was a brutal affair: some 11,000 Sudanese were killed, compared to just forty-eight British dead. The battle was a show of overwhelming modern technological know-how against almost medieval-style opposition, and the sheer killing power of the British, together with the desecration of the Mahdi's* tomb, left Kitchener open to criticism by no less than the young Winston Churchill*, who participated at Omdurman as both soldier and journalist. Kitchener shrugged off the criticism, however, and soon was on his way to South Africa* to take charge of the faltering war against the Boers* over regional paramountcy. Arriving in January 1900, at the war's low ebb for the British, as Commander-in-Chief Kitchener re-ordered Britain's fighting style, instituting a scorched-earth policy that destroyed the ability of the Boers to keep their highly effective commandos in the field. One element of the new policy was the construction of concentration camps used to house Boer prisoners, mainly women and children. The camps were a disgrace: more than 20,000 inmates died, most of them children and youths. Kitchener defended the camps, but he was decried in Parliament for employing 'methods of barbarism' and conditions in the camps thereafter improved markedly. Kitchener's reputation survived this episode, but it sullied him. The war against the Boers ended in 1902 and Kitchener departed for India*, where he took up the position of Commander-in-Chief of the 250,000-man Indian army. His relationship with the equally strong-willed Viceroy, Lord Curzon*, was prickly, and then became impossible and he resigned in 1904. The remaining years of Kitchener's life saw him occupy a number of leading military posts. Promoted field marshal in 1909, he later became Secretary of War in 1914, presiding over the British Army until his death by drowning two years later. Kitchener, with his ramrod stature, handlebar moustache, and unsmiling visage, was the epitome of the Imperial soldier, nowhere better reflected than on the famous 'Your Country Needs You' recruiting poster issued in the fall of 1914. He remains one of the most hotly debated of British Imperial military men.

Further Reading

Philip Magnus (1964). *Kitchener: Portrait of an Imperialist* (London, John Murray)

John Pollock (1998). *Kitchener: The Road to Omdurman* (London, Constable)

Klondike. One of the most famous gold rushes during the high period of Empire, gold found in 1896 on a tributary of the Klondike River in what is today Canada's Yukon* Territory touched off a frenzy of activity. Thousands of would-be prospectors headed north and for the next two years perhaps as much as $50 million in gold was taken from the aptly named Bonanza Creek. For most Canadians, as well as for others in the Empire, the Klondike gold strike marked the first time that the vast Canadian North had been considered anything other than a frozen wasteland.

Further Reading

Pierre Berton (1992). *Trails of '98* (Toronto, McClelland & Stewart)

J.A. Johnson (2001). *George Carmack: Man of Mystery who set off the Klondike Gold Rush* (Vancouver, Whitecap Books)

Kruger, S.J. Paulus (1825–1904). 'Paul' Kruger, President of the Boer Republic of the Transvaal* and, to many late-Victorian Imperialists, the British Empire's chief nemesis, was born in Cape Colony* and as a boy was part of the Great Trek*. He had almost no formal education, was married twice, and fathered seventeen children. He got involved in local politics through his initial service in the commandos and in 1874 he was elected to the executive council of the Transvaal, the next year becoming its Vice-President. He fiercely resisted Britain's annexation of the Transvaal in 1877 and was gratified to help defeat the British in the First Boer War* in 1880–1, and see the Transvaal's independence restored under British regional paramountcy. Partway through the war, Kruger was elected President of the Transvaal, a position he would hold until his death. The discovery of gold near Johannesburg in 1884 prompted a rush and Kruger feared that the Boer population would be swamped by *Uitlanders* (outsiders). As more and more miners and prospectors, financiers and outfitters flooded in, his fears became reality. By the 1890s, the British, especially Rhodes*, were looking at ways in which to overthrow Kruger's government, and in 1895 the Jameson Raid* proved an ill-fated attempt to do so. By the end of the decade and after many British imprecations, war between Britain and the Boers seemed inevitable. In September 1899, not long after scolding Colonial Secretary Joseph Chamberlain* that 'it is our country you want,' he sent Boer troops into Natal*, precipitating the Second Boer War*. The years that followed saw Kruger go into exile in the Netherlands, and in failing health he died while in Switzerland.

Further Reading

John Fisher (1974). *Paul Kruger: His Life and Times* (London, Secker & Warburg)

Johannes Meintjes (1974). *President Paul Kruger: A Biography* (London, Cassell)

Kuwait. In 1899, Britain became responsible for Kuwait's protection, a status maintained formally until 1961. British links with the tiny emirate at the head of the Persian Gulf stretched back to the days of the East India Company*, and throughout the early part of the twentieth century Kuwait was a convenient place for the British to formally discuss the future of the Middle East. The development of oil reserves in the 1930s made Kuwait of much greater importance to Britain, a situation that eventually provoked considerable controversy in Anglo-Kuwaiti relations.

Further Reading

Michael S. Casey (2007). *The History of Kuwait* (Westport, CT, Greenwood Press)

Simon C. Smith (1999). *Kuwait, 1950–1965: Britain, the al-Sabah, and Oil* (Oxford, Oxford University Press)

L

Laurier, Sir Wilfrid (1841–1919). Prime Minister of Canada from 1896 to 1911, Laurier was an important figure in developing the idea of 'Dominion autonomy' within the British Empire. Born in Canada East (Quebec*), he was educated at McGill University in Montreal and then practiced law in the city. He later engaged in journalism and was briefly a member of the provincial legislature before being elected to Parliament for the Liberals in 1874. In 1887, he was chosen to lead the Party, and did so until his defeat at the polls in 1911. In between, he led Canada for fifteen years, during which he staunchly resisted the movement for Imperial Federation*, navigated Canada's participation in the Second Boer War* (despite French Canada's vehement opposition to it), and introduced the Naval Service Bill in 1910, which proposed the construction of a Canadian navy to be at the service of the British Empire whenever and wherever required. Opposition to the bill in French Canada, as well as converse complaints by English-speaking Canadian Imperialists that it was not strong enough, contributed significantly to its defeat, along with that of the Laurier Liberals themselves in 1911.

Further Reading
Joseph Schull (1965). *Laurier: The First Canadian* (Toronto, MacMillan)
Oscar D. Skelton (1965). *Life and Letters of Sir Wilfrid Laurier* 2nd edn, 2
    vols (Toronto, McClelland & Stewart)

Lawrence, Sir Henry M. (1806–57). A heroic figure to the British community of the Indian Mutiny*, Lawrence was born in Ceylon*, educated at

Haileybury*, and in 1823 joined the Bengal Artillery stationed at Calcutta. He later served in Burma*, and in the First Afghan War*, as well as revenue surveyor in India. In 1846, he was made Resident of Lahore and Agent to the Governor-General for the North West Frontier. In 1856, on the eve of the Mutiny, Lawrence was named Chief Commissioner of the recently and controversially acquired province of Awadh. The next year its capital city of Lucknow was the site of a protracted siege by mutineers in which the 3,000 members of the British garrison and civilian population took refuge in the Residency. Fiercely defending his countrymen, Lawrence was killed early in the siege and was buried in the Residency garden, where his gravestone reads: 'Here lies Sir Henry Lawrence who tried to do his duty. May God have mercy on him.' His courage and sacrifice formed a key part of the British cultural residue of the Mutiny.

Further Reading

Henry Lawrence (1859). *Essays, Military and Political. Written In India* (London, W.H. Allen & Co.)

Harold Lee (2002). *Brothers in the Raj: The Lives of John and Henry Lawrence* (Oxford, Oxford University Press)

Lawrence, John, 1st Baron Lawrence (1811–79). Viceroy of India in the years shortly after the Indian Mutiny*, Lawrence pursued a conservative policy along India's borders, so as not to inflame Anglo-Russian tensions over Afghanistan. He arrived in India as an eighteen-year-old accompanying his older brother, Sir Henry Lawrence*, and followed a varied administrative and martial career, including the Sikh Wars of the 1840s. In 1849, he became a member of the Punjab Board of Administration and was integral in preventing the Mutiny from spreading to that province in 1857, the same year that he famously commanded the British troops that recaptured Delhi and the putative 'King of Delhi,' Bahadur Shah Zafar II*, from the rebellious sepoys. For this act he was made baronet. He became Viceroy in 1864, serving for five years until retiring to England.

Further Reading

Michael Edwardes (1958). *The Necessary Hell: John and Henry Lawrence and the Indian Empire* (London, Cassell)

R. Bosworth Smith (1883). *Life of Lord Lawrence*, 2 vols (London, Smith Elder)

Lawrence, T.E. (1888–1935). An enduringly romantic figure in the history of the Empire, Lawrence's place in the First World War's* Arab Revolt in the desert, at the negotiating table in its aftermath, his insistence on wearing Arab dress, and his obvious sympathy for Arab nationalism, made him both admired and controversial at a time when the Empire was very much a world-historical force. Lawrence's life began in the mysterious way it was always lived. Born in Wales, he was the illegitimate son of Thomas Chapman and his mistress, Sarah Junner, who settled finally in Oxford, beginning in 1896. The family was fairly well off: Thomas Lawrence, as the father renamed himself, supported them on a trust fund inherited from his own titled family. Lawrence and his four brothers all attended Oxford City High School for Boys. Characteristically, he did not like team sports, choosing instead to test himself against the elements in individual contests of physical endurance. He was a loner and a scholar. In 1907, he won a scholarship to Jesus College, Oxford, where he embarked on a degree in modern history. His academic progress was outstanding, to which can be added a strong youthful religiosity inherited from his mother whose own evangelical Christian faith frowned deeply on her conventionally immoral domestic status. He took a first-class degree in 1910, having by then already travelled to the Middle East. An appointment to the British Museum's archaeological dig at Carchemish, Syria soon followed and occupied him until 1914. Upon the outbreak of the First World War*, his specialist knowledge of the Middle East was tapped by the government and he was sent to Cairo as a member of Britain's new Military Intelligence Department. Life on camelback was just around the corner. Lawrence plunged into his new work in the Egyptian capital, bringing to bear on it a keen intellect and a deepening sympathy for Arab national aspirations. In January 1916, the Arab Bureau was formed, one of its main tasks being to gather information about the state of Arab readiness regarding a revolt against their Turkish overlords. Lawrence gradually saw his own work move explicitly in this direction, and in the fall of 1916 he was transferred to the Bureau. By that time, the Revolt was already underway in the Hejaz, a region along the Red Sea coast of today's Saudi Arabia. Lawrence was dispatched to Jiddah in the Hejaz, to report on the situation. His return to Cairo shortly thereafter was spent in writing up a report on the state of the Arab Revolt, what the Arabs themselves could do to bring it to fruition, and how both he and the British could best assist them in doing so. The eventual stirring success of the Revolt and the triumphant taking of Damascus in 1918 marked for Lawrence the end of the War. He returned to England immediately, and by the end of October was in talks about the right course for British policy in the Middle East. Lawrence's last piece of government work came in March 1921 at the Cairo Conference. In July he resigned from the Colonial Office. He was not quite thirty-four years old. Any number of people had him pegged for high and important office, but Lawrence would have none of it. He finished his history of the Arab Revolt, *The Seven Pillars of Wisdom*, and then sought a quieter life by enlisting in the Royal Air Force. The British government attempted to recruit him on various occasions, but he always refused. Changing his name legally to T.E. Shaw was an attempt at securing anonymity. But such never came in life, and certainly not in death. Lawrence was a liberal Imperialist. His greatest legacy is found in helping to initiate the drive for Arab independence. Dying in a motorcycle accident in 1935, Lawrence lived just long enough to see it begin to come to pass.

Further Reading

Malcolm Brown, ed. (1988). *The Letters of T.E. Lawrence* (London, J.M. Dent & Sons)

Jeremy Wilson (1990). *Lawrence of Arabia: The Authorized Biography of T.E. Lawrence* (New York, Atheneum)

Leakey, Louis S.B. (1903–72). Among the most famous of the twentieth century's archaeologists and palaeontologists, Leakey was born to Church of England missionary parents at Kabete in British East Africa*. Educated both locally and in England, he won a scholarship to Cambridge in 1922, intent on returning to Africa as a missionary. One of the few for whom

Darwin and Christianity posed no contradiction, he decided to become a 'fossil hunter' instead, securing a place on a British Museum expedition to the new British mandate of Tanganyika* in 1924. Upon his return to Cambridge, he read for a degree in anthropology and archaeology, and graduated with a double first in 1926. Cambridge sent him back to Africa on a research fellowship and, at length, in 1930, he earned a PhD. Many years of excavation and discovery followed. So, too, did politics, because his Kenyan birthright, fluency in Kikuyu, and ease of entry into the highest circles both in Britain and in Kenya, made Leakey an important, and some-times controversial, figure. From 1945 to 1961 he was curator of the Coryndon Memorial Museum in Nairobi, during which time he made his most famous discoveries of early hominid fossils at Olduvai Gorge in neigh-bouring Tanzania*. His wife, Mary, and son, Richard, became as well known as Leakey in the same fields, and for the latter, also in Kenyan wildlife conservation.

Further Reading

Mary Bowman-Kruhm (2005). *The Leakeys: A Biography* (Westport, CT, Greenwood Press)

Sonia M. Cole (1975). *Leakey's Luck: The Life of Louis Seymour Bazett Leakey, 1903–1972* (London, Collins)

Lennox-Boyd, Alan, 1st Viscount Boyd of Merton (1904–83). Colonial Secretary during a critical period of the Empire's decolonization, Lennox-Boyd was educated at Sherborne School and Christ Church, Oxford*. He eventually became a barrister, but not before gaining election to Parliament for the Conservatives in 1931. As a member of Churchill's* post-war govern-ment, he served as Minister for Transport and Civil Aviation and then, beginning in 1954, as Colonial Secretary. Under his watch the former colonies of Cyprus*, Ghana*, Iraq*, Malaya*, and Sudan* all achieved independence. His most difficult situation, however, emerged in Kenya*, with the Mau Mau* crisis of the mid- to late 1950s. In 1959, eleven detainees at the Hola detention camp were murdered, which led to a House of Commons debate and report censuring the government for having used excessive force. In the Cabinet re-shuffle following the general election of that fall, Lennox-

Boyd was replaced as Colonial Secretary by Iain Macleod*. The following year, he was raised to the peerage as Viscount Boyd of Merton. Popular with members of the Colonial Service*, he took up corporate directorship upon retirement, dying in 1983.

Further Reading

Alan Lennox-Boyd (1958). *Imperium et libertas* (London, Conservative Political Centre)

Philip Murphy (1999). *Alan Lennox-Boyd: A Biography* (London and New York, I.B.Tauris)

Lesotho. The Kingdom of Lesotho is landlocked, mainly agrarian, never witnessed European settlers, and is entirely surrounded by the Republic of South Africa*. As Basutoland*, it emerged under paramount chief Moshoeshoe I* in 1843, and in 1868 it was given British protection and became a High Commission Territory. The British move was disputed by the Cape Colony*, however, which absorbed it in 1871. Direct control from London was reinstituted in 1883. Autonomy was granted in 1965, and the next year Basutoland became independent under the name of Lesotho.

Further Reading

Elizabeth A. Eldredge (2007). *Power in Colonial Africa: Conflict and Discourse in Lesotho*, 1870–1960 (Madison, University of Wisconsin Press)

Judith M. Kimble (1999). *Migrant Labour and Colonial Rule in Basutoland, 1890–1930* (Grahamstown, SA, Institute of Social and Economic Research, Rhodes University)

Livingstone, David (1813–73). Famous as a missionary doctor and explorer, David Livingstone was born to working-class parents in the mill town of Blantyre, Scotland. Mostly self-taught until the age of twenty-three, he then enrolled at Anderson's College in Glasgow, where he received two years of rudimentary medical training. Deciding to devote his skills and his Christian faith to missionary service, he applied to the London Missionary Society and in 1840 was sent to South Africa. While there, he developed an intense interest in geographical exploration, discovering Lake Ngami in 1849, and then from 1852 until 1856, crossing the centre of the African continent from east to west, becoming the first white man to view what thereafter was called the Victoria Falls*. He returned to England in 1856 and was lionized by the mid-Victorian public, honoured by the Royal Geographical Society (RGS)*, and addressed large audiences, including at Oxford* and Cambridge, about the need to return to Africa in order to 'make an open path for commerce and Christianity.' His country-wide touring resulted in the founding of a new missionary society, the Universities Mission to Central Africa (UMCA), and the patronage of the RGS, which sent him back to Africa at the head of the Zambezi Expedition* in 1860. He did not return to England until 1864. The next year, he went to Africa for the final time. He was wracked now by personal sadness (his wife had died while with him on the previous expedition) and the privations of the explorer's life had damaged his health. Livingstone's final years in Africa were spent in a futile search for the headwaters of the Nile. Little was heard from him in the outside world, which piqued the interest of many, including the *New York Herald*, to 'find' him. To this end, Henry Morton Stanley* was dispatched to Central Africa, and in 1871 met up with Livingstone at Ujiji on the shores of Lake Tanganyika. Two years later, Livingstone died at Chitambo's Village (Zambia*), still searching fruitlessly for the source of the Nile. His body was brought home, and in April 1874 his funeral at Westminster Abbey was that of a hero of the Empire.

Further Reading

Dorothy O. Helly (1987). *Livingstone's Legacy: Horace Waller and Victorian Mythmaking* (Athens, OH, Ohio University Press)

Tim Jeal (1973). *Livingstone* (London, Heinemann)

Lobengula, Kumalo (c.1845–94). King of Matabeleland, located in today's Zimbabwe*, Lobengula was the last ruler of the Ndebele (usually pronounced Matabele in the colonial period) people and was a key figure in the events leading up to the Matabele Wars* of the 1890s. Born into royalty, Lobengula unexpectedly became king in 1868 and ruled until his death. Tall and muscular (although he became very overweight in his later years), Lobengula had little contact with the outside world until the 1870s, when he allowed the European search for gold to extend to a small part of Matabeleland. Pressure for additional concessions followed, especially after 1886 when gold was discovered on the nearby Rand. Two years later, and after much negotiation, Lobengula agreed to the Rudd Concession, which had a twenty-five-year lifespan and was the work of Cecil Rhodes* and his associates. Lobengula soon realized, however, that Rhodes' British South Africa Company* was determined to colonize the region. War broke out in the fall of 1893. Likely already ill, Lobengula died the next year. Not long afterwards, his people had been subjugated and Matabeleland subsumed by the new colony of (Southern) Rhodesia*.

Further Reading

Stuart Cloete (1969). *African Portraits: A Biography of Paul Kruger, Cecil Rhodes and Lobengula, Last King of the Matabele* (Cape Town, Constantia Publishers)

Gustav S. Preller (1963). *Lobengula: The Tragedy of a Matabele King* (Johannesburg, Afrikaanse Pers-Boekhandel)

London Declaration. Issued in 1949 by the Prime Ministers of what was then called the British Commonwealth of Nations, the London Declaration provided both symbol and substance to the passing of the Empire. Prodded by India's* wish to remain within the Commonwealth even though having recently declared itself a republic, the Declaration made clear the acceptance of the idea henceforth, as well as changing the body's name from 'British Commonwealth' to simply 'Commonwealth.'

Further Reading

R.J. Moore (1987). *Making the New Commonwealth* (Oxford, Oxford University Press)

Nicholas Mansergh (1982). *The Commonwealth Experience* (Toronto, University of Toronto Press)

Lower Canadian Rebellion. In November 1837, a Rebellion against the ruling elite of Lower Canada (Quebec*) broke out and lasted for about a year. It pitted a force of French-speaking Canadians – the *Patriote* movement – allied with some disenfranchised English-speaking merchants, against the so-called 'Château Clique,' the colony's ruling elite. The leading figure of the Rebellion was Louis-Joseph Papineau*, a *Patriote*, who sought a more equitable system of governance, which eventually was known as responsible government*. The local authorities resisted fiercely, although the rebels themselves were divided along political and religious lines in an age when the Roman Catholic Church wielded great power in the province. Parliamentary debates were followed by public protests, which led to violence. On the verge of arrest, Papineau fled to the United States. British forces defeated the rebels in two battles in December, and martial law was declared in Montreal. Further battles in 1838 were likewise fought and won by the British, who chose to solve the crisis by employing Lord Durham* to investigate its causes and recommend a solution, which he did, the result being the union of Upper and Lower Canada in 1841 and the implementation of responsible government later that decade. The Rebellion remains a contested part of Canadian history, especially its interpretation by some Quebeckers as a proto-nationalist event.

Further Reading

Allan Greer (1993). *The Patriots and the People: The Rebellion of 1837 in Rural Lower Canada* (Toronto, University of Toronto Press)

Fernand Ouellet (1980). *Lower Canada, 1791–1840: Social Change and Nationalism* (Toronto, McClelland & Stewart)

Lugard, Lord Frederick D. (1858–1945). In the list of British Imperial proconsuls, few surpass Lugard for length and variety of service. As soldier, governor, and theorist of Imperial rule, Lugard was the leading 'man on the spot' in British Africa during the early part of the twentieth century. Born in Madras in 1858, his childhood was passed there, and beginning in 1864 in Worcester, where his father had been appointed rector of an Anglican church. Educated locally, and then for a time near Manchester, in 1871 he was admitted to Rossall School, a Church of England establishment located in Lancashire. In time he began to think about a vocation, which led him to seek a place in the Indian Civil Service*. He failed to gain a place, however, but then sat the army examinations successfully. In February 1878, the now twenty-year-old Lugard arrived for a year's training at the Royal Military Academy, Sandhurst. Commissioned into the 9th Regiment, he served in India. In 1885, Lugard was sent along with his battalion to Africa. Then it was off to Burma* the next year, and as a reward the Distinguished Service Order in 1887. Devastated later that year by unrequited love, he resigned his commission and fled to Zanzibar and then Abyssinia, Aden*, and finally Mozambique. There, in the employ of the African Lakes Company, he was hired to hunt elephant. It was 1888, and Lugard was only thirty-years-old, but his career seemed over. Working at the rank of captain, however, Lugard quickly became an indispensable presence for the company and soon his anti-slavery exploits brought him to the attention of William Mackinnon* of the Imperial British East Africa Company*. Later, he would go to Uganda for the IBEAC, and then independently to Nigeria. The Conservative government of Lord Salisbury*, in office since 1895, thought it prudent to resist attempted French expansion in the region. Lugard was chosen by the government to do its bidding in this regard. In 1900, after Lugard had pushed hard to extend and consolidate the British presence in the area, the Salisbury government declared a Protectorate over Northern and Southern Nigeria, and Lugard was made High Commissioner of the Northern Protectorate. From then until 1906, Lugard led a lean but determined regime that brought all of the Islamic Protectorate's kingdoms under British control. In practice, this meant that its traditional chiefs and rulers came under the Indirect Rule* of the British. This system, with which Lugard became synonymous, was designed to leave in place most of the ruling structures of traditional Nigerian society, while erecting a British paramountcy to which all were accountable. As a colonial theorist, Indirect Rule became Lugard's cornerstone, and formed the basis of the two important books on the subject of European colonial rule in Africa he would later write: *Political Memoranda* (1919) and *The Dual Mandate in British Tropical Africa* (1922). In 1907, he was named Governor of Hong Kong*, a post he held until 1912. Lugard's Governorship there was something that never suited him, and so it was back to Africa in the fall of 1912, this time to draw up a plan to implement the government's desire to create an amalgamated colony of Nigeria. On New Year's Day 1914, the politically unified Nigeria was duly proclaimed, with Lugard as its Governor-General. In 1918, he was sixty years old, exhausted and ready to move on. Accordingly, he retired in November and returned to England. Lugard nonetheless would remain an active voice and a clear symbol of Empire until he died in 1945. Like most other Imperial proconsuls, his reputation is controversial: he is admired by some for the sheer fortitude of his character and the amplitude of his ideas; disdained or worse by many more for the unrepentant paternalistic superiority inherent in his words and actions.

Further Reading

Lord Lugard (1965). *The Dual Mandate in British Tropical Africa* (London, Frank Cass)

Margery Perham (1956, 1960). *Lugard: The Years of Adventure 1858–1898; Lugard: The Years of Authority 1898–1945* (London, Collins)

Lutyens, Sir Edwin L. (1869–1944). One of the leading British architects of the high period of Empire and responsible for many of its signature memorials and buildings, Lutyens was born in London and studied at the South Kensington School of Art before going into architectural practice. Late in the First World War*, he was appointed to the Imperial War Graves Commission. In this capacity he designed, among others, the Cenotaph, Westminster, and the Memorial to the Missing of the Somme at Thiepval, France. But his greatest achievement was to design some of the major public buildings required by the Raj when the decision was made to move its capital from Calcutta to 'New' Delhi in 1912. Lutyens worked on this project from then until 1929. The Viceregal Lodge (re-named the Rashtrapati Bhavan, it is now the home of India's President) became a spectacular example of his 'Delhi Order' of architecture, and together with other structures such as the India Gate located along New Delhi's Rajpath, Lutyens' work encapsulated British India in its final phase. Knighted in 1930, he later served as President of the Royal Academy. Together with Sir Herbert Baker*, Lutyens embodied the Imperial impulse set in stone.

Further Reading

Robert Grant Irving (1981). *Indian Summer: Lutyens, Baker, and Imperial Delhi* (New Haven, CT, Yale University Press)

Jan Morris (1983). *Stones of Empire: The Buildings of the Raj* (Oxford, Oxford University Press)

M

Maasai. A mainly Kenya*-based indigenous people, the Maasai are semi-nomadic and fiercely independent. Historically, feared for their prowess in war, they first encountered the British in the 1890s, and through treaties in 1904 and 1911 much of their land was acquired for white settlement. Despite being confined to reserves, the Maasai continued rather successfully in their pastoralist ways. Large herds of cattle were intrinsic to Maasai society, and their reserve lands, such as Maasai Mara, are situated in some of Africa's richest areas for wildlife. Maasai warriors, the *moran*, fought in the First and Second World Wars* for the British. Traditionally politically unengaged, they took little part in the Kenyan nationalist movement. Their distinctive brightly coloured clothing, cultural integrity (they were, for example, never enslaved) and fearsome reputation have long made the Maasai a greatly admired and written-about African people.

Further Reading
Elizabeth L. Gilbert (2007). *Tribes of the Great Rift Valley* (New York, Abrams)
Lotte Hughes (2006). *Moving the Maasai: A Colonial Misadventure* (New York, Palgrave Macmillan in association with St Antony's College, Oxford)

Macdonald, Sir John A. (1815–91). Canada's* first Prime Minister, Macdonald was the leading architect of Confederation, and afterwards fashioned the National Policy that saw a trans-continental railway span Canada and a tariff policy implemented, which allowed for the development of

Canadian industry over against the burgeoning American economy to the south. Born in Glasgow to an unsuccessful merchant and his wife, the family moved to Kingston, Upper Canada in 1820, where Macdonald grew up and was educated. As a young man, Macdonald moved to York (Toronto), where he articled to become a lawyer. He returned to Kingston in 1835 and the next year was called to the Bar. He practiced corporate law and then criminal law and made a name for himself as defence counsel for a number of those charged with treason during the Upper Canadian Rebellion* in 1837. He entered politics in 1843 as a Kingston alderman. The next year he was elected to the legislature of the Province of Canada, representing Kingston. His rise continued during the early 1850s, when he helped found the Liberal-Conservative Party, and in 1856 he became joint premier of Canada. From there he gradually began to advocate for the Confederation of all the British North American colonies. In 1867, the Dominion of Canada was formed, uniting Canada East and Canada West (Quebec* and Ontario*) with New Brunswick* and Nova Scotia*, and setting in motion the eventual creation of a continent-wide country. Macdonald took office as Canada's first Prime Minister and was knighted on 1 July 1867, which became the country's national day. He served until 1873, forced out by a railway scandal, before winning office for the Conservatives again in 1878 and holding it until his death in 1891. Macdonald was the most important political figure in early Canada and essentially established the role of the colonial Prime Minister.

Further Reading

Donald G. Creighton (1998). *John A. Macdonald: The Young Politician, The Old Chieftain* (Toronto, University of Toronto Press)

Richard Gwyn (2007). *John A.: The Man who Made us, the Life and Times of John A. Macdonald* (Toronto, Random House of Canada)

MacDonald, Malcolm J. (1901–81). A leading British politician and diplomat, MacDonald served in a number of Imperial and colonial offices as the Empire declined in the mid-twentieth century. Born the son of Labour Prime Minister Ramsay MacDonald, he was educated at Oxford* and elected to Parliament in 1929. Briefly Secretary of State for the Colonies* in 1935, he served in that capacity again from 1938 to 1940, as well as

Secretary of State for Dominion Affairs from 1935 to 1939. During these years he was involved in negotiations over the future of Northern Ireland and of Palestine*. His stance against the formation of an independent Jewish state was controversial in a number of quarters, including the Conservative Cabinet. He was High Commissioner to Canada from 1941 to 1946, and then Governor-General of Singapore* and Malaya* from 1946 to 1948. High Commissioner to India* from 1955 to 1960, he then went to Kenya*, where from 1963 to 1965 he was successively Governor, Governor-General, and High Commissioner during the former colony's independence period. MacDonald is seen rightly as a key figure in the closing days of Empire.

Further Reading

Elizabeth Cory and Sheila Hingley, eds (1988). *List of the Papers of Malcolm MacDonald* (Durham, University of Durham, Department of Palaeography and Diplomatic)

Clyde Sanger (1995). *Malcolm MacDonald: Bringing an End to Empire* (Kingston & Montreal, McGill-Queen's University Press)

Mackenzie, Sir Alexander (1764–1820). Mackenzie's fame rests on two late eighteenth-century intrepid expeditions through north-west Canada*, one leading to the Beaufort Sea in the Arctic and the other across the Continental Divide to the Pacific coast. Born in Scotland, he immigrated with his family to New York City in 1774 and a few years later, following the outbreak of the American War of Independence, he was sent to school in Montreal. He shortly entered the fur trade and by 1787 was a partner in the North West Company*, the Hudson Bay Company's* great Montreal-based rival. Together with a colleague, he theorized about possible routes to the Pacific, and in 1789 he started along the waterway that would later bear his name, the 2,600 mile-long Mackenzie River, the second-longest river in North America. Disappointed, however, that the river led ultimately to the Arctic Ocean and not to the Pacific, Mackenzie embarked on another expedition in 1793, which took him across a series of mountain ranges to the west coast. A remarkable efficient and resourceful explorer, Mackenzie never fired a shot in anger, despite numerous encounters with indigenous peoples. He was the first person to cross the continent north of Mexico. Knighted in 1802, Mackenzie retired to Scotland in 1812, where he died eight years later.

Further Reading

Barry M. Gough (1997). *First Across the Continent: Sir Alexander Mackenzie* (Toronto, McClelland & Stewart)

Derek Hayes (2001). *First Crossing: Alexander Mackenzie, His Expedition across North America, and the Opening of the Continent* (Vancouver, Douglas & McIntyre)

Mackenzie, Charles F. (1825–62). On New Year's Day 1861, in Cape Town, a thirty-five-year-old, Cambridge-educated, Scottish-born, Anglican high churchman was consecrated the first Church of England missionary bishop to Africa. In stark contrast to the more than forty years spent in India* by William Carey*, Bishop Charles Mackenzie survived barely one year in Central Africa. He died there, fevered and delirious, at the end of January 1862. But that lone year put Mackenzie directly in the path of a number of important streams that shaped mid- to late nineteenth-century missionary endeavour. Mackenzie's forlorn death – some called it martyrdom – represented to many the ultimate sacrifice that was always at least implicit in the service of the Victorian missionary. But it also came to signify an episode in church party politics, as well as a low-point in – until then – the celebrated career of the iconic missionary-explorer David Livingstone*. Mackenzie's brief life as a missionary provides a portal through which can be viewed the essence of the Victorian missionary imperative in the run-up to late nineteenth-century British Imperial expansion in Africa. And his lonely grave on Malo Island at the confluence of the Ruo and Shire Rivers in today's Malawi* is symbolic of the human cost of nineteenth-century missionary service. More broadly, the events that led up to his death speak clearly of the conflicting goals of Britain's mid-Victorian African Empire: In Livingstone we have the muscular Christian, impatient with both government and the church and ready to risk all to achieve the ideals of his own articulation of Britain's civilizing mission; In Mackenzie and his Universities Mission to Central Africa, on the other hand, can be seen the wholly socially respectable missionary, living and dying on the violent, slave-trading African frontier.

Further Reading

Owen Chadwick (1959). *Mackenzie's Grave* (London, Hodder & Stoughton)

C. Brad Faught (1997). 'Tractarianism on the Zambesi: Bishop Mackenzie and the Beginnings of the Universities Mission to Central Africa', *Anglican and Episcopal History*, vol. LXVI, no. 3, 303–28

Mackenzie, William Lyon (1795–1861). A pre-Confederation Canadian reformer who was a key influence on the ultimate adoption of responsible government, Mackenzie was born in Scotland, arriving in Upper Canada in 1820. Caught up quickly in the emergent political reform movement, he began publishing a newspaper, the *Colonial Advocate*, and in 1824 moved to York (Toronto), site of the provincial legislature. His fiery temperament and relentless criticism of the colony's ruling elite (the Family Compact, as it was known) led to his constant public denunciation. So provocative was Mackenzie that his printing press was wrecked by Family Compact vandals and the type thrown into Lake Ontario. Highly popular among the rural and non-Anglican population, however, Mackenzie was elected to the legislature several times, as well as becoming the first mayor of the re-named Toronto in 1834. But growing frustration at the inability to effect serious constitutional reform resulted in an ill-fated armed rebellion against the provincial government in 1837. Its failure led to Mackenzie's exile in the United States for ten years. Upon his return in 1849, he once again took up the banner of reform. By that time, however, responsible government had just come into effect, for which the earlier agitation by Mackenzie is rightly given considerable credit.

Further Reading

William Kilbourn (1956). *The Firebrand: William Lyon Mackenzie and the Rebellion in Upper Canada* (Toronto, Clarke, Irwin & Co.)

Anthony Rasporich (1972). *William Lyon Mackenzie* (Toronto, Holt, Rinehart & Winston of Canada)

Mackinnon, Sir William, 1st Baronet (1823–93). A leading financier of Empire whose influence was significant in late nineteenth-century East Africa, Mackinnon established both the British India Steamship Navigation

Company and the Imperial British East Africa Company*. Born in Scotland, he went to Calcutta in 1847 and a decade later founded his own company, carrying merchandise around the Bay of Bengal. Starting small, his company grew into the enormous BISNC, which extended its operations into Burma*, the Persian Gulf, and along the east coast of Africa. It was there in 1888 that Mackinnon established the IBEAC and was knighted the next year. Shortly thereafter he retired to England, dying in London.

Further Reading

John S. Galbraith (1972). *Mackinnon and East Africa, 1878–1895: A Study in the 'New Imperialism'* (Cambridge, Cambridge University Press)

J. Forbes Munro (2003). *Maritime Enterprise and Empire: Sir William Mackinnon and His Business Network, 1823–1893* (Woodbridge, Suffolk, Boydell Press)

Macleod, Iain N. (1913–70). Colonial Secretary during a period of intense decolonization in Africa, Macleod was born in Yorkshire and educated at Cambridge. Entering Parliament as a Conservative in 1950, Churchill* made him Minister of Health two years later. Appointed Secretary of State for the Colonies in 1959, for the succeeding two years Macleod presided over the independence of five African colonies, most notably Nigeria* and Tanzania*. He also ended the Mau Mau*-induced state of emergency in Kenya and freed Jomo Kenyatta* from seven years' incarceration. His noteworthy work at the Colonial Office* was the high-point of his career, although he held various other offices, including briefly Chancellor of the Exchequer in 1970, to which he had just been appointed prior to his early death.

Further Reading

Edward Pearce (1997). *The Lost Leaders* (London, Little, Brown)

Robert Shepherd (1994). *Iain Macleod* (London, Hutchinson)

'Mad Mullah' (Mohammed Abdullah Hassan) (1856–1920). An Islamic Somali nationalist, Mohammed Abdullah Hassan conducted a protracted resistance to British, Italian, and Ethiopian forces in the late nineteenth and early twentieth centuries. Born in northern Somaliland*, which at that time was a British Protectorate, he was shaped by the horse, by war, and by the Koran, and in the 1890s became a devoted follower of the Saalihiya order, which he vowed to spread throughout Somaliland. Alarmed at what he saw as the creeping Christianization of his homeland, he began to inspire a group of followers, 'dervishes', to withstand Ethiopian and British imprecations. Beginning in 1899, Hassan – known to the British as the 'Mad Mullah' – and his followers conducted an armed campaign, which was finally crushed in 1920. The British offered a settlement, which Hassan rejected, and he died at the end of the year.

Further Reading
Angus Hamilton (1970). *Somaliland* (Westport, CT, Negro Universities Press)
Douglas J. Jardine (1923). *The Mad Mullah of Somaliland* (London, Jenkins)

Mafeking, Siege of. Running for more than two hundred days from October 1899 to May 1900, the Siege of Mafeking became the most famous British action of the Second Boer War* and made a hero of Colonel Robert (later Lord) Baden-Powell*. The town of Mafeking in Natal* was selected by the British as an effective site to tie down the Boers upon their expected incursion. A defensive posture was adopted, which included trenches and gun emplacements, and when the Boer declaration of war duly came, Mafeking was ready to resist the onslaught of what proved to be a force of some 8,000 Boer troops. Baden-Powell had some 1,500 soldiers at his disposal, but the city was well-supplied with provisions and ammunition and together with his spirited leadership – he organized Sunday ceasefires, for example, during which the locals were able to play cricket and attend outdoor dramatic productions – the morale of the British was maintained. Eventually, the Boers tired of attacking what had turned out to be an impregnable redoubt. On 17 May 1900, a British relief column finally lifted the siege. In London and around the country, where Baden-Powell's breathless reports of the siege had been published in the papers, news of Mafeking's relief sparked enormous celebrations. 'Mafeking Night' became a byword for victory for the balance of the War and Baden-Powell the War's singular hero.

Further Reading

Malcolm Flower-Smith (2000). *Mafeking! The Story of a Siege* (Cape Town, Covos-Day)

Brian Gardner (1966). *Mafeking: A Victorian Legend* (London, Cassell)

Mahdi, The (Muhammad Ahmad) (1844–85). Claimant of a disputed position in Islamic (Shi'a) eschatology, the Mahdi is seen as a prophet of redemption. The designation was claimed by the Sudanese Muhammad Ahmad in 1882, sparking an Imperial crisis for the British. Over the course of the next three years, he defeated the armed forces sent to defend the Anglo-Egyptian Sudan*, culminating in the Siege of Khartoum and the death of General Gordon* in January 1885. Though Ahmad died later that year from illness, his victory established Mahdist rule in Sudan until 1898, when it was overthrown by the British re-conquest under the command of General Kitchener*.

Further Reading

P.M. Holt (1970). *The Mahdist State in the Sudan, 1881–1898* 2nd edn (Oxford, Clarendon Press)

Fergus Nicoll (2005). *The Mahdi of Sudan and the Death of General Gordon* (Stroud, Sutton Publishing)

Majuba Hill, Battle of. A small but decisive skirmish fought in February 1881, it occurred during the First Boer War* when the British were routed on a strategic hill in Natal*. Badly commanded by General George Colley, the British could not cope with the commando-style fighting of their enemy and they suffered 280 casualties to the Boers' six. Their defeat led to the treaty that ended the war and restored autonomy to the Boers' South African Republic. The humiliation of this defeat was sharp, and during the Second Boer War* 'Remember Majuba' was a rallying cry for British troops.

Further Reading

Oliver Ransford (1967). *The Battle of Majuba Hill: The First Boer War* (London, John Murray)

Mike Snook (2008). *Into the Jaws of Death: British Military Blunders, 1879–1900* (London, Frontline Books)

Malan, Daniel F. (1874–1959). Prime Minister of South Africa* from 1948 to 1954, Malan was the architect of the National Party's apartheid* policy, which would dominate the country until 1994. Born in the Cape Colony*, Malan was educated at Victoria College (later Stellenbosch University) and then entered a seminary to train for ministry within the Dutch Reformed Church. He obtained a doctorate in theology at the University of Utrecht in the Netherlands in 1905, and then returned home, where he became a champion of the Afrikaans language. He left the ministry in order to edit an Afrikaans newspaper, *Die Burger*, and in 1918 was elected to Parliament under the banner of the recently founded National Party. During the 1920s and 1930s, he held Cabinet office and ultimately became leader of a reformed, 'purified', National Party. Malan defeated Jan Christian Smuts* in the 1948 elections and during the ensuing six years the apartheid laws were gradually put in place. He retired in 1954 and died five years later. Malan's strident Afrikaner nationalism shaped the politics of multiple generations of people in South Africa.

Further Reading

Eric P. Louw (2004). *The Rise, Fall, and Legacy of Apartheid* (Westport, CT, Praeger)

Hendrik B. Thom (1980). *D.F. Malan* (Kaapstad, Boekhandel)

Malawi. An East-Central African country, Malawi was encountered first by the British in 1859, when the lake that dominates its geography was visited by David Livingstone*. Inspired by him, a number of Scots Presbyterian missionaries came to the region and in 1891 the British Central Africa Protectorate was established, which became, in 1907, the Nyasaland Protectorate. In 1953, Nyasaland federated with Northern and Southern Rhodesia*, but as the federation began to unwind, nationalists led by Dr Hastings Banda* campaigned for independence, which was achieved in 1964. Two years later, Malawi became a republic, choosing to remain within the Commonwealth*.

Further Reading

A.J. Hanna (1969). *The Beginnings of Nyasaland and North-eastern Rhodesia, 1859–95* (Oxford, Clarendon Press)

John McCracken, Timothy J. Lovering and Fiona Johnson Chalamanda, eds (2001). *Twentieth-Century Malawi: Perspectives on History and Culture* (Stirling, Centre of Commonwealth Studies)

Malaya (see Malaysia)

Malaysia. A Southeast Asian country formed from a number of British colonies dating back to the eighteenth century. The British established their first colony in the region at Penang upon its lease to the East India Company* in 1786. Various other trading settlements were founded over the following years, resulting in the Crown Colony of the Straits Settlements in 1826 comprised of Penang, Malacca, Singapore*, and Labuan. Throughout the nineteenth century, British regional influence widened to include a number of other settlements known as the Federated Malay States, as well as a group of un-federated states. Ultimately, following the Second World War*, the Malayan Union was established in 1946, which united all the British posses-sions in Malaya with the exception of Singapore. Many traditional Malayan rulers objected, however, and two years later the Union was dissolved and replaced by the Federation of Malaya, which recognized traditional local rulers. Malayan nationalists – especially Communists – objected strongly to the new Federation, however, and from 1948 until 1960 the Malayan Emergency witnessed a protracted insurgency. During the Emergency in 1957, independence for the Federation was achieved, and in 1963 Malaya, along with the remaining Crown Colonies in the region – Sabah*, Sarawak*, and Singapore – united to form Malaysia. Singapore subsequently left the union in 1965 to form its own sovereign city-state.

Further Reading

Virginia M. Hooker (2003). *A Short History of Malaysia: Linking East and West* (Crows Nest, NSW, Allen & Unwin)

A.J. Stockwell, ed. (2004). *Malaysia* (London, Stationery Office)

Maldives. An island nation located south-east of the Indian sub-continent, the Maldives is made up of a large number of atolls comprising in total some 115 square miles of land. An ancient ocean kingdom, which was always an important stopping-point for sailors and traders, the British declared a Protectorate over it in 1887, maintaining it until 1965, when the Maldive Islands achieved independence as the Maldives. Three years later, a republic was declared.

Further Reading

Max Beloff (1969, 1989). *Imperial Sunset*, 2 vols (London, Macmillan)

T.W. Hockley (2003). *The Two Thousand Isles: A Short Account of the People, History and Customs of the Maldive Archipelago* (New Delhi, Asian Educational Services)

Malta. A small island nation located in the Mediterranean Sea just south of Sicily, the British ruled it beginning in 1814 with the signing of the Treaty of Paris. Later, with the opening of the Suez Canal* in 1869, Malta proved a vital stop on the route to India* and for a time was home to the Royal Navy's Mediterranean Fleet. Malta lay under siege by the Axis powers from 1940 to 1943, and in the aftermath of the Second World War* there was a movement by some Maltese to 'integrate' with Britain, but nationalism proved stronger and in 1964 Malta gained its independence. Ten years later, Malta declared itself a republic but remained a member of the Commonwealth.

Further Reading

Douglas Austin (2006). *Churchill and Malta: A Special Relationship* (Stroud, Spellmount)

Simon C. Smith, ed. (2006). *Malta* (London, Stationery Office)

Mandela, Nelson R. (1918–). Former President of South Africa*, Mandela emerged from twenty-seven years in prison for opposing the apartheid* policies of the South African regime in 1990 as one of the great moral leaders of his time and, symbolically, the last of a kind of Imperial-era nationalist leader. Born in the Transkei to a Thembu royal family, he was educated locally by Methodist missionaries (who gave him the name Nelson after Admiral Horatio Nelson*) and then at Fort Hare University. He subsequently moved to Johannesburg and studied to become a lawyer. It was during these years that he began to become politically active, joining the African National

Congress (ANC)* and setting up a law firm devoted to representing disenfranchised blacks. He was first arrested in 1956 (for treason), and in 1961 he co-founded and became leader of the ANC's armed wing, *Umkhonto we Sizwe* (Spear of the Nation). Arrested again in 1962, he was convicted of sabotage and the long years of imprisonment began, much of which was spent on Robben Island off Cape Town. Ultimately released in 1990 after a concerted international campaign in his support, as well as reforms within the ruling National Party, Mandela won the leadership of the ANC. In 1994, after South Africa's first multi-racial elections, he became President, serving one term and retiring in 1999. Since then he has consolidated his position as a powerfully inspirational leader on a global scale.

Further Reading

Nelson Mandela (1994). *Long Walk to Freedom: The Autobiography of Nelson Mandela* (Boston, Little, Brown & Co.)

Martin Meredith (1997). *Nelson Mandela: A Biography* (London, Hamish Hamilton)

Manitoba. A province located at the geographical centre of Canada – although considered to be part of the West – the first European to encounter the territory that is now Manitoba was Henry Hudson, when he sailed into what was later named Hudson Bay in 1611. Not long afterwards in London, the Hudson's Bay Company* was chartered and for two centuries the vast watershed of the Bay supported a thriving fur trade. The territory under the HBC's control, known as Rupert's Land, was ceded to Canada in 1869 and became part of the Northwest Territories*. The next year a small portion of the land was used to form the province of Manitoba, the fifth province to enter the Canadian Confederation, which today covers some 250,000 square miles of prairie, forest, lakes, and granite shield.

Further Reading

Kenneth Coates (1987). *Manitoba: The Province and the People* (Edmonton, Hurtig)

W.L. Morton (1961). *Manitoba: A History* (Toronto, University of Toronto Press)

Manley, Norman W. (1893–1969). A Jamaican statesman, Manley presided over the Caribbean island's independence from Britain in 1962. Born of mixed-race parentage, Manley was educated locally before winning a Rhodes Scholarship to Oxford*, where he read law at Jesus College. During the First World War*, he served in the Royal Field Artillery, afterwards returning to Jamaica* to practice law and ultimately enter politics as founder of the People's National Party. From 1955 to 1959, he was Jamaica's Chief Minister, and then until 1962 its Premier. After shepherding the country through independence, he lost the ensuing election and closed out his public life as Leader of the Opposition. Posthumously he was named a National Hero of Jamaica.

Further Reading
Bill Schwarz, ed. (2003). *West Indian Intellectuals in Britain* (Manchester, Manchester University Press)
Philip M. Sherlock (1980). *Norman Manley* (London, Macmillan)

Maori. The indigenous people of New Zealand*, they first encountered the British in 1769 when Captain James Cook* visited the islands on his first Pacific voyage. Steady contact with European missionaries and whalers ensued and the first part of the nineteenth century saw the impact of European disease and weapons on Maori society. In 1840, the Treaty of Waitangi* was signed, the effect of which made the Maori British subjects. Throughout the balance of the century the 'land wars' saw the Maori turn over much of their traditional territory to British settlers. Combined with the impact of disease, Maori population numbers fell from about 100,000 to just 40,000, and it was thought by some that extinction was probable. But population numbers rebounded in the twentieth century, sparking a political and cultural revival, which included the recovery of disputed lands. Still, today the Maori on average are poorer than non-Maori New Zealanders and have a shorter life expectancy.

Further Reading
Harry Evison (1997). *The Long Dispute: Maori Land Rights and European Colonisation in Southern New Zealand* (Christchurch, Canterbury University Press)

Paul Moon (2007). *The Newest Country in the World: A History of New Zealand in the Decade of the Treaty* (New York, Penguin)

Maratha Wars. During the late eighteenth and early nineteenth centuries, the East India Company* fought three wars against the Maratha Empire of Central India*, the last of which broke its power and secured regional British paramountcy. The Third Maratha War, which began in 1817 and lasted for a year, saw the British greatly expand their territory, at the expense of a number of Maratha-ruled states, which subsequently became princely states* under the Raj. Resentment against the British for this defeat was strong, exemplified best by the last Peshwa (Prime Minister) of the Marathas, Nana Sahib, who later became one of the ringleaders of the Mutiny*.

Further Reading

R.J. Nadkami (1966). *The Rise and Fall of the Maratha Empire* (Bombay, Popular Prakashan)

Franklin R. Rogers (2002). *When the Fight was Done: A Novel of the Maratha Wars* (New York, Penguin)

Matabele Wars. Two wars fought in the 1890s between the Matabele (Ndebele) people of southern Africa and the British. In the summer of 1893, the Matabele under King Lobengula* attempted to subjugate their nearby rivals, the Mashona. While attempting to do so, armed columns of the British South Africa Company* (BSAC), whose eye was on the rich gold deposits of the region, took the opportunity to invade a mostly unprotected Matabeleland (today located in western Zimbabwe*). By November the Matabele had been overwhelmed by the terrific power of the Maxim gun, and the British occupied their capital city of Bulawayo. Lobengula fled and within a few months had died of disease. The Matabele were swiftly deprived of much of their land and livestock, many of them being employed now in the gold mines. Less than three years later, however, the Matabele revolted, sparking the Second Matabele War, which lasted from March 1896 until October 1897. Led by the Matabele spiritual leader Mlimo, he inspired both his own people and the neighbouring Mashona ('Shona') to rise up against the BSAC and its 4,000 settlers, blaming them for widespread drought and disease. At first successful because of the weak military position of the settlers – made acute by the continuing absence of most of the BSAC's troops and armaments, which had been used for the disastrous Jameson Raid* in the Transvaal a few months before – the British quickly sent reinforcements. The war was a protracted one, however, marked by long sieges, the assassination of Mlimo, and the involvement of Rhodes*, Selous*, and Baden-Powell.* It took Rhodes' personal diplomatic intervention in October 1897 to obtain the Matabele surrender, a harbinger of the disputed territory becoming Rhodesia* a short while later.

Further Reading
Robert Cary (1968). *A Time to Die* (Cape Town, H. Timmins)
Stafford Glass (1968). *The Matabele War* (Harlow, Longmans)

Mau Mau. A mainly Kikuyu-sponsored movement for land and freedom in pre-independence Kenya* that dated from the late 1940s, it became a crisis beginning in 1952. The assassination of the Paramount Chief of Kikuyuland, Waruhiu wa Kungu, in October of that year led quickly to the institution of a state of emergency in Kenya. Waruhiu had spoken out against the spate of killings of those Kikuyu who had refused to take the Mau Mau oath, as well as the murder of a small number of white farmers. During the last few months of 1952, over sixty such Kikuyu were murdered, many of them Christians who rejected the Mau Mau ideology and died as martyrs. The government then clamped down hard on suspected Mau Mau activists. The movement was branded terrorist and thousands of British troops were brought into Kenya and internment camps established. Mau Mau activists ranged through the Kikuyu highlands on the slopes of Mount Kenya and gradually were flushed out by the steady raiding of ground troops and through helicopter and airplane patrols. Jomo Kenyatta*, head of the Kenya African Union, was arrested, although his links to Mau Mau were later found to be tenuous. By 1955, Mau Mau had been largely contained and the next year its last important military leader, Dedan Kimathi, was captured. The movement sputtered on, however, and the state of emergency was not lifted until 1960. Mau Mau hastened the independence of Kenya but left a legacy of violence and atrocity that marked both Kikuyu society and the last years of colonial rule, a mark that remains controversial and, for many, unresolved.

Further Reading

David Anderson (2005). *Histories of the Hanged: Britain's Dirty War in Kenya and the End of Empire* (London, Weidenfeld & Nicolson)

David Throup (1987). *Economic and Social Origins of Mau Mau, 1945–1953* (Oxford, Oxford University Press)

Mauritius. An Indian Ocean island nation off the south-east coast of Africa, Mauritius saw Portuguese sailors visit in 1507 and then the arrival of Dutch settlers in 1638. Taken by France in 1715, the British seized it in 1810 during the Napoleonic Wars and ruled it until independence was achieved in 1968. Later, Mauritius became a republic, but remains within the Commonwealth. Historically, sugar-cane plantations dominated the economy. Mauritius was the only known habitat of the long-extinct Dodo bird.

Further Reading

Ashley Jackson (2001). *War and Empire in Mauritius and the Indian Ocean* (London, Palgrave)

Stephen Taylor (2007). *Storm and Conquest: The Battle for the Indian Ocean, 1808–10* (London, Faber & Faber)

Mboya, Tom (1930–69). An important Kenyan nationalist and later government minister in the 1960s, Mboya was murdered under suspicious circumstances that pointed to Jomo Kenyatta's* involvement. Born near Thika, Mboya received an education at various local Roman Catholic schools and in 1955 won a year's scholarship to study at Oxford*. While there he became a mentee of the leading Africanist, Margery Perham*, and they maintained a regular correspondence after Mboya's return to Africa. In the late 1950s and early 1960s, Mboya participated prominently in the Pan-Africa* movement and founded the People's Congress Party in Kenya, which later became part of the larger Kenya African National Union headed by Kenyatta. Upon Kenya's independence in 1963, Mboya became an MP and successively Minister of Justice and Constitutional Affairs, and Minister for Economic

Planning and Development. Popular and charismatic, it is believed that Mboya posed a threat to Kenyatta's Presidency, and as a result in 1969 was assassinated by Kikuyu loyalists who objected to his Luo ethnicity. The case has never been solved.

Further Reading

David Goldsworthy (1982). *Tom Mboya: The Man Kenya Wanted to Forget* (Nairobi, Heinemann)

Tom Mboya (1963). *Freedom and After* (London, A. Deutsch)

Milner, Alfred, 1st Viscount Milner (1854–1925). British High Commissioner to South Africa* during the Second Boer War*, and later, from 1918 to 1921, Colonial Secretary* in David Lloyd George's Liberal government, Milner was the most important Imperial administrator of his generation. Born in Germany and partially raised there, Milner was educated at Balliol College, Oxford*, and his cardinal philosophy was a commitment to the idea of the British Empire. If Lord Curzon* embodied the world-striding Imperialist, then Viscount Milner (as he became in 1902) was the Empire's Plato: thoughtful and ideological. His commitment to Imperialism as 'the highest development of patriotism' remained his lodestar. General Gordon's* death in the Sudan helped to crystallize Milner's pro-Imperial views, and in 1886, his political mentor, C.J. Goschen, recently named Chancellor of the Exchequer, appointed Milner his Principal Private Secretary. The next three years provided Milner with an indispensable training in finance and government, and prepared him for his first big post: Director-General of Accounts in Egypt* from 1889. Egypt was Milner's first hands-on experience of Empire and he thrived there, becoming convinced of the necessity of British Imperial power abroad to maintain international order and spread the principles of good (financial) government. The most important event for Milner in the next few years was his introduction to Cecil Rhodes* in 1895: 'a really *big* man', he later said of him. His desire for an active role in Imperial affairs now became acute. In 1897, he was offered the position of Governor of the Cape Colony and High Commissioner of South Africa. Milner's years as an Imperial proconsul were about to begin. For Milner, the Second Boer War* became his Imperial baptism of fire, and

173

his belief in and commitment to the Imperial idea was at this point given a sharp impetus by the men he chose to help him integrate the two Boer colonies into the South African Imperial structure. Nicknamed 'Milner's Kindergarten,' this group of young men, which included such later notables as Lionel Curtis* and John Buchan, was directed by Milner to bring about reform in a number of key areas. In Imperial terms, Milner's high-water mark had been reached. Still, having been named a trustee of the Rhodes Trust, Milner became a central figure in the establishment of the Scholarship, designed to spread abroad the Imperial gospel. The Rhodes Trust gave Milner a natural venue from which to plump for what was now being called Imperial union. He advocated closer co-operation between the leading Dominions and colonies of the Empire and the mother country. In December 1918, he was named Colonial Secretary, a position he held until February 1921. Milner's last years saw him continuing to champion the idea of Empire, now in a phase that used words like 'trusteeship' and 'development' to describe itself. To some extent, this brand of Imperialism was a long way from the grander idea, articulated as 'The Imperialist Creed,' of Milner's earlier vision of the Empire and for which he is remembered, not without debate, today.

Further Reading

A.M. Gollin (1964). *Proconsul in Politics: A Study of Lord Milner in Opposition and in Power* (London, Anthony Blond)

John Marlowe (1976). *Milner: Apostle of Empire* (London, Hamish Hamilton)

Missionaries. The sending of Christian missionaries to various parts of the Empire was a key feature of its global position from the early part of the eighteenth century, reaching a peak in numbers and popularity in the late-Victorian age. The phenomenon of the missionary abroad was never as unthinkingly hegemonic as post-colonialists have argued, but their impact on local peoples and societies was undoubtedly important and, in places, transformative. Beginning with the Baptist Missionary Society (1792), the non-denominational London Missionary Society (1795), and the (Anglican) Church Missionary Society (1799), the missionary imperative grew prodigiously in the years that followed. India was one of the first places to receive a British missionary with the arrival in Calcutta of William Carey*, a Baptist, in 1793. Carey's mantle would be taken up by many, although no one achieved the level of fame and recognition accorded David Livingstone* in the mid-nineteenth century. By that time the colonial churches, both established and free, in the older settler colonies of Canada* and Australia*, for example – themselves having been the recipients of missionaries and funds – were engaged in the sending of missionaries to the more recently acquired parts of the Empire. The Sudan Interior Mission was one such missionary society. Formed in Toronto in 1893, it grew into perhaps the largest inter-denominational missionary body in Africa, with some four hundred missionaries scattered across West Africa by the 1930s. Despite the some-time close relationship between colonial government and society, mission-aries were not necessarily the allies of British Imperialism, nor did they always endorse the commercial practices of their fellow countrymen. Nevertheless, the range of their impact – religious, educational, sociolog-ical, and medical – was immense and its legacy remains a lively source of debate and, for some, denunciation today.

Further Reading

Tom Hiney (2000). *On the Missionary Trail: The Classic Georgian Adventure of Two Englishmen, Sent on a Journey Around the World, 1821–29* (London, Chatto & Windus)

A.N. Porter (2004). *Religion versus Empire: British Protestant Missionaries and Overseas Expansion, 1700–1914* (Manchester, Manchester University Press)

Mitchell, Sir Philip E. (1890–1964). Colonial administrator from the period of the First World War* until the waning years of Imperial rule, Mitchell was born in London but his formative years were spent in Spain owing to his father's law practice in Gibraltar*. Later educated at St Paul's School and then at Trinity College, Oxford*, he joined the Colonial Service* in 1912 and was posted to Nyasaland*. He spent the War in the King's African Rifles* and in 1919 returned to civilian service and was transferred to Tanganyika*, where he would spend the next eight years as a district officer. Ideally suited to the job, Mitchell became Secretary of Native Affairs in the colony in 1928, rising to Chief Secretary in 1934. The next year he was appointed Governor of Uganda* and set to work trying to create an educated African elite suited to eventual self-government. To this end, he enlarged and strengthened the small Makerere College. Knighted in 1937, he moved on to Fiji* as Governor five years later, and then in 1944 happily returned to Africa as Governor of Kenya*. He remained in the post until 1952, presiding over Kenya as it moved into its nationalist period. Even though Mau Mau* exploded after his retirement, it is clear that he was aware of its growth and potential impact, and afterwards was criticized for having ignored it. He died in 1964 in Gibraltar*, where he had lived as a boy.

Further Reading

Richard Frost (1992). *Enigmatic Proconsul: Sir Philip Mitchell and the Twilight of Empire* (New York, The Radcliffe Press)

Sir Philip Euen Mitchell (1954). *African Afterthoughts* (London, Hutchinson)

Montserrat. Named by Columbus, Montserrat is a British Overseas Territory located in the Caribbean. It came under British control in 1632 when a group of exiled Irish Roman Catholic settlers arrived from nearby St Kitts and Nevis*. Historically, the production of sugar and rum dominated the island's economy, although in more recent years it has been tourism and music recording. Held briefly by the French during the American War of Independence, Montserrat reverted to the British afterwards and remains one of the last British-controlled Caribbean islands.

Further Reading

Donald H. Akenson (1997). *If the Irish Ran the World: Montserrat, 1630– 1730* (Kingston, ON, McGill-Queen's University Press)

Howard A. Fergus (2004). *Montserrat: History of a Caribbean Colony*, 2nd edn (Oxford, Macmillan Caribbean)

Moshoeshoe (c.1786–1870). King of the Sotho and founder of Basutoland* (modern-day Lesotho*), Moshoeshoe's great early rival, Shaka, King of the Zulu*, forced the Sotho people off their ancestral lands. Under Moshoeshoe's leadership they settled eventually at Thaba Bosiu and by the 1830s occupied much of what would later become Lesotho. The territory was contested, however, by both the British and the Boers. The British left the territory to the Boers in 1854, from which was created the Orange Free State*. A few years later, in 1858, the OFS-Sotho War erupted, which cost Moshoeshoe considerable land. The remaining territory was made a British Protectorate in 1868. Though disputed afterwards by the Boers, Basutoland's boundaries proved inviolable and have remained so. Shortly thereafter Moshoeshoe died, sparking a succession crisis unresolved until the 1880s.

Further Reading

Peter B. Sanders (1975). *Moshoeshoe: Chief of the Sotho* (London, Heinemann)
Leonard M. Thompson (1975). *Survival in Two Worlds: Moshoeshoe of Lesotho, 1786–1870* (Oxford, Clarendon Press)

Mountbatten, Louis, 1st Earl Mountbatten of Burma (1900–79). The last Viceroy of India*, Mountbatten was also Governor-General of India, Supreme Commander South-East Asia Theatre during the Second World War*, First Sea Lord, and Chief of the Defence Staff. Born Prince Louis of Battenberg at Windsor, he was a member of the Royal Family's German ancestry, the titles of which were formally dropped in 1917. A career naval officer, he served in both the First and Second World Wars*, famously orchestrating the disastrous Dieppe Raid in 1942, earning him the enmity of many Canadians whose troops paid a heavy price for what was then and has been ever since regarded as an unnecessary operation carried out against the impregnable German-held Normandy coastline. Appointed by Clement Attlee* as Viceroy of India in 1946, his six months there were extraordinarily hectic, as his sole mission was to ready the sub-continent for independence and, as became inevitable, partition. He carried out the task successfully, although not without severe controversy, especially over the vast number of deaths caused by Hindu-Muslim animosity made horrifically plain by partition. Mountbatten's later years were spent in pursuing a variety of charitable interests, but his career as a highly visible tribune of Empire ultimately made him a target for an IRA* assassination plot, which was carried out successfully near his summer home in County Sligo, Ireland* in 1979.

Further Reading

Stanley Wolpert (2006). *Shameful Flight: The Last Years of the British Empire in India* (New York, Oxford University Press)

Philip Ziegler (1985). *Mountbatten: The Official Biography* (London, Collins)

Mugabe, Robert G. (1924–). President of Zimbabwe* and before that a long-time advocate and soldier in the fight for independence from Britain. Mugabe is now one of the most heinous examples of the post-Imperial tyrant. But he was not always the favourite target of those who decry post-colonial ineptitude and human-rights violations. Twenty-five years ago and more, he was hailed as a freedom fighter, widely credited with bringing independence to his embattled former colony. Born in Southern Rhodesia* on a Jesuit mission where his father was the institution's carpenter, Mugabe received a good primary and secondary education and became a teacher locally and then for a time in Ghana*, where he was inspired by its independence in 1957. Upon his return home, he co-ordinated the Youth Wing of the National Democratic Party. The NDP was shortly banned, however, but then replaced by the swift creation of the Zimbabwe African Peoples Union (ZANU, later ZANU-PF), with Mugabe as its Secretary-General. The new party prepared itself for the likelihood of war by endorsing the use of violence against the white-run Rhodesian state. Promptly its leadership was jailed and for the next eleven years Mugabe remained behind bars. Escaping to Mozambique after his release in 1974, Mugabe led a sustained guerilla campaign against the Ian Smith* regime. Known as the 'Chimurenga' (war of liberation), it would last until 1979, when Smith agreed to negotiate an end to the war and the creation of a new regime. In due course, in April 1980, Mugabe and ZANU-PF won the British-supervised multi-racial elections prescribed by the Lancaster House Agreement of four months earlier, and he has never been out of power since, maintaining his position through violence, intimidation, and murder. He lives lavishly while much of Zimbabwe lies in ruins and most of its people live in dire poverty.

Further Reading

David Blair (2002). *Degrees in Violence: Robert Mugabe and the Struggle for Power in Zimbabwe* (London, Continuum)

Andrew Norman (2004). *Robert Mugabe and the Betrayal of Zimbabwe* (London, McFarland)

N

Nanking, Treaty of. Signed by the British and China's Qing Empire in 1842, the Treaty ended the First Opium* War that had been fought since 1839. The Treaty obliged the Chinese to pay a large sum of money (21 million silver dollars over three years) to the British as compensation for the opium confiscated since the start of the War, and for other debts and losses. Additionally, the port of Hong Kong was ceded to the British in perpetuity. The British agreed to evacuate their troops from Nanking and other locations. For the Chinese, the Treaty ultimately was seen as 'unequal' and lay at the root of much mistrust and their own sense of humiliation over the succeeding century.

Further Reading

P.D. Coates (1988) *The China Consuls: British Consular Officers, 1843–1943* (Oxford, Oxford University Press)

John K. Fairbank (1953). *Trade and Diplomacy on the China Coast: The Opening of the Treaty Ports, 1842–1854* (Cambridge, MA, Harvard University Press)

Napier, Sir Charles J. (1782–1853). A career soldier who rose to fame in India* as Commander-in-Chief, Napier was born into a noteworthy military family in Ireland*, served under Wellington in the Peninsular War against Napoleonic troops, and much later, in 1841, was posted to India. The next year he was promoted Major-General and given the command of the Bombay Presidency's army. His main task was to conquer Sindh* province, whose Muslim rulers had risen in rebellion against the British. He did so successfully and was subsequently made Governor of the Bombay Presidency, a post he held from 1843 to 1847. Two years later, he was appointed Commander-in-Chief, India, but after having quarreled with the Governor-General, Lord Dalhousie*, he resigned in 1851 and returned home, dying shortly thereafter. To his contemporaries Napier was a 'soldier's soldier' who once told a delegation of Hindu sati* supporters that their custom of burning a widow alive on the funeral pyre of her dead husband would be matched in turn by a British one: that of tying a rope around the neck of any such perpetrator and hanging them.

Further Reading

Byron Farwell (1985). *Queen Victoria's Little Wars* (New York, W.W. Norton & Co.)

Ian Hernon (2003) *Britain's Forgotten Wars: Colonial campaigns of the Nineteenth Century* (London, The History Press)

Natal. Today a province in South Africa* called KwaZulu-Natal and running inland from the Indian Ocean, Natal was made a British colony in 1843 when the antecedent Boer republic of Natalia was annexed, causing a quick exodus of most of the Afrikaner families in Natal to the Transvaal* and to the Orange Free State*. In 1897, it was enlarged with the addition of Zululand, and two years later witnessed the first fighting in the Second Boer War*. Natal was a founding member of the Union of South Africa* in 1910.

Further Reading

Bill Guest, ed. (1985). *Enterprise and Exploitation in a Victorian Colony: Aspects of the Economic and Social History of Colonial Natal* (Pietermaritzburg, University of Natal Press)

John Lambert (1995). *Betrayed Trust: Africans and the State in Colonial Natal* (Pietermaritzburg, University of Natal Press)

Nauru. The smallest island nation in the world at just 8 square miles, Nauru is a dot located in the South Pacific. First visited by a Westerner in 1798 when a British whaler landed there, it was made a colony by Germany in 1888. A large phosphate deposit was discovered a few years later and has since been the island's economic mainstay. At the outbreak of the First World War* in 1914, Nauru was captured by Australian troops. Subsequent to the Paris Peace Conference, the island became a League of Nations Mandate with co-trusteeship going to Britain, Australia*, and New Zealand*. Occupied by the Japanese from 1942 to 1945, afterwards the co-trusteeship was renewed. In 1966, Nauru became self-governing and two years later independence was declared.

Further Reading

Barrie Macdonald (1988). *In Pursuit of the Sacred Trust: Trusteeship and Independence in Nauru* (Wellington, New Zealand Institute of International Affairs)

Donald Denoon et al., eds (1997). *The Cambridge History of the Pacific Islanders* (Cambridge, Cambridge University Press)

Ndebele (see Matabele Wars)

Nehru, Jawaharlal (1889–1964). First Prime Minister of India*, Nehru was a leading Indian nationalist and a key figure in the independence movement. Born the son of a wealthy Brahmin lawyer in Allahabad, Nehru was educated in India and then sent to England to study, first at Harrow School and then at Cambridge. Becoming Westernized and, to the chagrin of his family, something of a dandy, he trained as a barrister at the Inner Temple in London and travelled the European continent. Returning to India during the First World War*, he joined the Indian National Congress*, with which his father had had a long association. Gandhi*, recently returned from South Africa*, had an immediate impact on Nehru, and the two men became close friends and strong political allies. In 1929, Nehru was elected the INC's President and was soon imprisoned as a result of the anti-salt tax campaign led by Gandhi. His growing political popularity coincided with the moral force of Gandhi, and the final drive to Indian independence. Re-elected Congress President in 1936, Nehru supported the British during the Second World War* in exchange for a promise of independence afterwards. In so doing he diverged from Gandhi, only to be re-united later. Reluctantly pulled into Gandhi's 'Quit India' campaign that began in 1942, Nehru nonetheless supported it and was duly imprisoned from then until the end of the war. Re-elected President of Congress in 1946, in anticipation of the transfer of power, he became India's first Prime Minister in August 1947 at independence. Still in office seventeen years later, he died and was succeeded by his daughter, Indira Gandhi. Disliked or worse by late-Raj Imperialists, Nehru's legacy is enduring in India's national life.

Further Reading

Judith M. Brown (2003). *Nehru: A Political Life* (New Haven, CT, Yale University Press)

Stanley A.Wolpert (1996). *Nehru: A Tryst with Destiny* (Oxford, Oxford University Press)

Nelson, Horatio, 1st Viscount Nelson (1758–1805). 'Britannia's God of War,' as one of his recent biographers has called him, Horatio Nelson is a supremely iconic figure in British history. For contemporaries, his victory over the combined fleets of France and Spain off the latter's Cape Trafalgar on 21 October 1805 ended the possibility of a Napoleonic invasion of Britain and ultimately paved the way for British Imperial sea-borne domination. The death of Nelson on board his aptly named flagship HMS *Victory* on the afternoon of the battle secured the nation and the Empire's safety, but at the cost of the life of its greatest hero. Born in 1758, in Norfolk, the son of a Church of England clergyman, he became a trainee on a line-of-battle ship in 1771. Six years later he was commissioned lieutenant and by 1784 he was captain and on station in the Caribbean, the so-called 'Hub of Empire.' Once returned from the West Indies in 1787, however, he became, like many of his peers, an out-of-work sea captain on half-pay. But in January 1793, when war against Revolutionary France was confirmed, Nelson got word that he would be in command of a sixty-four-gun ship of the line. The ensuing Mediterranean Campaign gave him an opportunity to regain his sea legs against a formidable French foe. Nelson's eventual arrival in Naples in September 1798 came following successive important victories. The year before he had been instrumental in the defeat of combined Spanish and French forces at Cape St Vincent, off the coast of Spain. That victory had come at a key moment for the British. The Mediterranean, by then, was even more of *le lac français* than before, and Nelson's heroic boarding of two Spanish vessels marked the beginning of a British comeback. Later in the campaign, Nelson would lose his right arm when it was shattered by a musket ball in an attack on Tenerife in the Spanish-held Canary Islands. Shortly thereafter he was promoted Vice-Admiral. His signal victory of the period, however, came in August 1798 in Egypt*. Long-standing British fears of a French attack on India* via Egypt began to be realized when Napoleon, accompanied by some 35,000 troops, arrived in Alexandria on 1 July. In the ensuing Battle of the Nile*, Nelson and his captains captured nine French battleships and destroyed two others. The victory re-asserted British dominion in the Mediterranean and pre-empted a potential attack on India. Victory at the Nile propelled Nelson into the front rank of British heroes, and a glorious welcome awaited him back home in England. In 1801, he was promoted Admiral and appointed to command the English Channel Fleet. The next year, the Peace of Amiens was signed, which offered a brief respite from warfare with the briefly checked French. But war resumed in 1803, setting in motion the final act of Nelson's career, the Battle of Trafalgar. His victory there consolidated the Royal Navy's dominance of the high seas, a position it would hold for the balance of the nineteenth century. Sea-power of this magnitude enabled the British Empire to expand and establish itself as the most extensive global trader of its time. Nelson himself was apotheosized as a result of Trafalgar, his death being interpreted by most as a sacrificial act for the greatness and glory of Britain and the Empire.

Further Reading

Andrew Lambert (2004). *Nelson: Britannia's God of War* (London, Faber & Faber)

Brian Lavery (2003). *Horatio Lord Nelson* (New York, New York University Press)

Newbold, Sir Douglas (1894–1945). Civil Secretary to the Sudan* government, Newbold was born at Tunbridge Wells and educated in classics at Oriel College, Oxford*. He served in the Middle East during the First World War*, and was wounded. In 1920, he joined the Sudan Political Service*.

He spent the decade as a district officer and in the secretariat at Khartoum, and in 1932 was made Governor of the province of Kordofan. Seven years later, he was appointed Civil Secretary, the highest-ranking British official in the Sudan. Made KBE in 1944, he met an untimely death the next year, which came after being thrown from a horse. Deeply sympathetic to the political, social, and economic aspirations of the Sudanese, he was preparing the way for their full self-government when he died. Similarly, Newbold had been the prime mover in the establishment of the University of Khartoum, the successor to Gordon College.

Further Reading

Robert O. Collins (1983). *Shadows in the Grass: Britain in the Southern Sudan, 1918–1956* (New Haven, CT, Yale University Press)

K.D.D. Henderson (1953) *The Making of the Modern Sudan: the Life and Letters of Sir Douglas Newbold* (London, Faber & Faber)

New Brunswick. A Canadian province located along the Atlantic coast, New Brunswick was first visited by a European when the French explorer, Jacques Cartier, arrived in 1534. The creation of the French colony of Acadia soon followed. The Treaty of Utrecht (1713) transferred the region to Britain and in 1755, just prior to the Seven Years' War*, the British chose to expel abroad the Acadian population, many of whom later returned. Loyalist refugees from the American War of Independence began to arrive in 1783, and the next year the colony of New Brunswick was established. Ongoing border disputes with the US state of Maine were resolved in 1842 with the signing of the Ashburton Treaty*. Heavily forested, New Brunswick was a key supplier of masts for the Royal Navy in the early part of the nineteenth century. In 1867, New Brunswick became one of the four original provinces to join the Canadian Confederation.

Further Reading

Phillip A. Buckner and John G. Reid, eds (1998). *The Atlantic Region to Confederation: A History* (Toronto, University of Toronto Press)

W.S. MacNutt (1984). *New Brunswick, A History: 1784–1867* (Toronto, Macmillan of Canada)

Newfoundland. A province of Canada and regarded as the first overseas British colony, Newfoundland is an enormous island (about 42,000 square miles) off the east coast of North America that was claimed for England by Sir Humphrey Gilbert in 1583 with a charter from Elizabeth I. Its seasonal fishery was dominated by merchants from the south-west of England for years, and as a consequence they opposed settlement, but in the 1600s several colonies were started on the Avalon Peninsula nonetheless. The French had never accepted England's claims to Newfoundland, however, but in 1713 the Treaty of Utrecht confirmed English sovereignty. Conditions for settlement improved, beginning in 1729 when a naval governor was appointed and gradually a courts system was established. In 1832, representative government was achieved and in 1855 full colony status was granted. The cod fishery, along with expanded timber cutting, mining, and agriculture, sponsored increased settlement. Newfoundlanders resisted overtures to join the Canadian Confederation in 1867. Dominion* status was achieved but then surrendered when the colony fell into bankruptcy in the 1930s. After the Second World War*, a debate was held on Newfoundland's future, which included a resumption of Dominion status or entering Canada as a province. The debate was fierce, resulting eventually in a referendum narrowly endorsing the Canadian option, and in 1949 Newfoundland became the country's tenth province. In 2001, the mainland territory of Labrador was formally added to Newfoundland, enlarging its territory to 156,000 square miles in total and changing the name of the province to Newfoundland and Labrador.

Further Reading

James K. Hiller, ed. (1980). *Newfoundland in the Nineteenth and Twentieth Centuries: Essays in Interpretation* (Toronto, University of Toronto Press)

Peter Neary (1988). *Newfoundland in the North Atlantic World, 1929–1949* (Montreal, McGill-Queen's University Press)

New South Wales. The first British colony in Australia*, and today the state with the country's largest population, New South Wales was given its name by Captain James Cook* in 1770. Established as a penal colony in 1788, the arrival of free settlers in the early part of the nineteenth century began to change the nature of the colony through the establishment of farms, towns, and the features of civil society, although convicts continued to arrive from Britain until 1840, accounting for about half of the colony's population of some 150,000. A legislative council was established in 1823, followed by an assembly in 1843. The gold rush of 1851 spurred further population and commercial expansion, and Sydney emerged as the state's most important urban centre, rivalling Melbourne in Victoria*. New South Wales entered the Commonwealth of Australia as an original member in 1901.

Further Reading

Beverley Kingston (2006). *A History of New South Wales* (New York, Cambridge University Press)

David Mackay (1985). *A Place of Exile: The European Settlement of New South Wales* (Melbourne, Oxford University Press)

New Zealand. An island nation in the south Pacific Ocean located some 1,200 miles south-east of Australia and comprised of two main islands (North and South) jointly covering about 103,000 square miles and separated by the narrow Cook Strait. The first European to visit New Zealand was Abel Tasman in 1642, the Dutch mariner for whom Tasmania* is named. The landing was not a success and several of Tasman's crew were killed by the indigenous Maori*. No further European contact was undertaken until Captain Cook* arrived on his first Pacific voyage in 1769. In the aftermath of Cook's visit, steady European contact ensued, initially through whaling, and then through trade and Christian evangelization. The British decided to separate New Zealand from New South Wales* in the late 1830s, and in 1840 the Treaty of Waitangi* was negotiated, symbolizing both continuing British control of the islands and their new status. A dozen years later, the British Parliament passed the New Zealand Constitution Act and the colony's first Parliament met in 1854. Responsible government* was granted in 1856 and full Dominion* status was attained in 1907. In 1947, after a protracted period of negotiation, the provisions of the Statute of Westminster (1931)* were ratified by the New Zealand Parliament, effectively giving the country its independence. Always an enthusiastic member of the Empire, a proportionately large number of New Zealanders fought in the Second Boer War* and the First and Second World Wars* and, like Canada* and Australia*, the Queen is head of state.

Further Reading

John Crawford and Ian McGibbon, eds (2003). *One Flag, One Queen, One Tongue: New Zealand, the British Empire, and the South African War, 1899–1902* (Auckland, Auckland University Press)

Philippa Mein Smith (2005). *A Concise History of New Zealand* (Melbourne, Cambridge University Press)

Nigeria. The most populous country in Africa (150,000,000), Nigeria is located on the western side of the continent and was first encountered by Europeans when visited by the Portuguese in the sixteenth century. British exploration (see Mungo Park*) and trade began in the nineteenth century, as did attempts at suppressing the slave trade, eventually from the British base established at Lagos in 1851. By the 1880s, the palm-oil trade was exciting considerable interest in the City of London, and in 1886 the Royal Niger Company under George Goldie* was chartered. Meanwhile, the Berlin West Africa Conference* of 1884–5 had led the British to establish a local Protectorate in 1891 named Oil Rivers, and another, the Niger Coast Protectorate, two years later. In 1900, the lands formerly held by the Royal Niger Company passed to the Crown and were re-organized as the Protectorate of Southern Nigeria (a few years later to include Lagos) and the Protectorate of Northern Nigeria. In 1914, the two Protectorates were unified as one colony. Made famous in Imperial circles by the working out of the British system of Indirect Rule* under the Governorship of Sir Frederick Lugard*, Nigeria was characterized by a north (mainly Muslim)-south (mainly Christian) divide. In the post-Second World War* period, sustained colonial nationalism hastened the arrival of independence, which occurred in 1960.

Further Reading

Michael Crowder (1970). *West Africa under Colonial Rule* (London, Hutchinson)

A.H.M. Kirk-Greene, ed. (1965). *The Principles of Native Administration in Nigeria: Selected Documents, 1900–1947* (London, Oxford University Press)

Niue. A tiny island nation in the South Pacific, it was sighted by Captain James Cook* in 1774, who considered it unfriendly and called it the 'Savage Island.' No further European contact was made until 1846, when missionaries from the London Missionary Society settled on the island. In 1900, Niue briefly became a British Protectorate, before being allowed annexation by New Zealand. In 1974, Niue became independent, although it remains in free association with New Zealand, with whom it shares Queen Elizabeth as head of state.

Further Reading

Terry M. Chapman (1976). *The Decolonisation of Niue* (Wellington, Victoria University Press)

Maihetoe Hekau et al. (1982). *Niue: A History of the Island* (Suva, Institute of Pacific Studies)

Nkrumah, Kwame (1909–72). One of the leading Pan-Africanists* of his day, and the first Prime Minister and then President of Ghana*, Nkrumah was a seminal figure in the decolonization of British Africa. Born in the Gold Coast*, he was educated in Accra and taught in a school before continuing his studies in the United States, where he earned four degrees and became deeply politicized. He moved to London in 1945, intending to continue his studies, and became involved in expatriate African politics, helping to organize the Fifth Pan-African Congress in Manchester. A committed socialist, he returned home in 1947 to become the General Secretary of the United Gold Coast Convention, whose main goal was national independence. Briefly imprisoned in 1948, Nkrumah built on his growing popularity around the colony, the result of which was a new political coalition, the Convention People's Party (CPP). Using it as his political instrument, and with the gradual acceptance of the colonial state, Nkrumah slowly moved the Gold Coast towards self-government and then independence. In 1951, free elections were held, which saw the CPP sweep almost every seat in the assembly. Released from prison after the result, Nkrumah formed a government and within two years he was Prime Minister of the Gold Coast. From 1953 to 1957, Nkrumah crafted the rudiments of the new state of Ghana out of the old colony of the Gold Coast. Independence was declared in the latter year and in 1960 Ghana became a republic, remaining within the Commonwealth. Nkrumah held power until a military coup in 1966, which, it was later revealed, was likely backed by the Central Intelligence Agency. He went into exile in Guinea, dying six years later while seeking medical treatment in Europe.

Further Reading

David Birmingham (1998). *Kwame Nkrumah: The Father of African Nationalism* (Athens, Ohio University Press)

Marika Sherwood (1996). *Kwame Nkrumah: The Years Abroad 1935–1947* (Legon, Ghana, Freedom Publications)

North Borneo (see Sabah)

Northern Territory. An Australian federal territory, the Northern Territory occupies almost 548,000 square miles of the harsh north-central part of the country. Though it briefly gained colonial status as North Australia (1846), it was under the control of New South Wales* from 1825 to 1863, at which time it became part of South Australia*, remaining under its control until 1911, when taken over by the Australian government, whose constitutional power over the Northern Territory remains in effect today.

Further Reading

Ernestine Hill (1995). *The Territory: The Classic Saga of Australia's Far North* (Sydney, Angus & Robertson)

Deryck M. Schreuder and Stuart Ward, eds (2008). *Australia's Empire* (Oxford, Oxford University Press)

North West Company. One of the great Canadian fur-trading companies, the North West Company operated from 1779 until 1821, when it merged with its powerful rival, the Hudson's Bay Company*. Formed in Montreal by a group of Scottish-born entrepreneurs, including Simon McTavish and James McGill, the NWC fought steadily against the HBC's fur trade monopoly, and by the late 1780s was exporting annually some 20,000 beaver pelts to Europe from its main trapping and trading area of the Athabasca (today's northern Manitoba*, Saskatchewan*, and Alberta*) region. Clashes between the two companies grew in number and ferocity, climaxing in the years from 1815 to 1819, causing the NWC's partnership to fray. During this period, the Colonial Office* was lobbied for support from a number of quarters and wished to see the situation resolved. In 1821, the British Parliament passed an Act granting the HBC exclusive trading rights in the region, but requiring the inclusion of a couple of leading 'Nor'Westers' as governors. This new coalition acted under the old HBC charter and the Company grew apace, its dominance of the Canadian west assured until its vast landholdings were purchased by the Canadian government in 1869–70.

Further Reading

Jennifer S.H. Brown (1980). *Strangers in Blood: Fur Trade Company Families in Indian Country* (Vancouver, University of British Columbia Press)

M.W. Campbell (2002). *The Nor'Westers: The Fight for the Fur Trade* (Calgary, Fifth House Publishers)

North-West Frontier Province. Today a province in Pakistan*, during the late nineteenth century the NWFP became a battleground between British India and Afghanistan. Finally, in 1893, the British succeeded in implementing the Durand Line (named for Sir Mortimer Durand, Foreign Secretary at the time), which in the view of the British alone divided the two territories from each other. Granted its own commissioner and formally inaugurated by Lord Curzon* in 1902, the NWFP was given a legislative council in 1932 and a governor three years later. At the time of Indian independence, the NWFP became part of the new state of Pakistan, which would struggle for control of the region with Afghanistan. Home to the Khyber Pass* and the Pashtun (Pakhtun) people, the NWFP was always considered by the British to be a wild and violent place, and its supposed romanticism in this regard was written about by Kipling*, among others.

Further Reading

Rudyard Kipling (1888). 'The Man Who Would Be King,' in *The Phantom Rickshaw and other Eerie Tales* (Allahabad, Wheelers)

Lawrence James (1997). *Raj: The Making and Unmaking of British India* (London, Little, Brown & Co.)

Northwest Territories. One of three Canadian federal territories, the NWT occupies about 520,000 square miles of the country, reaching from the provincial boundaries along the sixtieth parallel of British Columbia*, Alberta*, and Saskatchewan* up to the High Arctic. Created in 1870, following the transfer of the Hudson's Bay Company's* vast Rupert's Land to the Canadian government, the NWT has seen its size diminish steadily as pre-existing provinces expanded and new provinces and territories were created, the latest being Nunavut in 1999. Its population is just 42,000, a little over half of which is Native Indian, Inuit, or Métis.

Further Reading
Pierre Berton (1989). *The Mysterious North* (Toronto, McClelland & Stewart)
William R. Morrison (1998). *True North: The Yukon and Northwest Territories* (Toronto, Oxford University Press)

Nova Scotia. An Atlantic coast province of Canada, Nova Scotia was settled initially by the Scots, beginning in 1621. The area was long contested, however, owing to the small French settlement at Port Royal dating from 1604. In 1713, the Treaty of Utrecht confirmed mainland Nova Scotia as British, to which Cape Breton Island was added (it became a separate colony from 1784 to 1820) after the French were defeated there in 1758 at Louisbourg, and then in 1759–60 at Quebec and Montreal. Marked by the expulsion of the Acadians in 1755, Nova Scotia was given a legislative assembly in 1758. The western, mainland portion of the colony became the separate colony of New Brunswick* in 1784. Thousands of Americans, both white and black, immigrated to Nova Scotia in the ensuing years, as did Highland and Ulster Scots. In 1848, Nova Scotia was the first British colony to achieve responsible government, and in 1867 it joined the Canadian Confederation.

Further Reading
John Grenier (2008). *The Far Reaches of Empire: War in Nova Scotia, 1710–1760* (Norman, University of Oklahoma Press)

Phillip A. Buckner and John G. Reid, eds (1994). *The Atlantic Region to Confederation: A History* (Toronto, University of Toronto Press)

Nyasaland (see Malawi)

Nyerere, Julius K. (1922–99). First President of Tanzania* (Tanganyika) and a leading African nationalist, Nyerere emerged as one of the most eloquent and thoughtful statesmen of his time. Born into a chiefly family in Tanganyika not long after it became a British mandate, Nyerere was educated by Roman Catholic missionaries and then in Tabora, before winning a scholarship to Makarere College in Uganda*. Later returning to Tabora to teach in a school, in 1949 he won a scholarship, which he used to attend the University of Edinburgh, where he earned an MA degree in economics and history. His time abroad exposed him to more advanced socialist thinking, which he combined with his own socially progressive Roman Catholicism to fashion a distinctive ethic of African communitarianism, which he called *Ujamaa*. He returned to Tanganyika in 1952, and the next year became the President of the Tanganyikan African Association. In 1954, this body became the more politically oriented Tanganyikan African National Union, and a concerted drive for independence began. In 1958, Nyerere was elected to the Legislative Assembly, where he became Leader of the Opposition. Self-government was granted to Tanganyika in 1961, with Nyerere as Chief Minister. The next year Tanganyika achieved its independence, with Nyerere as Prime Minister, and when the country declared itself a republic in 1962, Nyerere was elected President. He held the position until stepping down without bloodshed in 1985. Regarded as the 'Father of the Nation,' most of his socialist economic planning did not work – which he admitted freely – but he was highly respected nonetheless. He lived simply in retirement in his home village, but travelled widely as an advocate of his continent's countless poor and as an esteemed African statesman.

Further Reading
B.G. Petruk (2005). *Julius Nyerere: Humanist, Politician, Thinker* (Dar es Salaam, Mkuki na Nyota Publishers)

Nyerere, Julius K.

Cranford Pratt (1976). *The Critical Phase in Tanzania, 1945–1968: Nyerere and the Emergence of a Socialist Strategy* (New York, Cambridge University Press)

O

Obote, A. Milton (1924–2005). First Prime Minister of independent Uganda*, Obote was mission-educated and later graduated from Makarere College. He lived and worked in Kenya* for a time in the 1950s, where he became politicized. Returning to Uganda in 1956, he joined the political party Uganda National Congress (UNC), and the next year was elected to the legislative council. Party amalgamations and much internecine political jockeying took place over the next five years in the run-up to independence. As leader of the Uganda People's Congress (UPC), Obote became Prime Minister in the spring of 1962, and President the next year. He ruled in an increasingly hegemonic fashion until 1971, years marked by an ongoing struggle with the traditional ruler of Buganda*, the *Kabaka*, the result of which was the abolition of Uganda's federal structure and the creation of an executive presidency in 1967. Obote's power was maintained by the Ugandan military, which was under the control of Idi Amin*. Relations between the two men soured in the late 1960s, however, and in 1971 Amin conducted a successful coup while Obote was out of the country. After eight years of terror and misrule, Amin himself was ousted from power and in the election that followed in 1980, Obote's UPC garnered the most votes, propelling him back into office for the next five years. The result of the election was hotly contested, however, and a guerilla war ensued between Obote's Uganda National Liberation Army and the National Resistance Army led by Yoweri Museveni. Perhaps as many as 100,000 people died before Obote was overthrown for the second time in 1985. He spent the next twenty years in exile in Tanzania* and Zambia*. Obote's record, at least during his first years in power, was reasonably free of taint, but then slipped into the all-too-familiar one in post-colonial Africa of violence and corruption.

Further Reading
Vijay Gupta (1983). *Obote: Second Liberation* (New Delhi, Vikas)
Kenneth Ingham (1994). *Obote: A Political Biography* (London, Routledge)

Oldham, J.H. (1874–1969). A missionary, Oldham was born in India* to a military family. Educated in Edinburgh and then at Trinity College, Oxford*, he was intent upon a career in the Indian Civil Service* but, following a decisive Christian conversion experience, decided to become a missionary instead. In 1897, he went to Lahore in the service of the Scottish YMCA. Returning to Edinburgh three years later, he studied theology, followed by further study in missions theory in Germany. In 1908, he became the organizing secretary of the World Missionary Conference, which was held in Edinburgh two years later and proved a turning-point in his life. In 1912, he became editor of the new and soon to be highly regarded journal, *International Review of Missions*, a post he held until 1927. During these years, he advocated missionary ecumenism and championed the rights of colonial native peoples, especially those in India and Africa. In Kenya*, for example, his insistence that African interests must be paramount over those of the white settlers was instrumental in the British government's adoption of such a policy in 1925. In this vein, he had worked to convince the Colonial Office* to engage more fully in the expansion of African education, the result of which was the establishment of the Advisory Committee on Native Education in Tropical Africa in 1923. He was a fierce opponent of racism, calling it 'the deadliest enemy of a humane civilization,' and dedicated much of his long life to this cause as a chief feature of his Christian faith.

Further Reading
Keith Clements (1999). *Faith on the Frontier: A Life of J.H. Oldham* (Edinburgh, T. & T. Clark)
J.H. Oldham (1924). *Christianity and the Race Problem* (London, Student Christian Movement)

Omdurman, Battle of. The last great British imperial battle involving cavalry, it sealed the re-capture of Mahdist Sudan after Gordon's* defeat of thirteen years before. Commanded by General Kitchener*, the battle took place on 2 September 1898 at Omdurman, the Mahdist capital, across the Nile from Khartoum. The Anglo-Egyptian force under Kitchener numbered some 25,000 troops and included a devastatingly effective gunboat flotilla. The Sudanese – Ansar or Dervishes, as they were usually called – numbered twice as many, but were lightly equipped and suffered massive casualties: as many as 11,000 killed as opposed to just some fifty killed on the Anglo-Egyptian side. The battle broke the power of the Mahdists, restoring Anglo-Egyptian rule, which would last until Sudanese independence in 1956. Kitchener's ferocious treatment of the Ansar and the desecration of the Mahdi's tomb came in for immediate criticism by soldier-journalist Winston Churchill*. But as Lord Kitchener of Khartoum, his reputation as the leading military man of empire was sealed by the comprehensive victory at Omdurman and the subsequent forcing out of the region of the French at Fashoda*.

Further Reading
John C. Pollock (1998). *Kitchener: The Road to Omdurman* (London, Constable)
Philip Ziegler (1973). *Omdurman* (London, Collins)

Ontario. The largest province in Canada by population, modern Ontario was founded formally in 1791 when the Constitutional Act divided the Province of Quebec* into Upper and Lower Canada. As Upper Canada, Ontario's first Lieutenant Governor, John Graves Simcoe, developed a legal and legislative system. The province's first immigrants, Loyalists from the American colonies who fled as refugees from the War of Independence, had begun to arrive in 1784, gradually creating agricultural land out of the immense primeval forest that blanketed the colony. York (Toronto) was named its capital and the province grew quickly, especially after the conclusion of the War of 1812*. The Upper Canada Rebellion* in 1837 resulted in the re-ordering of the colony's politics, issuing later in the adoption of responsible government*, which would have a significant impact on colonial governance throughout the Empire. In 1841, as suggested by Lord Durham's Report*, the Act of Union united Upper and Lower Canada as the Province of Canada. As Canada West, Ontario was now one-half of a thriving British colony in North America. In 1867, the achievement of Canadian Confederation was driven largely by politicians from 'Ontario' – as the province was known henceforth – with the help of their London counterparts. The provincial motto, 'Loyal She Remains,' speaks to Ontario's deep attachment to the Crown, which during the later years of Victoria's reign especially was manifest in a strong endorsement of the Empire. As the industrial and population heartland of Canada, Ontario has been at the centre of the country's politics and economics for most of its history, although in recent years the rise of the West – especially Alberta* – has meant a partial shift in the national locus of power away from it.

Further Reading

Robert Bothwell (1986). *A Short History of the Province of Ontario* (Edmonton, Hurtig)

Gerald M. Craig (1963). *Upper Canada: The Formative Years, 1784–1841* (Toronto, McClelland & Stewart)

Opium Wars. Also known as the Anglo-Chinese Wars, the Opium Wars were fought between 1839 and 1842 and again between 1856 and 1860, largely over the importation of opium into Chinese treaty ports from British India*. The wars were the culmination of a long period of forced trade between Britain and China. Always reluctant to trade with the West, China grudgingly opened one port (Canton) to western trade in the sixteenth century. Chinese exports such as tea, porcelain, and silk were valued highly by western countries, notably Britain, but goods going the other way were not. Consequently, the British built up a large trade deficit with China, which had to be covered with silver. In an attempt to staunch the flow of silver, the British began to export opium to China instead, and by the early part of the eighteenth century addiction had begun to be a serious social problem in Canton and beyond. In 1729, the wide-scale importation of opium was banned by the Chinese emperor and the British took to smuggling. The East India Company* gained a monopoly over opium's production and sale in the 1770s and profited enormously from the illicit trade for the next half-century. China protested vigorously, re-issuing the ban in 1799, but to no avail. Finally, in 1839, the Chinese trade commissioner at Canton imposed a trade embargo on the British. The British reluctantly complied, promising an end to the illicit opium trade, but those merchants who had become rich off the trade rejected the stance and were outraged when a large quantity of the drug was destroyed by the Canton authorities. In an attempt to avoid having to pay its traders a huge liability for their loss, the British government decided to force a war with the Chinese, the result of which was the Treaty of Nanking in 1842, the restoration of the (illegal) opium trade, and the forcing open of a number of additional treaty ports, such as Hong Kong*. In 1856, war broke out again between Britain and China. This time France joined in, spurred by the killing of a French missionary. Hostilities ceased in 1858, followed by the signing of the Treaty of Tianjin. While the Treaty languished unratified by the Chinese, the British and the French renewed hostilities in an attempt to force the Chinese to act. In 1860, the Chinese gave way, ratifying the Treaty at the Convention of Peking. A series of new ports was opened up to Anglo-French trade, freedom of movement for missionaries in China was guaranteed, and a large indemnity in silver was paid by the ruling Qing dynasty. For the Chinese, the Treaty of Tianjin set in place the loathsome treaty system, a sign of their humiliation by the West and a flash-point in Sino-Western relations that lasted until the handover of Hong Kong to the People's Republic of China in 1997.

Further Reading

Gerald S. Graham (1978). *The China Station: War and Diplomacy, 1830–1860* (Oxford, Oxford University Press)

Carl A. Trocki (1999). *Opium, Empire and the Global Political Economy: A Study of the Asian Opium Trade, 1750–1950* (London, Routledge)

Orange Free State. A state in the Republic of South Africa*, the OFS originated in the early part of the nineteenth century when a small number of Boers began to migrate north of the Orange River. In 1836, the numbers increased dramatically with the commencement of the Great Trek* by disaffected Boers from Cape Colony* seeking to escape British sovereignty. These settlers formed a republican assembly, which after much negotiation with the British pertaining to claims made by existing tribal groups, proclaimed the independence of the OFS in 1854. For the next half-century, however, sovereignty continued to be contested, especially after the discovery of diamonds in territory contiguous to the OFS and claimed by it. In 1900, the British annexed the OFS, re-naming it the Orange River Colony. Following the conclusion of the Boer War* in 1902 the British negotiated the Colony's future. In 1907, it gained self-government and three years later it joined the new Union of South Africa bearing its original name of the Orange Free State.

Further Reading

G.H.L. Le May (1965). *British Supremacy in South Africa, 1899–1907* (Oxford, Oxford University Press)

Colin Murray (1992). *Black Mountain Land: Land, Class, and Power in the Eastern Orange Free State, 1880s to 1980s* (Washington, Smithsonian Institution Press)

Outram, Sir James (1803–63). A prominent general in the Indian Mutiny*, Outram was a hero to his contemporaries. Born in Derbyshire and educated in Aberdeen, he became a cadet in the army of the East India Company* in 1819. During the 1820s and 1830s, Outram was part of various campaigns culminating in the First Afghan War*, during which he distinguished himself and was promoted major. Service in Sindh* and then in Hyderabad, where he defended the Residency against the attack of some 8,000 Baluchis (Sikhs), led to further promotions, a sterling reputation, and in 1854, appointment as Resident of Lucknow. By then known as the 'Bayard of India', Outram campaigned successfully against the Persians and then returned to India in time to take a leading role in resisting the Indian Mutiny* in the summer of 1857. Ultimately ensuring the relief of the besieged Lucknow, he was rewarded with promotion to Lieutenant-General and made baronet. The quintessential soldier of empire, upon Outram's death he was buried at Westminster Abbey.

Further Reading

Roy D. Thomas (2007). *Outram in India: The Morality of Empire* (Bloomington, IN, Authorhouse)

Lionel J. Trotter (1909). *The Bayard of India: A Life of Sir James Outram* (London, Dent)

Oxford, University of. No university was associated more closely with the Empire than Oxford. Exemplified most clearly by the creation of the Rhodes Trust and the establishment of the Beit Chair in the History of the British Commonwealth (as its title became), during the latter nineteenth century and for much of the twentieth Oxford and Empire were linked inextricably. Benjamin Jowett, master of Balliol College from 1870 to 1893, saw himself as the creator of Imperial statesmen, such as Curzon*, and earlier in the 1850s had been a member of the commission on the Indian Civil Service*, which had opened it up to competitive examination. In the establishment of the Indian Institute at Oxford in 1884, the creation of courses for Colonial Service cadets in the 1920s, and the building up of a cadre of scholars working on the history of the British Empire, Oxford became the epicentre of Imperial studies and, to some extent, administrative training.

Further Reading

Frederick Madden and D.K. Fieldhouse, eds (1982). *Oxford and the Idea of Commonwealth: Essays Presented to Sir Edgar Williams* (London, Croom Helm)

Richard Symonds (1986). *Oxford and Empire: the Last Lost Cause?* (Oxford, Clarendon Press)

P

Pakistan. A republic within the Commonwealth, Pakistan formerly was part of British India*, gaining its independence in 1947. As the Mughal Empire declined in the eighteenth century, the East India Company* moved to fill the vacuum, ultimately ruling much of the region along with client princes. Later, in train with the rise of nationalism that marked the waning years of the Raj, a movement for an independent state for India's Muslims grew. Channelled by the All-India Muslim League* and led ultimately by M.A. Jinnah*, the idea was formalized in 1940 when the League adopted the 'Lahore Resolution.' As Indian independence neared, and despite objections to a separate Muslim state by Gandhi*, the British agreed to partition, whereby two independent states would emerge from Imperial India. In August 1947, such is what happened when both India* and Pakistan achieved independence. Pakistan itself covered two territories in the east and northwest, divided by India. The period of independence was marred by violence and death as millions of Muslims left India to take up residence in Pakistan, and a similar number of Hindus left what was now Pakistan to enter the new India. Jinnah became Pakistan's Governor-General and the country held Dominion* status within the Commonwealth until 1956. In that year it became a republic. In 1971, East Pakistan seceded to become the independent state of Bangladesh*.

Further Reading

Ayesha Jalal (1985). *The Sole Spokesman: Jinnah, the Muslim League and the Demand for Pakistan* (Cambridge, Cambridge University Press)

Ian Talbot (1988). *Provincial Politics and the Pakistan Movement: The Growth of the Muslim League in North-West and North-East India, 1937–47* (Karachi, Oxford University Press)

Palestine. The name given to what essentially comprises the modern state of Israel, Palestine passed into British hands in 1917 after four hundred years of Ottoman rule. The First World War* occasioned the dissolution of the Ottoman Empire and in 1916 the Sykes-Picot Agreement negotiated between the British and the French envisaged Palestine as an international zone. The next year the Balfour Declaration* made plain Britain's desire that a Jewish homeland be established in Palestine. That December, the Turks were driven out of Jerusalem by General Allenby* and by October 1918 their regional control was lost and they surrendered. In 1920, acting on the Paris Peace Conference's decision to enact an international mandate system over many former colonial territories, the British moved to assume control of Palestine (Palestine and Transjordan), a process finalized in 1923. The British occupation and the sponsorship of a Jewish homeland in the midst of an Arab region grew in controversy and violence in the 1930s. The conclusion of the Second World War* increased the pressure on Britain and in the face of attacks on British soldiers and military installations, the cost of maintaining the mandate, and managing the flood of Jewish refugees who wanted to immigrate to Palestine, the British decided to terminate their mandate. It took effect in 1948, the day after the State of Israel was proclaimed. Immediately, Israel was attacked by its regional enemies. The Arab-Israeli War ensued, which spelled the end of Palestine as a territorial designation.

Further Reading

Wm. Roger Louis (1984). *The British Empire in the Middle East, 1945–1951: Arab Nationalism, the United States, and Post-War Imperialism* (Oxford, Oxford University Press)

Bernard Wasserstein (1991). *The British in Palestine: The Mandatory Government and the Arab-Jewish Conflict*, 2nd edn (Oxford, Oxford University Press)

Pan-African Congress. Begun in 1909 as the Pan-African Conference, the Congress was a series of five meetings held in 1919, 1921, 1923, 1927, and 1945 that revolved ultimately around how to speed up the end of European colonial occupation of most of Africa and the West Indies. In particular, the fifth Congress held in Manchester at the end of the Second World War* was a key moment in the history of decolonization. Attended by a number of African and West Indian nationalist leaders such as Jomo Kenyatta*, Kwame Nkrumah*, and George Padmore, the Congress passed resolutions demanding the end of Imperial rule and racial discrimination and the implementation of universal suffrage throughout Africa and the Caribbean. The many African nationalist movements that led to independence in the 1950s and '60s were inspired by the Congress.

Further Reading

Hakim Adi (1995). *The 1945 Manchester Pan-African Congress Revisited* (London, New Beacon Books)

George Padmore, ed. (1963). *History of the Pan-African Congress: Colonial and Coloured Unity, A Programme of Action* (London, Hammersmith Bookshop)

Papineau, Louis-Joseph (1786–1871). A French-Canadian nationalist and politician during the first half of the nineteenth century, Papineau argued forcefully in favour of his countrymen seizing the reins of government in Lower Canada (Quebec*) from British control. As leader of the *Parti Canadien*, afterwards the *Parti Patriote*, Papineau was a prominent voice in the colonial assembly, eventually being named its Speaker. Later becoming a republican, he and his colleagues demanded the implementation of the 'Ninety-two Resolutions,' in 1834, designed broadly to bring about responsible government* in the colony. They were rejected by the British, and in the aftermath Papineau helped to organize and lead the Lower Canadian Rebellion* of 1837–8. In the midst of the Rebellion's failure, he fled to the US and then to France, where he remained until being granted amnesty. Returning home in 1845, he re-entered politics. In exile he had been deeply opposed to the Act of Union in 1841 that bound Upper and Lower Canada together as the Province of Canada, advocating instead French Canada's annexation to the US. But his political voice became increasingly margin-alized and he retired from politics in 1854. Still, Papineau was the first French-Canadian nationalist who commanded a wide following and his legacy was taken up vigorously in Quebec politics in the late nineteenth and early twentieth centuries.

Further Reading

Alfred D. Decelles (1964). *The 'Patriotes' of '37: A Chronicle of the Lower Canadian Rebellion* (Toronto, University of Toronto Press)

Fernand Ouellet (1961). *Louis-Joseph Papineau: A Divided Soul* (Ottawa, Canadian Historical Association)

Papua New Guinea. Located in the South Pacific near Australia* and home to a staggeringly rich variety of some eight hundred indigenous languages, it was first encountered by Europeans in the sixteenth century. Germany, in its inaugural flush of Imperial expansion, occupied the northern part of it beginning in 1884, but after the conclusion of the First World War* the British were mandated to administer New Guinea, as the former German possession was now known. They assigned it to Australia, which, since 1906, had been administering the other, southern part of the contiguous territory, Papua. Following the Second World War*, the mandate was renewed by the UN and from 1949 to 1973 the unified Papua New Guinea continued to be administered by Australia. In the latter year, it was granted self-government, and in 1975 full independence was achieved. PNG is a clear example of sub-Imperialism within the Empire, whereby Australia acted on behalf of Britain, whose ultimate sovereignty prevailed.

Further Reading

W.J. Hudson (1974). *New Guinea Empire: Australia's Colonial Experience* (Melbourne, Cassell Australia)

Peter Maiden (2003). *Missionaries, Headhunters and Colonial Officers* (Rockhampton, Central Queensland University Press)

Park, Mungo (1771–1806). One of the early British explorers of Africa, Park was born and educated in Scotland. He trained as a surgeon in Selkirk and then at the University of Edinburgh, where he also became highly interested in botany and natural history. Through a family connection he came to know Sir Joseph Banks*, who obtained a post for him as assistant ship's surgeon on an East Indiaman sailing for Sumatra in 1793. Inspired by his time in the South Pacific, having returned home Park again found a supporter in Banks, who recommended him to the African Association for a journey to explore the course of the great Niger River of West Africa. He was appointed to head the expedition in 1794, and in June 1795 found himself in The Gambia* about to head inland, which he commenced doing in December. For the next eighteen months he followed the course of the Niger River, visiting its cities, trading with the local peoples, and enduring a four-month-long captivity at the hands of a Muslim chieftain. He returned to England in late 1797 and immediately wrote a book about his experiences, *Travels in the Interior Districts of Africa* (1799), which became an instant travel classic. But once tasted, the explorer's life could not be resisted and in 1805 he said goodbye to his wife and three children and set out for yet another arduous journey to and along the Niger. According to his instructions from the British government, he was to follow the river to its end. Much disease and death accompanied the expedition, including his own. Park either drowned or died at the hands of attacking villagers about 300 miles above where the Niger spills into the Bight of Benin. Park's explorations were essential in establishing the British presence in West Africa, especially in Nigeria* and the Gold Coast*, and to his contemporaries, as well as successive generations, his name became synonymous with intrepid African exploration.

Further Reading

Richard Lupton (1979). *Mungo Park the African Traveller* (Oxford, Oxford University Press)

Mungo Park (2000). *Travels in the Interior Districts of Africa*, Kate Ferguson Marsters, ed. (Durham, NC, Duke University Press)

Parkin, Sir George R. (1846–1922). Self-described as the 'wandering evangelist of Empire,' Parkin was a prominent advocate of Imperial Federation* and the first Secretary of the Rhodes Trust. Born in New Brunswick*, he was educated there and at Oxford*, before returning home to become a teacher and headmaster. In 1889, at the behest of the Imperial Federation League, he made a lecture tour of the Empire, advocating closer ties among its leading colonies and the mother country, from which came one of his many books, *Round the Empire* (1892). In 1902, he resigned from Upper Canada College in Toronto where he had been Principal, in order to head the Rhodes Trust, which he did for twenty years. Knighted in 1920, he died two years later.

Further Reading

Anthony J.P. Kenny, ed. (2001). *The History of the Rhodes Trust* (Oxford, Oxford University Press)

Sir John Willison (1929). *Sir George Parkin: A Biography* (London, Macmillan)

Peninsular & Oriental Steam Navigation Company. The shipping line that grew famous transporting all manner of passengers to British India* and to other points in Southeast Asia, the P&O was founded by Brodie Wilcox and Arthur Anderson in 1822. A few years later, they were joined by Richard Bourne and together the three men began a regular steamer service to the Iberian Peninsula, hence the first part of its name. In 1840, the Company was contracted by the British Admiralty to deliver mail to Alexandria, thus adding Oriental to its name, now incorporated under Royal Charter. The P&O grew apace on the strength of mail delivery, commercial carriage, passenger transport, and corporate takeovers, peaking in size after the First World War*, when it had nearly five hundred ships in service.

Further Reading

David Howarth and Stephen Howarth (1986). *The Story of P&O: the Peninsular and Oriental Steam Navigation Company* (London, Weidenfeld & Nicolson)

Stephen Rabson and Kevin O'Donoghue (1988). *P&O: a Fleet History* (Kendal, World Ship Society)

Perham, Dame Margery F. (1895–1982). A major figure in the history of twentieth-century British colonial administration, especially in Africa,

Perham was born as the Empire approached its climax and lived through the era of its decline and effective disappearance from world affairs. Her direct experience of Imperial life in the field, together with many years of research, writing, and teaching – mainly at Oxford* – gave her an unparalleled knowledge of British affairs in Africa and made her a public figure in this regard far beyond the walls of Nuffield College, where she spent most of her professional career. Perham lived a long and remarkable life, an Imperial life that bears some resemblance to those of other notable women of Empire, such as Mary Kingsley* and Gertrude Bell*. From the moment she first set foot on African soil as a leave-taking Sheffield history lecturer in 1921, to her death over sixty years later, Perham's whole life was focussed on the ways and means of Britain's African Empire: its systems of governance and those who administered them; its economic impact; its geostrategic implications; its effect on native Africans, including nationalism and the end of Empire. From the 1930s to the 1960s, it is unlikely that anyone in the administrative apparatus of the British Empire, and almost assuredly anyone in the world of scholarship, had as nuanced an understanding of how Britain's African Empire actually worked as did Perham. Her road into Africa led from British Somaliland* in 1921, where she went on leave with her sister, the wife of the local British district commissioner. From those simple beginnings was spawned a career at the centre of the British governance of Empire. Appointed Fellow and Tutor in Modern History at St Hugh's College, Oxford in 1924, her teaching and research focussed on Imperial history, the League of Nations mandates system, and, from 1926, Colonial Service officer training. In 1928, the Rhodes Trust awarded her a travelling fellowship, which she used to go around the world studying how the British and American governments handled 'native administration.' So long and so thorough was her tour that she had to sacrifice her teaching post at St Hugh's, but so expert did she become in colonial administration that in 1935 Oxford appointed her research lecturer in the field, and a few years later, when Nuffield College was being endowed, she was appointed the first official and only woman fellow of the new foundation. For the next quarter-century or so, Perham delved deeply into every aspect of British Africa. She was an advisor to the Colonial Office*; she was heavily involved in the Oxford summer school for Colonial Service cadets; she became Director of Oxford's Institute of Commonwealth Studies; she wrote the two-volume magnum opus biography of Lord Frederick Lugard*, the leading theoretician and practitioner of Britain's Indirect Rule* method of governing much of its African Empire; she publicly debated the future of African Empire in the pages of *The Times* and elsewhere. Then, as the era of African independence and decolonization began, she advised newly independent governments about post-colonial governance and corresponded with leading African nationalists such as Tom Mboya* of Kenya*. Reflecting her resurgent Christian faith, she even served as President of the Universities' Mission to Central Africa for a year, and finally, in her last significant public act, she flew out to Nigeria* in 1968 in the midst of a civil war to advise its President. Appointed dame commander three years earlier in 1965, Perham's life provides a unique window into the workings of the British Empire in Africa for most of the time it was fully operational.

Further Reading

C. Brad Faught (forthcoming). *Into Africa: The Imperial Life of Margery Perham* (London and New York, I.B.Tauris)

Alison Smith and Mary Bull, eds (1991). 'Margery Perham and British Rule in Africa,' *The Journal of Imperial and Commonwealth History*, vol. 19, no. 3

Pitcairn Island. The end-point of the most famous ship's mutiny in British history, Pitcairn is a rocky outcrop in the South Pacific, north-east of New Zealand* and south-east of Tahiti. Pitcairn is the second-largest of a group of four volcanic islands, and the only inhabited one, which today forms a British Overseas Territory. Known about by the British since 1767 but uninhabited, in 1790 Pitcairn saw the arrival of nine mutineers led by Fletcher Christian and a small group of Tahitian accomplices after they had committed mutiny on board the HMS *Bounty* under the command of Lieutenant William Bligh* the previous year. They burned the stolen ship in what became called Bounty Bay and then set about establishing a settlement. The fate of the mutineers was not discovered until 1806. In 1838, Pitcairn became a British colony. The population has always been small, although in the mid-nineteenth century the government mandated a mass emigration to the better-endowed Norfolk Island. However, many of those who immigrated decided later to return to Pitcairn. The names of the chief mutineers, Christian and Adams, continue to dominate on Pitcairn among a population that today has dwindled to about fifty.

Further Reading

Maurice Allward (2000). *Pitcairn Island: Refuge of the Bounty Mutineers* (Stroud, Tempus)

Robert B. Nicolson (1997). *The Pitcairners* (Honolulu, University of Hawai'i Press)

Plains of Abraham, Battle of the. The most important battle in the Anglo-French struggle for North America during the Seven Years' War*, Britain's victory on 13 September 1759 at Quebec* harkened the end of New France and the beginning of what would become modern Canada*. Under the command of General James Wolfe*, the battle required three months of laying siege to the walled city of Quebec, located on a promontory high above the St Lawrence River*, but less than an hour for its successful execution. In total, some 9,000 troops on both sides took part, with casualty figures of about 650 each being almost exactly equal. The French fought under the command of General Louis-Joseph, Marquis de Montcalm, who was wounded during the battle and died the next morning. Wolfe's death came on the field when he was struck in the stomach and the chest, dying after he had been informed that the French had broken and run. A few days after the battle, the French formally capitulated and turned over Quebec to the British. The onset of winter meant that the campaigning season was over until the next year, but in September 1760 Montreal fell to the British also, signalling the collapse of New France. In 1763, the Treaty of Paris formally gave possession of it to Britain.

Further Reading

Fred Anderson (2000). *Crucible of War: The Seven Years' War and the Fate of Empire in British North America, 1754–1766* (New York, Alfred A. Knopf)

Stuart Reid (2003). *Quebec 1759: The Battle that Won Canada* (Oxford, Osprey Publishing)

Plassey, Battle of. Fought on 23 June 1757 in Bengal*, victory for the East India Company* under the command of Colonel Robert Clive* broke the regional power of the Mughal Nawab, Siraj-ud-Daula, and his French allies, and portended the rise of British India*. The Battle of Plassey represented the Bengali theatre of the Seven Years' War* and the culmination of a protracted struggle between the EIC and the French-backed Mughals for regional ascendancy. A relatively small engagement, Clive had at his disposal some 3,000 troops in total, compared to the Nawab's 50,000, of whom just 5,000 actually took part in the battle. Clive's tactical brilliance and the superior firepower of the British meant that victory was achieved with the death or wounding of just 75 men, compared to the 500 casualties suffered by those of the Nawab. The spoils of victory for both the EIC and for Clive were enormous. The EIC established a trade monopoly and Clive was launched into a life of power and luxury (and controversy), while his bank account bulged with the immediate addition of some £234,000 from the Nawab's treasury. Though some later scholars have played down the intrinsic importance of the Battle of Plassey, it nevertheless consolidated Britain's pre-eminent position in India's richest region and opened the way for British domination of the sub-continent for most of the next two centuries.

Further Reading

Sushil Chaudhury (2000). *The Prelude to Empire: Plassey Revolution of 1757* (New Delhi, Manohar Publishers & Distributors)

Michael Edwardes (1969). *Plassey: The Founding of an Empire* (London, H. Hamilton)

Pretorius, Andries W.J. (1798–1853). A Boer* leader who was instrumental in the founding of the Transvaal*, Pretorius was born in the Cape Colony* and became a farmer. He joined the Great Trek* and in 1838, as Commandant-General of the Boers in Natal*, participated in the Battle of Blood River, in which a small number of them were attacked by thousands of Zulus* but emerged victorious nonetheless. For the next fifteen years until his death, he was a prominent Boer leader, especially in negotiations with the British over territory. In 1848, he moved north of the farthest line of British sovereignty, the Vaal River, and stayed. Eventually, in 1852, the independence of the Transvaal Boers was recognized by the British. Pretorius died the next year, a hero to his countrymen, a scourge to others. His lasting memorial is the name given to the capital of the Transvaal, Pretoria.

Further Reading
B. J. Liebenberg (1977). *Andries Pretorius in Natal* (Pretoria, Academica)
Oliver Ransford (1972). *The Great Trek* (London, John Murray)

Primrose, Archibald, 5th Earl of Rosebery (1847–1929). Prime Minister and Foreign Secretary, Primrose was the leader of the Liberal Imperialists. Born in London and educated at Eton and Christ Church, Oxford*, the aristocratic and wealthy Primrose became Lord Dalmeny in 1851 and then Earl of Rosebery in 1868. He was instrumental in organizing Gladstone's* victorious Midlothian Campaign of 1879, which helped propel Gladstone back into office the next year. Rosebery would be rewarded by twice being named Foreign Secretary by Gladstone, but they fell out over their different conceptions of Empire, decisively so in 1894 over whether or not to make Uganda* a Protectorate. Gladstone's resignation of the premiership that year had much to do with Uganda. But even though Rosebery won the day in Cabinet over the issue, his victory would be brief. His own administration lasted just fifteen months, and once out of office in June 1895, he never regained it. His later political life was conducted from the margins. In 1918, he suffered a stroke and his last years, before his death in 1929, were difficult and sad.

Further Reading
Gordon Martel (1986). *Imperial Diplomacy: Rosebery and the Failure of Foreign Policy* (Kingston, ON, McGill-Queen's University Press)
Leo McKinstry (2005). *Rosebery: Statesman in Turmoil* (London, John Murray)

Prince Edward Island. The smallest province in Canada, at just some 2,200 square miles, Prince Edward Island lies a short distance off the Atlantic coast near New Brunswick* and Nova Scotia*. As Île St Jean, PEI was settled by the French in the 1720s. In 1763, the Treaty of Paris ceded it to Britain and its name was anglicized to the 'Island of Saint John.' The land was divided into large townships, held mostly by absentee British landlords. For most settlers, land tenure was a crying grievance left largely unsettled until Confederation in 1867. The island population grew nonetheless, through a mixture of immigrants from the British Isles and Loyalists from the American War of Independence. In 1769, the island was granted its own governor, council and assembly, and in 1799 its name was changed to Prince Edward Island to honour a son of George III*. Responsible government* was granted in 1851. A lively sense of their own identity led Islanders to resist joining Canada in 1867, but within a few years a growing colonial debt, pressure from Britain, promises of financial support from Canada, and the example of the other Maritime colonies convinced Islanders that joining Confederation was the right way forward. Accordingly, they did so in 1873.

Further Reading
J.M. Bumsted (1987). *Land, Settlement and Politics on Eighteenth-Century Prince Edward Island* (Kingston, ON, McGill-Queen's University Press)
E.R. Forbes and D.A. Muise, eds (1993). *The Atlantic Provinces in Confederation* (Toronto, University of Toronto Press)

Princely States. The term used to describe hundreds of territories in British India* where various degrees of princely autonomy prevailed. The British divided them into three classes or orders, based upon size and importance, and recognized by greater or lesser gun salutes, and within these realms local rule prevailed over certain jurisdictional matters. Some '21-gun' princely states, such as Hyderabad or Jammu and Kashmir, were virtually autonomous, and while under British paramountcy their Nizam and Maharajah respectively enjoyed great wealth and power. Others, especially those in the third tier, usually were comprised of significant landowners but carried no civil or criminal authority. In the 1850s under Lord Dalhousie*, the Governor-General, the British intensified the controversial doctrine of lapse. This policy saw seven leading princely states fall under East India Company* control when their rulers' line of descent ended. Beginning in 1921 until independence in 1947, a permanent Chamber of Princes existed to advise the government on matters of concern to the Princely States. In the years following the establishment of the new states of India and Pakistan*, the princely order was gradually abolished.

Further Reading

Charles Allen (2005). *Maharajas: Resonance from the Past* (Noida, Brijbasi)

Ernst Waltrand (2007). *India's Princely States: People, Princes, and Colonialism* (Abingdon, Routledge)

Q

Quebec. The key to the Empire's late eighteenth-century presence in North America and today Canada's largest province by territorial size, Quebec was French-held until 1759, when the colony of New France began its fall into British hands after the Battle of the Plains of Abraham*. The French had arrived in 1534, when Jacques Cartier sailed up the St Lawrence River*. In 1608, the village of Quebec was established by the explorer Samuel de Champlain. The colony took a long time to grow, reaching a population of perhaps 60,000 by the time of the British Conquest begun under General James Wolfe*. In 1760, the old colony of New France was re-organized as the British colony of Quebec. Legislation in the form of the Quebec Act (1774) established Quebec's boundaries, and in 1791 the Constitutional Act divided the colony into Upper and Lower Canada, each with a governor, a legislative council and a legislative assembly. This configuration stood until the 1840s when, after the Rebellions of 1837, Lord Durham's* Report recommended that the two colonies be unified as the Province of Canada. Lower Canada (the original colony of Quebec) now became Canada East, and in 1867 entered the Canadian Confederation as a province under its old name of Quebec. For the Empire, absorbing Quebec's 60,000 French-speaking and Roman Catholic colonists was the first major attempt at assimilation, and was resented bitterly by those effected. Though such a policy was formally tried directly following the Conquest and again, though less strenuously, after the Act of Union in 1841, the British moved away from this line after the implementation of responsible government* in 1849, and such was never the stated aim of the Imperial government again.

Further Reading

Hilda Neatby (1972). *The Quebec Act: Protest and Policy* (Scarborough, ON, Prentice-Hall of Canada)

Fernand Ouellet (1980). *Lower Canada, 1791–1840: Social Change and Nationalism*, trans. Patricia Claxton (Toronto, McClelland & Stewart)

Queensland. An Australian state, the first British contact with it came in 1770 when Captain Cook* visited its coastline during his first voyage. Settled originally as a penal colony, general settlement began in 1841. In 1859, the Colony of Queensland was established, with Canadian-style responsible government*. Its economy revolved largely around the production of wool, fruit, and beef. In 1901 it joined the Australian Federation.

Further Reading

Raymond Evans (2007). *A History of Queensland* (Cambridge, Cambridge University Press)

Bill Thorpe (1996). *Colonial Queensland: Perspectives on a Frontier Society* (St Lucia, Queensland, University of Queensland Press)

R

Raffles, Sir T. Stamford B. (1781–1826). Significant as the founder of Singapore* and a prominent British presence in Southeast Asia, Raffles was born on board ship off the coast of Jamaica*. His father was a slave-ship captain, but died when Raffles was just fourteen, forcing the family into dire financial straits and he into a clerkship with the East India Company*. In 1805, Raffles was sent to Penang, where he became assistant secretary to the Governor, got married, and began to make a name for himself as someone with considerable linguistic and administrative skill. In 1811, acting with the approval of the EIC, he decided to campaign against Dutch-held Java. The invasion was successful and Raffles was named Lieutenant-Governor of Java as a reward. In 1816, following the conclusion of the Napoleonic Wars and the return of Java to the Dutch, Raffles sailed back to England, wrote a book, the *History of Java and its Dependencies* (1817), a powerful indictment of Dutch colonialism, was knighted, and in October 1817 departed for the important EIC post of Bencoolen as its new Governor-General. Attempting to maintain harmony in Anglo-Dutch relations comprised the bulk of Raffles' work, but in 1819 such did not preclude his founding of Singapore. Located at the southern tip of the Malay Peninsula, the area was devoid of a Dutch presence. In a short span of time Singapore thrived and in 1824 the Anglo-Dutch Treaty settled all of their outstanding regional grievances. By then, however, Raffles was on his way home for the last time, where he would throw his remaining energies into the Zoological Society of London (of which he was the first President) and in founding the London Zoo. Worn out by years of enduring the stifling Southeast Asian climate, he died aged just forty-five.

Further Reading

Maurice Collis (1966). *Raffles* (London, Faber & Faber)

Charles E. Wurtzburg (1986). *Raffles of the Eastern Isles* (Oxford, Oxford University Press)

Raj (see India)

Red River Rebellion. The first major crisis faced by the new Canadian government after Confederation in 1867, the Red River Rebellion began in 1869 in what is now the province of Manitoba* and lasted until the following year. Inter-racial strife between the French-speaking and English-speaking inhabitants of the colony of Red River was at the heart of the rebellion, but it was sparked by the arrival of William McDougall as Governor. He sent surveyors to the colony in advance of the official transfer of land from the Hudson's Bay Company* to the Canadian government in 1870, and they proceeded to divide up the land based on the Ontario* township system. This survey was deemed unlawful by the majority Métis (mixed French and Indian blood) population of Red River, and led by Louis Riel* they refused to allow McDougall to enter the territory, establishing their own provisional government instead. This new government of 'Assiniboia' then proceeded to arrest anyone who was opposed to them, namely a group of loud and abusive Canadian government supporters, one of which, Thomas Scott, was eventually executed. In the aftermath of his execution, the Canadian government negotiated the creation of the new province of Manitoba, in which some of the provisional government's demands, such as separate Roman Catholic and French-speaking schools, were established. To enforce Canadian sovereignty, an Anglo-Canadian military expedition under Colonel (later Sir) Garnet Wolseley* was sent to Manitoba. By now, however, there was much outrage in Ontario over the death of Scott, and fearing that he would be arrested and executed, Riel fled to the United States. Wolseley's arrival in Manitoba in August 1870 marked the end of the Rebellion, but similar grievances would surface again fifteen years later during the Northwest Rebellion in Saskatchewan*.

Further Reading

J.M. Bumsted (1989). *The Red River Rebellion* (Winnipeg, Watson & Dwyer)

George F.G. Stanley (1989). *Toil & Trouble: Military Expeditions to Red River* (Toronto, Dundurn Press)

Responsible Government. Used to denote a government responsible to the assembled representatives of the people and given impetus in British North America by Lord Durham's* Report following the Upper and Lower Canadian Rebellions* of 1837. An old British Parliamentary principle, when transferred across the Atlantic in the mid-nineteenth century, responsible government gave the colonists control of their domestic affairs. First enacted in Nova Scotia and in the Province of Canada, it was implemented by degrees elsewhere in British North America and gradually became the form of government aspired to and achieved by many of the Empire's other colonies.

Further Reading

Phillip Buckner (1985). *The Transition to Responsible Government: British Policy in British North America, 1815–1850* (Westport, CT, Greenwood Press)

J.M.S. Careless (1967). *The Union of the Canadas: The Growth of Canadian Institutions, 1841–1857* (Toronto, McClelland & Stewart)

Rhodes, Cecil J. (1853–1902). Probably the most famous British Imperialist of the nineteenth century, Rhodes' legacy extends from Africa to the Oxford* Scholarship that bears his name. Born in the East Anglian town of Bishop's Stortford, Rhodes considered the Church and the law as career possibilities, but what enticed him most was the prospect of joining his eldest brother who had gone to South Africa* in 1868 in order to grow cotton. Accordingly, in September 1870, Rhodes arrived in Natal*, but he spent only one year on his brother's farm. He found farming and its small financial rewards unappealing and was much more interested in the possibility of quick riches in the new diamond diggings 400 miles away near the Vaal River. For Rhodes, the next decade of his life was transformational. From staking claims at Kimberley, to initial wealth, to mergers and consolidation and the formation of De Beers Consolidated Mines Ltd*, Rhodes lived an out-sized life while still in his twenties. These were the years in which he came to understand his motivations and convictions as enunciated in his 'Confession of Faith.' This document, which he penned in 1877, spelled out clearly the ways in which Rhodes had come to define his life's mission. For British Imperial history in Africa there are few documents of a personal nature as important as Rhodes' Confession and its 'Big Idea,' which aspired to British world domination. In 1881, Rhodes was elected to the Cape Colony's House of Assembly and quickly increased his public profile. During the mid- to late 1870s, Rhodes had attended Oxford University, from where, at length, he graduated in 1881. At twenty-eight years of age, Rhodes was one of a handful of highly influential men in South Africa, but unlike most of them, he had a plan. Beginning in 1884, Rhodes was successful in folding the territory of Bechuanaland (today's Botswana*) into the Cape. Pushing north by means of railway building was the key to Rhodes' strategy of Imperial acquisition, but the overwhelming impediment to such a plan was the existence of Britain's white co-occupants of South Africa, the Boer republics of the Transvaal* and the Orange Free State*. For Rhodes, the Boers were an unfortunate inconvenience. They needed to be 'squared.' As a result, in the 1880s Rhodes worked as much as possible in co-operation with the leading Boers in the Cape Assembly to do just that. Rhodes saw the Cape Colony*, united between Boer and Briton, as the persuasive means by which to ensure that the Boer Republics would not inhibit Rhodes' eventual plan for a British-dominated South African federation. In the meantime, Rhodes became even richer through the opening up of gold mines in the Transvaal. For Rhodes, the main problem with the Transvaal's President, Paul Kruger*, was that he could not be 'squared.' So obstinate was the Boer leader, in his view, that Rhodes did something highly controversial in 1895. He allowed a devoted subordinate, Dr Leander Starr Jameson*, to lead an ill-advised assault on the Transvaal capital of Pretoria in an attempt to overthrow the government. The Jameson Raid* was a disaster, however. A Parliamentary enquiry ensued, which found Rhodes responsible for it, and Jameson went to prison. Rhodes resigned the Prime Ministership of the Cape in disgrace, but it did not stop his expansive plans otherwise. In 1896, the Ndebele* in Southern Rhodesia* rose in rebellion against the British South Africa Company*, which eventually put them down. Out of office, but not out of the House of Assembly, when war inevitably came between the British and the Boers in 1899, Rhodes rallied the 50,000 people of Kimberley to withstand their attackers. Rhodes died in 1902, the year the Boer War* ended. His legacy was controversial then, and he remains a highly disputed figure today, by turns loathed and admired.

Further Reading

John Flint (1974). *Cecil Rhodes* (London, Hutchinson)

Robert I. Rotberg (1988). *The Founder: Cecil Rhodes and the Pursuit of Power* (Oxford, Oxford University Press)

Rhodesia, Northern (see Zambia)

Rhodesia, Southern (see Zimbabwe)

Riel, Louis (1844–85). One of the most controversial figures in Canadian history, Riel was executed for treason following the Northwest Rebellion in 1885. Long regarded by his people, the mixed-blood Métis, and by French-speaking Canadians as a cultural hero, most others in Canada regarded him as at best a flawed hero, and at worst a tangible threat to the young Canadian state who got what he deserved. During the years following the Red River Rebellion* in 1870, Riel lived in various places, including the United States and Quebec*. Elected MP on three occasions, he never was able to take his seat. Troubled by financial concerns and mental instability, Riel eventually got married and in 1883 took a job teaching at a school in Montana. From there, in 1884, he was asked by the Métis people of Saskatchewan* district to assist them in their political and legal grievances. Riel moved north that summer and for the ensuing months he canvassed local opinion, which, in the form of a petition, was sent to Ottawa in December. Riel, however, began to doubt that anything would come of it, and acting upon his own exalted sense of self as the 'Prophet of the New World', he took up arms in March 1885. The insurrection was put down swiftly, however, Riel was captured and in July was put on trial for treason. Defense counsel argued unsuccessfully that he was insane and Riel was found guilty. The verdict was appealed to the Judicial Committee of the Privy Council*, which dismissed it. Political considerations delayed Riel's execution, but on 16

November he was sent to the gallows. His reputation has been much rehabilitated in the years since his death, but Riel's name still elicits heated debate in Canada, both academic and popular.

Further Reading

Louis Riel (1985). *The Collected Writings of Louis Riel*, George F.G. Stanley, ed. (Edmonton, University of Alberta Press)

Maggie Siggins (1994). *Riel: A Life of Revolution* (Toronto, HarperCollins)

Roberts, Frederick S., 1st Earl Roberts (1832–1914). One of the best known and most popular of Victorian military commanders, the diminutive Roberts (or 'Bobs,' as he was affectionately called) spent over half a century on active service and was in the adulatory public spotlight for much of it. Born into a prominent military family in Cawnpore, India*, Roberts was educated at Eton and Sandhurst before being commissioned into the Bengal Artillery in 1851. He fought in the Indian Mutiny*, and later served in Abyssinia before being promoted Major-General and commanding the Kuram field force in the Second Afghan War*. Success there led to his command of the Kabul and Kandahar field force, and the relief of the latter city. A series of honours were bestowed on him for these victories, culminating in 1881 with a baronetcy. Throughout the 1880s, he served in various capacities and theatres, including Commander-in-Chief of the Indian Army. He was made Field Marshal in 1895, and in 1899 commanded the British forces at the outset of the Boer War*. Success did not come during that first year in South Africa, however, and in 1900 he was replaced by Kitchener*. Lionized and loved nonetheless, from 1901 until 1904 Roberts was Commander-in-Chief of the British Army. His last years were full of adulation and appointments, and upon his death he was accorded the signal honour of lying in state in Westminster Hall. He was buried at St Paul's Cathedral.

Further Reading

Walter Jerrold (1900). *Lord Roberts of Kandahar, VC: The Life-Story of a Great Soldier* (London, S.W. Partridge)

Frederick S. Roberts (1911). *Forty-one Years in India: From Subaltern to Commander-in-Chief* (London, Macmillan)

Robinson and Gallagher. Two names synonymous with twentieth-century theorizing about the nature of (British) Imperialism, Ronald E. Robinson (1920–99) and John A. Gallagher (1919–80) were a pair of Oxbridge iconoclastic historians who helped re-invigorate the study of Empire beginning in 1953. In that year they published a provocative article in the *Economic History Review*, 'The Imperialism of Free Trade,' in which they argued against the view held by most of their contemporaries that Europe had embarked on an age of 'New Imperialism' during the closing years of the nineteenth century, epitomized by the partition of Africa. Robinson and Gallagher rejected this thesis, arguing instead that British Imperial policy demonstrated 'continuity' both before and during the Victorian era and that at the end of the century the only thing new about Imperial expansion was its location. Their trenchantly argued article was decried by many, especially Marxist and socialist historians, who held the view that late-Victorian Imperial expansion was of a qualitatively different kind than that seen earlier. Robinson and Gallagher followed up their 1953 article in 1961 with what became a similarly influential book, *Africa and the Victorians*. Through this book, and other later writings, many of their ideas became central to debates about the causes, nature, and extent of Imperialism: 'Formal and informal Empire,' the 'official mind,' 'collaboration,' the 'Egyptian Crisis,' and 'the metropole and the periphery' entered the lexicon of Imperialism, where they have remained ever since.

Further Reading
John Gallagher and Ronald Robinson (1953). 'The Imperialism of Free Trade', *The Economic History Review*, Second Series, vol. VI, no. 1
Ronald Robinson and John Gallagher with Alice Denny (1985). *Africa and the Victorians: The Official Mind of Imperialism*. 2nd edn (Basingstoke, Macmillan)

Rorke's Drift, Battle of. Fought in January 1879 in Natal* as an immediate supplementary to the nearby Battle of Isandlwana*, Rorke's Drift became a byword for heroism in the British Army, as a record eleven Victoria Crosses were awarded for actions on that day. The overwhelming British defeat by the Zulu* at Isandlwana on 22 January 1879 was followed later that day and the next by a desperate defence of the mission station and garrison at Rorke's Drift. Just 139 soldiers were stationed there, as against some 4,500 Zulu impis. Run by a Swedish missionary, Rorke's Drift had been turned into a small fortress by the British, garrisoned by an infantry company from the 24th Foot. The Zulu, led by the younger brother of King Cetshwayo*, Dabulamanzi, launched a fierce attack that lasted until the early morning of 23 January. But the garrison resisted doggedly and in light of the later arrival of a British relief column the Zulu chose not to continue the attack. The British suffered about thirty casualties compared to over five hundred for the Zulu.

Further Reading

Adrian Greaves (2002). *Rorke's Drift* (London, Cassell)

Donald R. Morris (1986). *The Washing of the Spears: A History of the Rise of the Zulu Nation under Shaka and its Fall in the Zulu War of 1879* (New York, Simon & Schuster)

Round Table Conferences. Three conferences held in London from 1930 to 1932, in which India's* constitutional future was discussed, the immediate result being the reformist Government of India Act of 1935. Under Ramsay MacDonald, the British government met with nationalist leaders such as Gandhi* and Jinnah*. The Conferences were the first time that the British and Empire public really got a sense of the urgency of Indian nationalism, and the benign, dogged, and simply dressed Gandhi as its most prominent face. It was at this time that Churchill* famously voiced his dislike of Gandhi as a 'half-naked' fakir who had come, just as in India, in his traditional garb to 'parley' with the representatives of the King-Emperor.

Further Reading

S.M. Burke and Salim Al-Din Quraishi (1995). *The British Raj in India: An Historical Review* (Karachi, Oxford University Press)

Lawrence James (1997). *Raj: The Making and Unmaking of British India* (London, Little, Brown & Co.)

Royal Canadian Mounted Police. The best known of the Imperial-era national police forces, the RCMP, known as the 'Mounties,' was formed in

1873 in an attempt to put an end to incursions by American whisky traders in the Canadian west and the havoc and violence they were causing, especially in the lives of native Indians. The Northwest Territories*, acquired by the Canadian government from the Hudson's Bay Company* just three years earlier, would see the extension of Canadian sovereignty through the signing of a series of treaties with Indian tribes over the next quarter of a century. Charged with enforcing these treaties, the RCMP was seen by most as just and incorruptible, and the Mounties' scarlet tunic was modelled on that worn by the British Army. Evolving into Canada's national police service, the RCMP continues to harken back to its founding as a frontier force and to the enduring myths of the Canadian west.

Further Reading

William R. Morrison (1985). *Showing the Flag: The Mounted Police and Canadian Sovereignty in the North, 1894–1925* (Vancouver, University of British Columbia Press)

Keith Walden (1982). *Visions of Order: The Canadian Mounties in Symbol and Myth* (Toronto, Butterworths)

Royal Geographical Society. Founded in 1830, the RGS grew out of the African Association and other small London learned societies of the time. One of its founders was Sir John Franklin*, and in 1859 it was granted a Royal Charter by Queen Victoria*. During the nineteenth century, the RGS sponsored a number of important expeditions, including those undertaken by Charles Darwin, David Livingstone*, John Hanning Speke*, and Sir Richard Burton*. Sir Roderick Murchison was its most influential President during this period and helped to make the Society well known both within Britain and beyond. In the twentieth century, the RGS continued to sponsor expeditions, notably to the polar regions, such as that undertaken by Robert Falcon Scott and (later Sir) Ernest Shackleton in 1901. In 1994, the RGS merged with the Institute of British Geographers and today forms the largest geographical society in Europe.

Further Reading

Christopher Ondaatje (1998). *Journey to the Source of the Nile* (Toronto, HarperCollins)

Royal Geographical Society (2005). *To the ends of the Earth: Visions of a changing world: 175 years of exploration and photography* (London, Bloomsbury)

Royal Niger Company (see Sir George Goldie)

Royal Titles Act. An Act of Parliament proclaimed on 1 January 1877 adding 'Empress of India' to the list of Queen Victoria's titles. As Prime Minister, Disraeli* had engineered the formal adoption of the new royal title, much to the consternation of his political nemesis, Gladstone*, who thought it pure political flattery and was loud in his denunciation of it.

Further Reading

Christopher Hibbert (2004). *Disraeli: A Personal History* (London, HarperCollins)

Elizabeth Longford (2000). *Victoria RI* (London, Abacus)

Royal West African Frontier Force. A field force designed by the Colonial Office* in 1897 to garrison Nigeria*, Sierra Leone*, the Gambia*, and the Gold Coast* from the threat of French imperial expansion in the region. In 1898, then-Colonel Frederick Lugard* arrived in Nigeria to raise it. Under his command until the end of the next year and the dissipation of the French threat, the West African Field Force then became the RWAFF, with Nigeria supplying the majority of its battalions. During the First World War*, it saw action against the Germans in Cameroon, as well as in East Africa. From 1939 until 1947, control of the RWAFF was transferred from the Colonial Office to the War Office. During the War it fought in North Africa, as well as in Burma*. The RWAFF disbanded gradually in accordance with the independence of its constituent colonies, and 1960 marked its complete dissolution.

Further Reading

Austin Haywood and F.A.S. Clarke (1964). *The History of the Royal West African Frontier Force* (Aldershot, Gale & Polden)

Margery Perham (1956, 1960). *Lugard: the Years of Adventure, 1858–1898; Lugard: the Years of Authority, 1898–1945* (London, Collins)

Rum. The drink that kept the British Empire afloat, in the view of some, rum is distilled from the by-products of sugar cane and historically its production was centred in the Caribbean. Its formal association with the Royal Navy began in 1655, when Jamaica was captured by the English, and because of the plentitude of rum the daily liquor ration for seamen was changed from French brandy to rum. Powerfully alcoholic, the Royal Navy at the behest of Admiral Sir Edward Vernon began to water down rum around 1739 in order to limit drunkenness and thereby improve the fighting spirit and competence of the men. Known as 'Old Grog,' it was the basis for the sailors' daily half pint – increasing later to a pint – rum ration (a 'tot'), a practice that lasted in the Royal Navy until 1970.

Further Reading

Arthur Herman (2004). *To Rule the Waves: How the British Navy Shaped the Modern World* (New York, HarperCollins)

A.J. Pack (1982). *Nelson's Blood: The Story of Naval Rum* (Havant, Hants, K. Mason)

S

Sabah. A Malaysian state formerly called North Borneo, Sabah was part of the Sultanate of Brunei* before coming under British control. In 1761, the East India Company* established a trading post in the region. Not much came of it, however, and later, in 1881, the British North Borneo Company was formed to successfully exploit Sabah's rich timber stands and rubber plants, which led in 1888 to its being accorded Protectorate status. Administration of the territory was left in the hands of the Company, which continued until 1942, when Sabah was invaded and occupied by the Japanese. Following the end of the Second World War* and the expulsion of the Japanese, in 1946 Sabah was made a Crown Colony. In 1963, independence was achieved as part of the Federation of Malaysia*, in which Sabah formed a province.

Further Reading

K.G. Tregonning (1965). *A History of Modern Sabah, North Borneo, 1881–1963* (Singapore, University of Singapore Press)

Leigh R. Wright (1970). *The Origins of British Borneo* (Hong Kong, Hong Kong University Press)

Saint Christopher (Kitts) and Nevis, Federation of. A tiny two-island nation in the Caribbean, St Kitts and Nevis is the smallest country in the Americas. Sighted and named by Columbus in 1493, St Kitts was colonized by the British in 1624 and Nevis, located across a narrow strait of water, four years later. Together, they were the first British colonies in the

Caribbean and became an integral part of the plantation sugar economy beginning in the 1640s. Admiral Lord Nelson* was married to Frances (Fanny) Nisbet on Nevis in 1787, while on station in the Caribbean. Independence as a member of the Commonwealth was achieved in 1983.

Further Reading
Brian Dyde (2005). *Out of the Crowded Vagueness: A History of the Islands of St Kitts, Nevis & Anguilla* (Oxford, Macmillan Caribbean)
Verna P. Moll (1995). *St Kitts and Nevis* (Oxford, Clio)

Saint Helena. A small, volcanic island in the South Atlantic Ocean, St Helena is a British Overseas Territory (which includes Ascension Island and Tristan da Cunha) made famous by being the site of Napoleon's post-Waterloo incarceration from 1815 until his death in 1821. Discovered by the Portuguese in 1502, St Helena became known to other Europeans by the end of the century, including the English. In 1659, the East India Company* built a fort on the island and two years later was granted a Royal Charter. Company rule passed to the Crown in 1834. Never greatly prosperous, the British continued to use St Helena as a coaling station and island prison: some 5,000 Boers were shipped there during the Second Boer War*. In 1981, St Helena was made a British Dependent Territory, before giving way to its current status in 2002.

Further Reading
Julia Blackburn (1991). *The Emperor's Last Island: A Journey to St Helena* (New York, Vintage Books)
Stephen A. Royle (2008). *The Company's Island: St Helena, Company Colonies & the Colonial Endeavour* (London and New York, I.B. Tauris)

Saint Lawrence River. Gateway to North America and the most important waterway in Canadian history, the St Lawrence was named and navigated by Jacques Cartier in 1534–5. It flows for some 744 miles from the Great Lakes region to the Atlantic Ocean, and drains over a million square miles of territory in several Canadian provinces and American states. From the days of the fur trade forward, the St Lawrence has been an essential artery for Canadian trade. Strategically, its importance was vital to the British Conquest of New France in 1759, and the subsequent struggle with first the French, and then with the Americans, over sovereignty in North America. During the Second World War*, German U-Boats launched attacks in the lower St Lawrence, sinking several Royal Canadian Navy vessels and merchant ships. In 1959, the Queen together with US President Dwight Eisenhower opened the St Lawrence Seaway, which links a series of canals and locks, making the river navigable by ocean-going ships all the way to Lake Ontario. The Laurentian Thesis, articulated by historian Donald Creighton and political economist Harold Innis, argues that the St Lawrence River made Canada's upper North American, east-west economic and political orientation viable and legitimate, as against the continentalist pressure of the United States.

Further Reading

Donald Creighton (2002). *The Empire of the St Lawrence: A Study in Commerce and Politics* (Toronto, University of Toronto Press)

Frank Mackey (2000). *Steamboat Connections: Montreal to Upper Canada, 1816–1843* (Montreal and Kingston, McGill-Queen's University Press)

Saint Lucia. An island nation in the Caribbean first successfully colonized by the French in 1660. Lost to the British three years later, it was fought over continuously until finally becoming permanently British in 1814 with the signing of the Treaty of Paris ending (it was thought) the Napoleonic Wars. Representative government was granted in 1924. St Lucia gained internal self-government in 1967. Independence as a member of the Commonwealth was achieved in 1979.

Further Reading

Jean Besson, ed. (2007). *Caribbean Land and Development Revisited* (Basingstoke, Palgrave Macmillan)

H.A. Will (1970). *Constitutional Change in the British West Indies, 1880–1903* (Oxford, Oxford University Press)

Saint Vincent and the Grenadines. Located in the Caribbean and comprised of the main island of St Vincent and most of the nearby Grenadines chain, it was colonized by the French beginning in 1719 and then ceded to Britain in 1763 by the Treaty of Paris, which formalized the British conquest of New France. A representative assembly was established in 1776. The French reclaimed the islands in 1779 during the American War of Independence, but it reverted to permanent British control in 1783 and the signing of the next Treaty of Paris. Crown Colony status was attained in 1877, and a legislative council in 1925. Internal self-government was granted in 1969, and ten years later came independence.

Further Reading

Jill Bobrow and Dana Jinkins (1985). *St Vincent and the Grenadines* (Waitsfield, VE, Concepts Publishing Co.)
Robert B. Potter (1992). *St Vincent and the Grenadines* (Oxford, Clio Press)

Salisbury, 3rd Marquess of (Robert A.T. Gascoyne-Cecil) (1830–1903). Three-time Tory Prime Minister, Lord Salisbury was associated particularly with British Imperial expansion near the end of the nineteenth century and early in the twentieth. Firmly aristocratic in mien and educated at Eton and Christ Church, Oxford*, he entered Parliament in 1853 and as the Marquess of Salisbury became a member of the House of Lords in 1868. He served briefly as Secretary of State for India* in the government of Lord Derby, doing so again for Disraeli* from 1874 to 1878, followed by his appointment as Foreign Secretary until 1880. Leadership of the Conservatives ensued after Disraeli's death, and Salisbury's first administration from 1885 to 1886. Regaining office the next year, Salisbury was Prime Minister until 1892. His third and final administration ran from 1895 to 1902. As Prime Minister, he usually retained the duties of Foreign Secretary and was exercised most by Britain's place in the world. Employing the vehicle of the chartered company when possible, he presided over much of the country's expansion abroad during the partition of Africa, including the Fashoda* incident, and later the execution of the Second Boer War*. Along with Disraeli, he was seen to have consolidated the Tories as the party of Empire.

Further Reading

Paul R. Brumpton (2002). *Security and Progress: Lord Salisbury at the India Office* (Westport, CT, Greenwood Press)

Andrew Roberts (1999). *Salisbury: Victorian Titan* (London, Weidenfeld & Nicolson)

Sarawak. Contiguous to Sabah*, it is the largest state in Malaysia*, rich in timber and rubber. Controlled by the Sultan of Brunei in the early part of the nineteenth century, order broke down, only to be restored at the hands of the intrepid James Brooke*, whose reward was to be made Rajah of Sarawak by the Sultan in 1841. Thereafter, Brooke established a family dynasty. Status as a Protectorate was granted to Sarawak by the British government in 1888. The Brooke era lasted formally until 1946, when Sarawak became a British colony. By that time, Malay nationalism was strong and British control was resisted. In 1963, Sarawak became independent as part of the new Federation of Malaysia.

Further Reading

Nigel Barley (2002). *White Rajah* (London, Little, Brown & Co.)

Steven Runciman (1960) *The White Rajahs: A History of Sarawak from 1841 to 1946* (Cambridge, Cambridge University Press)

Saskatchewan. A province in western Canada*, Saskatchewan entered Confederation in 1905. Occupied for thousands of years by Plains Indians, it had been held as part of the Hudson Bay Company's* vast territory of Rupert's Land, before being transferred to the Canadian government in 1870. In 1882, it became an administrative district. Expansive prairie dominates the southern part of the province, while forests and lakes cover the north. It was the site of the violent Northwest Rebellion in 1885. Long regarded as Canada's grain-growing breadbasket, it is rich also in minerals, as well as in oil and natural gas. Immigrants began to arrive in large numbers at the beginning of the twentieth century, eventually pushing the province's population to over a million. During the Second World War*, it was a key site for pilot training in the British Commonwealth Air Training Plan*.

232

Further Reading

W.A. Waiser (2005). *Saskatchewan: A New History* (Calgary, Fifth House)

David E. Smith, ed. (1993). *Building a Province: A History of Saskatchewan in Documents* (Saskatoon, Fifth House)

Sati (Suttee). An ancient religious practice of (voluntary) self-immolation engaged in by recently widowed Hindu women who would place themselves on the funeral pyre of their dead husbands, it was abhorred by the British and after years of campaigning against it by missionaries and administrators was finally outlawed in the Bengal* Presidency by Lord Cavendish Bentinck* in 1829. The other East India Company* territories followed suit shortly thereafter, although it remained legal in some Princely States* until 1846.

Further Reading

Andrea Major (2006). *Pious Flames: European Encounters with Sati, 1500–1830* (Oxford, Oxford University Press)

Clare Midgley (2007). *Feminism and Empire: Women Activists in Imperial Britain, 1790–1865* (London, Routledge)

Schumpeter, Joseph A. (1883–1950). A Moravian-American economist, Schumpeter integrated sociology into his economics, including a theory of Imperialism, which has since been an important strand in the broader understanding of its nature. Born in the Austro-Hungarian Empire, Schumpeter taught at university in Graz before becoming briefly the Austrian Minister of Finance in 1919. Later he moved to the University of Bonn, and then, with the rise of the Nazis, he emigrated to the US, where he held a professorial appointment at Harvard from 1932 until his death eighteen years later. Though not published in English until after his death, Schumpeter's *Imperialism and Social Classes* (1951) offers an important and influential theory about the nature of Imperial expansion. Arguing that Imperialism was the 'objectless disposition on the part of the state to unlimited forcible expansion,' he maintained that it was grounded in a nation's history, in its national sentiment, in patriotism; in short, Schumpeter defined Imperialism as a social atavism, a kind of hangover from the autocratic history shared by most of the Imperial states of Europe. The logical conclusion he arrived at was that as older ideas of overlordship, male supremacy, and glory dissipated, so too would Imperialism.

Further Reading
Yuichi Shionoya and Mark Perlman, eds. *Schumpeter in the History of Ideas* (Ann Arbor, University of Michigan Press)

Richard Swedberg (1991). *Schumpeter: A Biography* (Princeton, Princeton University Press)

Scott, Paul (1920–78). A British novelist, playwright and poet, Scott's fictional accounts of British India* offer a superb rendition of the last years of the Raj. Born and educated in London, Scott served in the British Army during the Second World War*, and in 1943 was posted to India. After the War, he remained in India, working as an accountant before returning to live in England in 1950. Two years later, his first novel, *Johnny Sahib* (1952), was published. Throughout the decade and into the 1960s, Scott met with little literary success, but in 1966 he published *The Jewel in the Crown*, a book that started with slight sales but grew steadily. Soon after came three more novels (*The Day of the Scorpion; The Towers of Silence; A Division of the Spoils*), in what became the Raj Quartet. These books sealed Scott's reputation as the leading fictional chronicler of the Raj, especially when in 1984 they were turned into one of the most popular television series in British history. His last novel on what he called 'the extended metaphor' of British India was *Staying On*, which was awarded the 1977 Booker Prize. By then already ill with cancer, Scott died the next year.

Further Reading
Hilary Spurling (1990). *Paul Scott: A Life* (London, Hutchinson)

Patrick Swinden (1980). *Paul Scott: Images of India* (London, Macmillan)

Second World War (1939–45) Just as in the First World War*, troops from the Empire – particularly the Canadians – were mobilized from near the outbreak of hostilities, this time in September 1939. A truly global conflict, the Empire's far-flung nature meant that theatres of war included Hong

Kong*, Malaya*, Singapore*, Burma*, and North Africa. Australians and New Zealanders fought in Greece, Canadians in Europe and Hong Kong, South Africans in Italian-held Ethiopia, and native Kenyans as well as other African troops in Ethiopia, as well as some in Burma. Meanwhile, the British Commonwealth Air Training Plan* saw the training of thousands of aircrew in Canada, Australia and elsewhere in the Empire. The staggering cost of the Second World War, the anti-Imperial stance of the United States, Britain's desperate financial shape, and the rise of colonial nationalism, combined to bring a swift contraction of the Empire in the generation after 1945, some arguing that the War in fact had sounded its death-knell.

Further Reading

Glen St J. Barclay (1976). *The Empire is Marching: A Study of the Military Effort of the British Empire, 1800–1945* (London, Weidenfeld & Nicolson)

Wm. Roger Louis (1977). *Imperialism at Bay, 1941–45: The United States and the Decolonization of the British Empire* (Oxford, Oxford University Press)

Seeley, Sir John Robert (1834–95). An historian and writer, Seeley's *Expansion of England* (1883) was one of the most important books of the latter nineteenth century in attempting to explain – and provide a rationale for – Britain's steady acquisition of overseas territories. Educated at the City of London School and at Cambridge, Seeley became professor of Latin at University College London in 1863. Famous for his phrase that Britain had acquired an Empire in 'a fit of absence of mind', Seeley's essentially liberal Imperialist views intersected favourably with growing public and party polit-ical opinion at the time, and re-affirmed the then almost universal idea that Britain ruled her Empire in the best interests of her subjects. He was knighted in 1894, the year before his death.

Further Reading

Sir John Robert Seeley (1971). *The Expansion of England* (Chicago, University of Chicago Press)

Deborah Wormell (1980). *Sir John Seeley and the Uses of History* (Cambridge, Cambridge University Press)

Selborne, 2nd Earl of (William Waldegrave Palmer) (1859–1942). A key Imperial administrator around the turn of the twentieth century, Selborne was educated at Winchester and Oxford*, and entered Parliament as a Liberal in 1885. In 1895, he became Under-Secretary of State for the Colonies and thereby Colonial Secretary Joseph Chamberlain's* right-hand man. Five years as First Lord of the Admiralty from 1900 to 1905 were followed by five years in South Africa* as High Commissioner and sometime Governor of the Transvaal* and the Orange River* colonies. Especially through his 'Selborne Memorandum,' he was instrumental in moving both colonies toward self-government in anticipation of the creation of the Union of South Africa* in 1910.

Further Reading

D. George Boyce, ed. (1990). *The Crisis of British Power: The Imperial and Naval Papers of the Second Earl of Selborne, 1895–1910* (London, Historians' Press)

David E. Torrance (1996). *The Strange Death of the Liberal Empire: Lord Selborne in South Africa* (Kingston, ON, McGill-Queen's University Press)

Selkirk, 5th Earl of (Thomas Douglas) (1771–1820). Well known in Canada as the Scottish sponsor of pioneering immigrant communities in various parts of the country, Selkirk inherited enormous wealth, which he used to send thousands of Scots 'crofters' (tenants on his land) to British territories in early nineteenth-century Canada. In 1803, Selkirk-sponsored immigrants in Prince Edward Island*. The next year another group arrived in Upper Canada, north of present-day Toronto. Later, and after considerable persuasion and expenditure to buy Hudson's Bay Company* shares, Selkirk acquired an enormous 116,000 square-mile tract in Rupert's Land. The colony, which saw its first settlers arrive in 1812, came to be called Red River (the forerunner of today's Winnipeg, Manitoba*). The colony was contested, however, by the HBC's main competitor, the Northwest Company*, whose trade routes the new colony bisected. The Métis people of the region also disliked the new colony, and matters turned violent in 1816 with the Battle of Seven Oaks, in which twenty-five of the colonists were killed, including the Governor. Selkirk visited his embattled colony in the aftermath of the killings, but his peremptory arrest of those Northwest Company men he believed were responsible led to their accidental deaths and a protracted court battle. He died a short time later, and his colonizer's dream – for a time, at least – died along with him.

Further Reading

J.M. Bumsted, ed. (1988). *The Collected Writings of Lord Selkirk, 1810–1820* (Winnipeg, Manitoba Record Society)

John M. Gray (1963). *Lord Selkirk of Red River* (Toronto, Macmillan)

Selous, Frederick C. (1851–1917). Probably the most famous of colonial Africa's 'White Hunters,' Selous was born in London and educated at Rugby, before setting off for southern Africa, reaching today's Zimbabwe* in 1872. For the rest of that decade and all of the next, Selous became intimately familiar with South-Central Africa, ranging far and wide to shoot game and explore the varied topography. He also became a dedicated naturalist, and in later years a conservationist who oversaw a burgeoning collection of specimens, many of which were given to museums or sold to private collectors. In 1890, he ceased the intensely peripatetic life of his youth and took employment with the British South Africa Company*, whose 'pioneer column' he led north to establish what would become the colony of Southern Rhodesia*. By this time his contemporary reputation was great, and in 1892 the Royal Geographical Society* awarded him its Founder's Medal in recognition of his intrepid ways. Later in the 1890s, he fought in the Matabele Wars*, which confirmed British sovereignty in Southern Rhodesia. Afterwards he returned to hunting and leading or participating in expeditions, including Theodore Roosevelt's gigantic safari in British East Africa in 1909, during which the former US President shot game by the hundreds. During the First World War*, Selous was a captain in the Royal Fusiliers in BEA, and in 1916 was awarded the Distinguished Service Order. He was killed by a German sniper the next year.

Further Reading

John G. Millais (1919). *Life of Frederick Courteney Selous* (New York, Longmans, Green)

Stephen Taylor (1989). *The Mighty Nimrod: A Life of Frederick Courteney Selous, African Hunter and Adventurer, 1851–1917* (London, Collins)

Seven Years' War. Called by some the first 'world war', the Seven Years' War (1756–63) ended the French Imperial presence in North America and made Britain Europe's leading colonial power, with vast holdings in North America and the consolidation of East India Company* rule in Bengal.* There was also a continental theatre of war in which Prussia and Austria, among other states, fought. Altogether, the War involved fifteen belligerents. It began with skirmishes between the French and the British in North America, provoked by the westward expansion of the colonies of Virginia and Pennsylvania into the Ohio Valley, which was claimed by the French. For the British Empire, the two signal battles of the War took place at Plassey* in 1757 and at Quebec* two years later. Victory at both meant British Imperial ascendancy, confirmed by the Treaty of Paris in 1763 and re-orienting the Empire in ways not fully realized until after the loss of the American colonies a generation later.

Further Reading

William H. Fowler (2005). *Empires at War: The Seven Years' War and the Struggle for North America* (Vancouver, Douglas & McIntyre)

Frank McLynn (2004). *1759: The Year Britain became Master of the World* (London, Jonathan Cape)

Sex and Empire. One of the newer areas of Imperial studies, it is an important but strongly debated field. Examining sexuality as a means for motivation, sublimation, or subjugation in the history of the British Empire, more recently the field has begun to examine, for example, the impact of prostitution and transmittable diseases on the lives of British soldiers abroad. Whether it was in the establishment of regimental brothels in pre-Mutiny India, or the pederasty scandal and subsequent suicide of Sir Hector MacDonald, Commander-in-Chief of British forces in Ceylon in 1903, sexuality and gender is an increasingly studied field of enquiry in the history of Empire.

Further Reading

Ronald Hyam (1990). *Empire and Sexuality: The British Experience* (Manchester, Manchester University Press)

Philippa Levine, ed. (2004). *Gender and Empire* (New York, Oxford University Press)

Seychelles. An archipelago island nation located in the Indian Ocean some thousand miles off the coast of Kenya* and heavily dependent upon tourism and tuna fishing, the Seychelles were first seen by a European when Vasco da Gama passed by in 1502. In 1609, an East Indiaman landed, but it was the French who claimed the islands first in 1756. The British vied for control nonetheless, succeeding formally in 1814 with the signing of the Treaty of Paris. Linked administratively for years with Mauritius*, the Seychelles became a separate Crown Colony in 1903. In 1976, independence was achieved as a republic within the Commonwealth.

Further Reading

William McAteer (1990). *Rivals in Eden: A History of the French Settlement and British Conquest of the Seychelles* (Sussex, Book Guild)

Deryck Scarr (2000). *Seychelles since 1770: History of a Slave and Post-Slavery Society* (London, Hurst & Co.)

Shaka (c.1787–1828). Regarded as the founder of the Zulu* nation in southern Africa and a great chieftain and military leader, Shaka united various of the Zulu sub-tribes in the early part of the nineteenth century, resulting in a nation of some 250,000 people, 50,000 of which were warriors. Both brutal and innovative, Shaka's military reforms would come to have a serious impact on the British later in the nineteenth century. In particular, his creation of the 'buffalo horns' formation played havoc with the British troops at Isandlwana* in 1879, resulting in one of their most famous defeats.

Further Reading

Carolyn Hamilton (1998). *Terrific Majesty: The Power of Shaka Zulu and the Limits of Historical Invention* (Cambridge, MA, Harvard University Press)

E.A. Ritter (1978). *Shaka Zulu* (Markham, ON, Penguin)

Sierra Leone. Located on the west coast of Africa, Sierra Leone was the site of intensive transatlantic slave trade* shipments until 1787, when

Freetown was founded as a refuge for former slaves by the St George's Bay Company, comprised of a number of British abolitionists and philanthropists. Of the first group to come to Freetown, most were former American slaves from London. Subsequently, a large number of former American slaves who had previously been living in Nova Scotia* were brought over. The philanthropic roots of Sierra Leone showed themselves again in the establishment of Fourah Bay College in 1827, the oldest institution of higher education in West Africa. Made a Crown Colony in 1808, the remainder of the territory was given Protectorate status in 1896. Two years later, the 'Hut Tax War' broke out and for several months the British faced armed opposition to the tax regime they had installed in 1893. Twentieth-century economic development was slow and centred on the diamond trade, both legal and illegal. Gradual constitutional development resulted in the creation of a legislative council in 1924, and the granting of local ministerial responsibility in 1953. Sierra Leone became independent in 1961. Ten years later it became a republic, choosing to remain within the Commonwealth.

Further Reading

C. Magbaily Fyle (2006). *Historical Dictionary of Sierra Leone* (Lanham, MD, Scarecrow Press)

Simon Schama (2006). *Rough Crossings: Britain, the Slaves, and the American Revolution* (New York, Ecco)

Sikh. An important minority population in India, throughout the period of British India* the Sikhs were both foe of and then friend to the Crown. Long opposed to the Mughal dynasty, the Sikhs looked upon British nineteenth-century expansion in the same light, and in 1845 sparked the first Anglo-Sikh War, which lasted until the next year, only to resume for a second time in 1849. Decisive victories by the British in the Sikh heartland of the Punjab led to its annexation to British India that same year. Thereafter, Sikh martial traditions were employed by the Raj, especially on the North-West Frontier. Sikhs were well represented in both the First and Second World Wars*, during which over 80,000 were killed fighting for the Allies. At the time of Indian Independence in 1947, there was heavy conflict between Sikh and Muslim in the Punjab, and calls for an independent Sikh state of Khalistan continue to this day.

Further Reading

J.S. Grewal (1998). *The Sikhs of the Punjab* (Cambridge, Cambridge University Press)

Andrew J. Major (1996). *Return to Empire: Punjab under the Sikhs and British in the Mid-Nineteenth Century* (New Delhi, Sterling Publishers)

Simon Commission. Known officially as the Indian Statutory Commission (which included Burma), the Simon Commission was comprised of seven British Parliamentarians appointed in 1927 by the Baldwin Tory government to examine Indian constitutional affairs stemming from the reformist Government of India Act of 1919. Chaired by Sir John Simon, one of the Commission's members was Clement Attlee* who, twenty years later, would preside over Indian independence. The Commission received stiff opposition from the Indian National Congress* as well as from the All India Muslim League*, both of whom believed that they were being shut out of the process. Met by loud protests at its hearings in India, the Commission finally published its report in 1930, which recommended that full representative government be established at the provincial level in India to replace the old form of dyarchy, in which some departments of government were responsible to the provincial legislature and others to the Governor. Dominion* status for India would be the natural outcome of the process of reform, stated the British government, and the Government of India Act passed in 1935 reflected the recommendations of the Simon Commission.

Further Reading

Shiri Ram Bakshi (1977). *The Simon Commission and Indian Nationalism* (New Delhi, Munshiram Manoharlal Publishers)

Edward Cadogan (1933). *The India We Saw* (London, John Murray)

Sindh. A province in modern Pakistan*, Sindh comprised part of British India* after being conquered in 1843 by forces under the command of General Sir Charles Napier* who, apparently, reported his victory to the Governor-General,

Lord Ellenborough, by using a single word in Latin: 'Peccavi', translated as 'I have sinned'. Ruled by the British until Indian independence in 1947 and the creation of Pakistan, Sindh became known to the Victorian public through Sir Richard Burton's* peregrinations there in the 1840s and, later, as the heartland of India's Muslims led by Sindh native Muhammad Ali Jinnah*.

Further Reading

Suhail Zaheer Lari (1994). *A History of Sindh* (Karachi, Oxford University Press)

Christopher Ondaatje (1996). *Sindh Revisited: A Journey in the Footsteps of Captain Sir Richard Francis Burton: 1842–1849, The India Years* (Toronto, HarperCollins)

Singapore. A Southeast Asian city-state at the tip of the Malay Peninsula, Singapore was founded in 1819 by Sir Stamford Raffles* on behalf of the East India Company*. He saw the island location as strategically ideal for the spice trade. Five years later, Singapore was made a British colony. Governed briefly by the India Office beginning in 1858, it became a Crown Colony in 1867. The latter nineteenth century saw Singapore emerge as one of the most important British outposts in its Asian Empire, with much of local high colonial society based at the famous Raffles Hotel. During the Second World War*, Singapore fell to the Japanese, causing Churchill* to remark that it was 'the worst disaster and largest capitulation in British history'. Re-possessed by Britain in 1945, Singapore became self-governing in 1959. Four years later, it declared unilateral independence before joining the new Malay Federation*. In 1965, Singapore left the Federation, becoming one of the world's last sovereign city-states. It is a parliamentary democracy within the Commonwealth.

Further Reading

Maya Jayapal (1992). *Old Singapore* (Singapore, Oxford University Press)

Peter A. Thompson (2005). *The Battle for Singapore: The True Story of Britain's Greatest Military Disaster* (London, Portrait)

Slave Trade and Slavery. The twin scourges of transatlantic commerce from the sixteenth to the nineteenth centuries, the British went from being the world's leading slave trade practitioner to its chief enemy. By the middle of the eighteenth century, Liverpool had emerged as the centre of the slave trade, engaged in the 'triangular trade': the other points being the African west coast and the West Indies and North America. The plantation economy – involving mainly sugar of the British Caribbean – was enormously profitable. At home, Britons became large consumers of sugar. Slavery itself was prohibited in Britain after the Mansfield court decision of 1772, but these were the years of greatest export: perhaps as many as 40,000 slaves per year travelled the Middle Passage on British slavers from Africa to plantations in Jamaica*, Barbados*, and elsewhere. These years also, however, saw the rise of a sustained campaign against the trade, beginning formally with William Wilberforce's* abolition bill introduced in 1787, which, after twenty years of public and Parliamentary debate, yielded an Act outlawing the slave trade within the British Empire in 1807. Thereafter, the movement continued until slavery itself was similarly abolished in 1834.

Further Reading

Roger Antsey (1975). *The Atlantic Slave Trade and British Abolition, 1760–1810* (London, Macmillan)

Adam Hochschild (2005). *Bury the Chains: Prophets and Rebels in the Fight to Free an Empire's Slaves* (New York, Houghton Mifflin)

Smith, Ian D. (1919–2007). Prime Minister of Southern Rhodesia* and then of Rhodesia, Smith was at the eye of the protracted controversy over white minority rule there in the 1960s and '70s. Born in Southern Rhodesia, he was educated locally and then at Rhodes University in South Africa*. He served in the Royal Air Force during the Second World War*, and afterwards returned to Southern Rhodesia to a farm near his hometown of Selukwe. Elected to the Southern Rhodesian Parliament in 1948, he became a supporter of the short-lived Federation* of the two Rhodesias and Nyasaland*. Later, and in increasing disagreement with Britain's insistence that Rhodesian independence could not come until the introduction of majority rule, he helped form the Rhodesian Front party. As one of its chief representatives, he was re-elected to the Southern Rhodesia Parliament in 1962. Two years later, he became Prime Minister, vowing never to allow black majority rule, 'not in a thousand years.' Black nationalist leaders such as Robert Mugabe* and Joshua Nkomo were imprisoned during these years. In 1965, Smith's government issued a Unilateral Declaration of Independence (UDI)*. Rejected by Britain and most of the world, Smith defiantly remained Prime Minister of Rhodesia until 1979. Several attempts at negotiating Rhodesia's constitutional future were made in the midst of what became a civil war, but no settlement was reached until 1979–80 under the provisions of the Lancaster House agreements. In the aftermath of the 1980 multi-racial elections, Smith became Leader of the Opposition in the new Parliament of Zimbabwe*. He remained in that position until 1985, before retiring to his farm. His last years were spent in writing books that heaped scorn on the successor Mugabe regime. He died in Cape Town, where he had gone to seek medical treatment.

Further Reading

Dickson A. Mungazi (1998). *The Last Defenders of the Laager: Ian D. Smith and F.W. de Klerk* (Westport, CT, Praeger)

Ian Douglas Smith (1997). *The Great Betrayal: The Memoirs of Ian Douglas Smith* (London, Blake Publishing)

Smuts, Jan Christian (1870–1950). A prominent military leader and statesman from South Africa*, Smuts was born into a prosperous Afrikaner farming family in the Cape Colony*. A brilliant student, he was educated at Victoria College, Stellenbosch, leading to a scholarship he used in order to read law at Christ's College, Cambridge. Graduating with a first-class degree in 1893, he went up to London to begin a career in law. He decided, however, not to remain in England and, passing up an offer to become a fellow in law at his old Cambridge college, returned to the Cape Colony in 1895. The next years were highly eventful. He practiced law briefly, but soon found himself caught up in the drive for South African federation. Initially admiring of Rhodes*, for whom he worked for a short time, he quickly rejected his Imperial machinations, especially the Jameson Raid*. Smuts served with distinction in the Second Boer War* as a commando leader, and then in the negotiations to end the War and, eventually, those that led to the creation of the Union of South Africa* in 1910. As South

Africa's Minister of Defence from 1910 to 1924, he led the allied forces in East Africa during the First World War*, also becoming the country's Prime Minister between 1919 and 1924. In 1939, he became Prime Minister again, followed two years later by his being made Field Marshal. He was defeated in the 1948 elections that brought the National Party to power with its policy of apartheid. He was made Chancellor of Cambridge University in 1948, an example of his marked internationalism, but he never rejected the belief in Afrikaner white superiority inculcated in his youth.

Further Reading
O. Geyser (2001). *Jan Smuts and his International Contemporaries* (Johannesburg, Covos Day)

Kenneth Ingham (1986). *Jan Christian Smuts: The Conscience of a South African* (New York, St Martin's Press)

Sobers, Sir Garfield (Garry) (1936–). Arguably the greatest cricket all-rounder in the history of the quintessential British Imperial game, Sobers was born in Barbados*. A natural athlete who excelled at a number of sports, in cricket he was a uniquely outstanding batsman, bowler, and fielder. He played his first Test Match aged just seventeen in 1953, and his last in 1974. Knighted in 1975, Sobers is a revered figure in his home country, as well as throughout the Caribbean and the cricket-playing world. In 1998, he was named a National Hero of Barbados.

Further Reading
Hilary Beckles (1994). *An Area of Conquest: Popular Democracy and West Indies Cricket Supremacy* (Kingston, I. Randle)

Sir Garfield Sobers (2002). *Garry Sobers: My Autobiography* (London, Headline)

Solomon Islands. An island state located in the South Pacific near Papua New Guinea*, the Solomons are comprised of some 1,000 islands, of which the main one is Guadalcanal. European contact began with the Spanish in 1568. Christian missionaries began to arrive in the nineteenth century, and in 1893 the British declared a Protectorate over the islands. During the

Second World War*, the Solomons became the scene of heavy fighting between the Allies and the Japanese, especially the Battle of Guadalcanal from 1942 to 1943. After the War, British rule resumed, and in 1974 parliamentary democracy and ministerial government were adopted. Two years later, the Solomons became self-governing, and in 1978 independence was achieved.

Further Reading

Judith A. Bennett (1987). *Wealth of the Solomons: A History of a Pacific Archipelago, 1800–1978* (Honolulu, University of Hawai'i Press)

Ben Burt (1994). *Tradition and Christianity: The Colonial Transformation of a Solomon Islands Society* (Philadelphia, Harwood Academic Publishers)

South Africa. Formed in 1910 from the Cape Colony*, Natal*, Orange Free State*, and the Transvaal*, the Union of South Africa is a republic located at the southern tip of the African continent. A British presence was established in 1795 at Cape Town, where the Dutch had been settled since 1652. In 1806, the East India Company* annexed the Cape Colony. Frontier wars against the Zulu*, Xhosa*, and the Boers* especially were fought during the nineteenth century, exacerbated by the discovery in the interior of diamonds in 1867 and gold in 1884. The last of these, the Second Boer War* from 1899 to 1902, set in motion the eventual unification of the four colonies as set out by the Selborne* Memorandum of 1907. As a Dominion*, the country played a key role in the twentieth-century constitutional evolution of the Empire-Commonwealth and participated fully in the First and Second World Wars*. In 1948, the election of the National Party inaugurated the intensification of racial segregationist laws, collectively called apartheid*. Amid increasing pressure from fellow Commonwealth members over its racial policies, South Africa became a republic and left the Commonwealth in 1961. In 1990, the National Party allowed for the legality of opposition parties such as the African National Congress and began to dismantle apartheid. In 1994, multi-racial elections were held and the ANC came to power under the Presidency of Nelson Mandela*. In that year, South Africa was re-admitted to the Commonwealth.

Further Reading

T.R.H. Davenport (2000). *South Africa: A Modern History* (Toronto, University of Toronto Press)

Deborah Posel (1991). *The Making of Apartheid, 1948–1961* (Oxford, Oxford University Press)

South Australia. The fourth-largest state in the Australian* federation, it was planned as a colony of free settlement, as opposed to transported convicts, and was proclaimed in 1836 along the lines theorized by Edward Gibbon Wakefield*. In 1834, the South Australia Act had been passed by the British Parliament, which led to the colony's proclamation two years later. In 1843, a legislative council was created. Always progressive politically, in 1861 partial women's suffrage was introduced, a process completed in 1894 when universal suffrage was adopted and women were allowed to stand for election to Parliament. In 1901, South Australia entered the Commonwealth of Australia as a founding state.

Further Reading

F.K. Crowley, ed. (1974). *A New History of Australia* (Melbourne, Heinemann)

Ronald H. Parsons (1999). *Migrant Ships for South Australia, 1836–1860* (Gumeracha, Gould Books)

South Georgia and the South Sandwich Islands. A British Overseas Territory located in the remote South Atlantic, icy South Georgia was probably sighted by seafaring Englishmen in 1675. Exactly one hundred years later, Captain James Cook* landed, claimed it for Britain, and named it for King George III*. Used primarily as a sealers' base throughout the nineteenth century and then that for whalers in the twentieth, British sovereignty was upheld through a series of Letters Patent and resident administration and magistrate. Its current status was designated in 1985. Cook also surveyed and claimed the South Sandwich Islands in 1775, naming them after the First Lord of the Admiralty, the Earl of Sandwich. Annexed in 1908, both South Georgia and the South Sandwich Islands were for a time administratively part of the Falkland Islands*. Their sovereignty long contested by Argentina, they were occupied briefly by Argentine forces during the Falklands War*. South Georgia was the site of Sir Ernest Shackleton's emergency landfall during his Antarctic expedition of 1916. Later, in 1922, he died on board ship near the island and is buried on it.

Further Reading
Alan E. Day (1996). *The Falkland Islands, South Georgia and the South Sandwich Islands* (Oxford, Clio Press)
Robert Headland (1985). *The Island of South Georgia* (New York, Cambridge University Press)

Speke, John Hanning (1827–64). A mid-Victorian explorer of Central Africa and discoverer of the source of the Nile*, Speke was born in Somerset, served in the Bengal Native Infantry, and while on leave in 1854 joined an expedition to the Horn of Africa led by Sir Richard Burton*. Narrowly avoiding death when attacked by Somali clansmen, he returned to England to convalesce. Speke and Burton then planned another expedition to Africa, this time to search for the Nile's elusive headwaters. Setting out from Zanzibar* in 1857, they trekked inland as far as Lake Tanganyika, the first Europeans to see this vast inland sea. Suffering from disease and privation, they separated temporarily, during which time Speke journeyed north and in the summer of 1858 discovered and named Lake Victoria, which he concluded had to be the source of the Nile. Returning to the east African coast, Speke sailed for London in advance of Burton, and by the time the latter man had returned, Speke was being hailed as the solver of the Nile puzzle, the greatest geographical mystery of the age. An unfortunate falling out between the two men ensued, in large part the workings of an unscrupulous publisher, and they never reconciled. Speke's third and final expedition to Africa was from 1860 to 1863, during which time he explored Lake Victoria. In September 1864, while preparing to debate Burton (who held a contrary view of the source of the Nile) at a meeting of the British Association in Bath to be chaired by David Livingstone, Speke was killed in a shooting accident that was possibly suicide.

Further Reading
Alexander Maitland (1971). *Speke* (London, Constable)

John Hanning Speke (1996). *The Journal of the Discovery of the Source of the Nile* (Mineola, NY, Dover Publications)

Sri Lanka. Located just off the south-east coast of India, Sri Lanka (formerly Ceylon*) is a lush island of about 25,000 square miles that was annexed by the East India Company's* Madras Presidency in 1796, thereby squeezing out long-time Dutch trading interests. British colonial status was declared in 1802 in the midst of a continuing struggle to pacify the ancient Sinhalese Kingdom of Kandy. Success in this regard came in 1815, and over the next half-century colonial settlement ensued, which resulted in the creation of commercial tea plantations and the large-scale production of rubber. The Second World War* and action in the Pacific emphasized Ceylon's importance as a British naval base, with Trincomalee becoming the home port of the Royal Navy's Eastern Fleet. Lord Mountbatten* used Kandy as his headquarters for most of the time that he was Supreme Allied Commander, Southeast Asia. Shortly after the end of the War, Dominion status was granted, and in 1948 Ceylon became self-governing. In 1972, Ceylon became a republic within the Commonwealth and changed its name to Sri Lanka in the midst of ongoing political strife between the Sinhalese and the island's other major ethnic group, the Tamils.

Further Reading
E.F.C. Ludowyk (1966). *The Modern History of Ceylon* (New York, Praeger)
Patrick Peebles (2006). *The History of Sri Lanka* (Westport, CT, Greenwood Press)

Stanley, Henry Morton (1841–1904). One of the greatest explorers of nineteenth-century Africa, Stanley was born John Rowlands in Wales to an unmarried mother and an unknown father. Raised initially by his grandfather, he spent the bulk of his youth until aged fifteen in a workhouse. After teaching at a school briefly, in 1859 he sailed for the United States. Beginning in New Orleans, he re-invented himself. He fought in the Civil War (for both sides) and then became a journalist, first in St Louis and then later New York. In 1869, he was hired by the *New York Herald* to 'Find Livingstone', who had been in Africa for the previous three years with almost no word of his whereabouts. Outfitting an expedition in Zanzibar* early in 1871, he located

Livingstone that October or November at Ujiji on the shores of Lake Tanganyika. His most recent biographer doubts that Stanley met Livingstone with the phrase that was mocked by many at the time but became famous as 'Dr Livingstone, I presume?' But, regardless, the two men became great friends over the course of the next four months and Stanley esteemed Livingstone and his memory for the rest of his life. In 1874, Stanley led another expedition to Africa, this time to follow the course of the Congo River. For a thousand days, and in the midst of severe hardship, disease, and death, Stanley explored the course of the river. Stanley's fame was widespread by this time and Leopold II, King of the Belgians, employed him to open up the Congo to European commerce. His last African foray came in 1886, when he led the Emin Pasha* Relief Expedition. Retiring to Surrey, Stanley entered Parliament in 1895, and in 1899 was knighted. An undeserved reputation as a disreputable adventurer dogged him always, colouring his historical reputation.

Further Reading

Tim Jeal (2007). *Stanley: The Impossible Life of Africa's Greatest Explorer* (London, Faber & Faber)

James L. Newman (2004). *Imperial Footprints: Henry Morton Stanley's African Journeys* (Washington, Potomac Books)

Straits Settlements. A collection of territories in Southeast Asia originally under East India Company* control and based at Singapore*. In 1826, they were unified, and Singapore was made their capital in 1836. The other major members were Penang and Malacca. In 1867, the Straits Settlements was made a Crown Colony, which lasted until 1946. Singapore became independent soon thereafter, while Penang and Malacca would become part of the Malayan (Malaysian)* Federation.

Further Reading

Hai Ding Chiang (1978). *A History of Straits Settlements Foreign Trade, 1870–1915* (Singapore, National Museum)

Colin M. Turnbull (1972). *The Straits Settlements, 1826–67: Indian Presidency to Crown Colony* (London, Athlone Press)

Sudan. A republic in North Africa. British rule lasted from 1899 to 1956 in a joint Anglo-Egyptian administration. Before that, beginning in 1882, the British gained control of Egypt*, which in turn made Britain ultimately responsible for the vassal state of the Sudan. A Sudanese Islamist uprising culminated in 1884–5 with the forced evacuation of the Anglo-Egyptian garrison and the death of General Gordon* at Khartoum. From then until 1899, Mahdist rule prevailed before the British re-conquest of the Sudan under the command of Lord Kitchener*. Ruled effectively as a British colony, the Crown's administrative arm, the Sudan Political Service*, was known for the scrupulous efficiency of its mostly Oxbridge-educated officers. Sudanese independence aspirations first surfaced clearly in 1924. The Egyptian Revolution of 1952 heralded an onrush of Sudanese nationalism, resulting in the arrival of independence on the first day of 1956.

Further Reading

Robert O. Collins (1967). *Egypt and the Sudan* (Englewood Cliffs, NJ, Prentice-Hall)

Wm. Roger Louis (2006). *Ends of British Imperialism: The Scramble for Empire, Suez and Decolonization* (London and New York, I.B.Tauris)

Sudan Political Service. Administrators of colonial Sudan*, the SPS – formally, the Sudan Civil Service – was created in 1899, following the re-conquest of the previous year. Over its fifty-seven-year existence until Sudan's independence in 1956, almost four hundred officers served in this elite administrative corps. Comprised significantly of Oxbridge graduates, many of whom held sporting Blues awarded for playing in the 'Varsity Match in any of a variety of sports,' the land of Blacks ruled by Blues, as Sudan came to be called by those in colonial circles, operated much like its larger counterparts, the Colonial Service* and the Indian Civil Service*. Sudan's vast geography – almost a million square miles – was administered by rarely more than about 125 SPS officers at any given time. As an administrative body it established a reputation for high-mindedness and incorruptibility.

Further Reading

Robert O. Collins (1972). *The Sudan Political Service: A Portrait of the Imperialists*, African Affairs, vol. 71, 293–303

A.H.M. Kirk-Greene (1982). *The Sudan Political Service: A Preliminary Profile* (Oxford, Parchment)

Suez Canal. A North African waterway built mainly by the French between 1854 and 1869 linking Port Said on the Mediterranean Sea with Suez on the Red Sea, it became vital to British trade and strategic thinking, almost halving the travel distance by steamship between Britain and India and influencing significantly the move to partition Africa. Within a few years of its opening, the British were convinced of the Canal's importance, epitomized by Benjamin Disraeli's* purchase of nearly half the shares in the Suez Canal Company for the British government in 1875. Beginning in 1882, British troops were stationed along the Canal and remained until 1956, the last ones being removed just weeks in advance of the Egyptian government's nationalization of the Suez Canal Company, which provoked the Suez Crisis*.

Further Reading

D.A. Farnie (1969). *East and West of Suez: The Suez Canal in History, 1854–1956* (Oxford, Clarendon Press)

Zachary Karabell (2003). *Parting the Desert: The Creation of the Suez Canal* (New York, A.A. Knopf)

Suez Crisis. One of the last great Imperial crises, which came to signify the end of British power in the Middle East, the Suez Crisis began on 29 October 1956, when British, French, and Israeli troops launched an attack on the Canal Zone in order to inhibit Egypt's nationalization of the Canal, which had been declared in July. American support for Britain's position as chief stockholder in the canal company was not forthcoming, and the Conservative government of Anthony Eden*, in conjunction with the French and then the Israelis, decided on an invasion of the Canal Zone in order to restore its ownership and the free passage of ships. Convinced that the United States would ultimately support this military attack, the tripartite powers proceeded with the invasion. The operation was highly successful in military terms but it provoked great opposition from the US, as well as from certain members of the Commonwealth. Threatening to take financial action that would bring about the collapse of the British currency, the Americans forced a ceasefire on the aggressors and demanded that they evacuate the Canal Zone. Eden announced the ceasefire on 6 November and the Anglo-French Task Force was pulled out completely by the end of December. In its place came the first detachment of United Nations Emergency Force 'peacekeepers,' an idea suggested by Canadian External Affairs Minister, Lester Pearson, for which he would win the Nobel Peace Prize. Eden's resignation spelled the end of his political career, while Britain's humbling at the hands of the United States demonstrated its loss of decisive power in international affairs.

Further Reading

L.J. Butler (2002). *Britain and Empire: Adjusting to a Post-Imperial World* (London and New York, I.B.Tauris)

John Darwin (1988). *Britain and Decolonisation: The Retreat from Empire in the Post-War World* (London, Palgrave Macmillan)

Swaziland. A tiny, landlocked African kingdom surrounded by South Africa* and Mozambique, Swaziland was able to maintain a degree of independence from both Briton and Boer in the 1880s through a fierce sense of identity based on a stable monarchy. It consolidated its semi-independent status, and following the Second Boer War* a Special Commissioner was designated by the British to oversee its affairs, although the Transvaal* played a practical role in its administration until South Africa* left the Commonwealth in 1961. In 1967, Britain accorded Swaziland internal self-government, which became independence the next year.

Further Reading

D. Hugh Gillis (1999). *The Kingdom of Swaziland: Studies in Political History* (Westport, CT, Greenwood Press)

Hilda Kuper (1986). *The Swazi: A South African Kingdom* (New York, Holt, Rinehart & Winston)

T

Tagore, Rabindranath (1861–1941). The first Indian poet and writer to become well known in Britain and a trenchant critic of the Raj, Tagore won the Nobel Prize in Literature in 1913. Born in Bengal* to a leading Brahmin family, Tagore is credited with sponsoring the Bengali renaissance in the arts. Educated locally and then for two years in law at University College London, Tagore returned to Bengal in 1880 and took up the life of a gentleman landowner, supervising his family's estates in Shilaidaha. He wrote throughout this period of his life, and in 1901 established an ashram to confirm his contemplative life. Well-published in the years before the First World War*, Tagore was the first Asian to be awarded the Nobel Prize. His works included *Naivedya* (1901), *Gitanjali: Song Offerings* (1912), and *Chitra* (1914), which were read in translation in the West. In 1915, he was knighted, but four years later, in the aftermath of the Amritsar Riots*, he renounced the honour. His status both at home and abroad grew in the 1920s and 1930s. His path diverged from that of Gandhi*, whom he criticized for emphasizing symbol and protest against the British instead of education and action. At his death, he was mourned as the supreme champion of Bengali literature, art, and music.

Further Reading

Kalyan K. Sengupta (2005). *The Philosophy of Rabindranath Tagore* (Aldershot, Ashgate)

Rabindranath Tagore (2004). *Rabindranath Tagore: Selected Poems* (Oxford, Oxford University Press)

Tanganyika (see Tanzania)

Tanzania. Located in East Africa, Tanzania covers 365,000 square miles and contains most of the vast, game-rich Serengeti Plain and the continent's highest mountain, Kilimanjaro. Explored by European (German) missionaries beginning in the mid-nineteenth century, the territory was annexed by Germany in 1885, which proceeded to penetrate the interior by rail as far as Lake Tanganyika. During the First World War*, there was considerable military action between the contiguous German Tanganyika and British East Africa*, and afterwards the colony was awarded to Britain as a League of Nations Mandate. Under British control, Tanganyika eventually followed a similar path to independence as that of other African territories. Julius Nyerere* and the Tanganyika African National Union led the nationalist movement, which culminated with independence in 1961. Three years later, newly independent Zanzibar* joined Tanganyika in a union, known henceforth as the United Republic of Tanzania.

Further Reading

Ralph Austen (1968). *Northwest Tanzania under German and British Rule, 1889–1939*, 2 vols (New Haven, CT, Yale University Press)

John Iliffe (1979). *A Modern History of Tanganyika* (Cambridge, Cambridge University Press)

Tasmania. An Australian island state, located south of the mainland, the Dutch explorer Abel Tasman sighted it in 1642, naming it Van Diemen's Land after the Governor of the Dutch East India Company. The British arrived in 1803, and shortly thereafter settled at Hobart, the future capital. Most early settlers were convicts or prison guards, and for years the island was known principally for its penal colonies. In 1825, after having been constitutionally part of New South Wales, Van Diemen's Land became a separate colony. Responsible government was initiated in 1856, the same year that the colony was re-named in honour of Tasman, and it was a founding member of the Australian federation in 1901.

Further Reading

L.L. Robson (1983). *A History of Tasmania. Volume I. Van Diemen's Land from the Earliest Times to 1855* (Melbourne, Oxford University Press)

_____ (1991). *A History of Tasmania. Volume II. Colony and State from 1856 to the 1980s* (Melbourne, Oxford University Press)

Thatcher, Margaret H., Baroness Thatcher (1925–). British Prime Minister from 1979 until 1990, Margaret Thatcher presided over a Conservative government charged with some of the last acts of Empire, including the creation of Zimbabwe* from the former colony of Southern Rhodesia*. Born in Lincolnshire and educated there and at Somerville College, Oxford*, she qualified as a barrister in 1953. Politically active since her undergraduate days, she was elected MP in 1959. She rose in the Conservative Party, and achieved Cabinet rank under Edward Heath in the early 1970s. In 1975, she became Leader of the Opposition, and four years later was elected the first woman Prime Minister in British history. Dealings with the IRA* over the future of Northern Ireland* were a key part of her first government, including surviving a bomb attack in 1984. By that time she had presided over the Lancaster House Agreement that created the framework for the founding of Zimbabwe, directed Britain's victorious effort in the Falklands War* against Argentina, and negotiated the Sino-British Joint Declaration setting out the terms for the handover of Hong Kong*, which would come in 1997. A staunch supporter of free-market economics and a crusading anti-Communist, she eventually faced a revolt in her Cabinet, which culminated in her fall from power in November 1990. In spirit, Thatcher was a throwback to the Imperial days of her Tory predecessors, Disraeli and Salisbury.

Further Reading

Anthony Seldon and Daniel Collings (1999) *Britain Under Thatcher* (London, Longman)

Margaret Thatcher (1993). *The Downing Street Years* (London, HarperCollins)

Thuggee. Meaning thief in Hindi, the 'thugs' operated as a network of robbers and murderers in India*, which the British attempted to suppress.

Groups of thugs operated as far back as the thirteenth century and were comprised of Hindus, Muslims, and Sikhs*. They owed obeisance to the Hindu goddess Kali, and in many respects were a cult. They preyed on travellers, luring them in through false kindness until choosing the right moment for an undetected robbery and murder. Long opposed by the British, a concerted campaign was undertaken against thuggery in the 1830s by William Sleeman, Superintendent of the newly created Thuggee and Dacoity Department in Bengal*. Eradication of the cult came slowly, but by the 1870s it was achieved. Figures as to how many people were killed by thugs are unreliable, but one of the best estimates is approximately 50,000 during the British period.

Further Reading

Martine van Woerken (2002). *The Strangled Traveller: Colonial Imaginings and the Thugs of India* (Chicago, University of Chicago Press)

Kim A. Wagner (2007). *Thuggee: Banditry and the British in Early Nineteenth-Century India* (Basingstoke, Palgrave Macmillan)

Thuku, Harry (1895–1970). Recognized as the first Kenyan nationalist, Thuku was a Kikuyu* who worked as a clerk for the colonial government in Nairobi. In 1921, he founded the East African Association, the first political society of its kind in Kenya, as a protest against the labour control system symbolized by the hated *kipande* identity and pass card. Eventually arrested the next year, his detention by the police sparked a riot involving as many as 7,000 people in the streets of Nairobi. The police responded by trying to break up the demonstration using guns, and at least twenty-five people were killed. Thuku spent the next nine years in government exile. Upon his release in 1931, he resumed his activism but it never became violent, and he was wholly against the Mau Mau* movement of the 1950s. By that time he was a successful coffee farmer. Hailed by most as a father figure in the history of Kenyan nationalism, he was eclipsed by others, especially Kenyatta*.

Further Reading

Jack R. Roelker (1966). *The Genesis of African Protest: Harry Thuku and the British Administration in Kenya, 1920–1922* (Syracuse, Syracuse University Press)

Harry Thuku (1970). *Harry Thuku: An Autobiography* (Nairobi, Oxford University Press)

Tilak, Lokmanya Bal G. (1856–1920). A key Indian nationalist leader, Tilak was part of the first wave of those who came to demand independence from Britain. Born into a middle-class family in Maharashtra, he received a college education and became a schoolteacher, and then a crusading journalist demanding immediate self-government for India. Increasingly radical, Tilak rejected what he saw as the soft-nationalism of the Indian National Congress in the 1890s, preferring *swaraj* (self-rule) as the only proper end for true Indians. He became an inspiration to Hindu nationalist radicals, adopting, for example, the socially retrograde position of decrying a new British law that made the marriageable age of a child bride twelve instead of ten in the name of Hindu orthodoxy. Arrested for sedition in 1908, he served the next six years in prison. Upon his release, he co-founded the All-India Home Rule League with Annie Besant* and Jinnah*, and continued to agitate for India's freedom, which, he argued under Marxist influence, would not result from the non-violent campaign then just beginning under Gandhi*. At his death, Tilak was acclaimed a Hindu hero, although later his legacy was largely subsumed by Gandhi and Jinnah.

Further Reading

Ganesh P. Pradhan (1994). *Lokmanya Tilak* (New Delhi, National Book Trust)

Shanta Sathe (1994). *Lokmanya Tilak: His Social and Political Thought* (New Delhi, Ajanta)

Tippu Tip (*c.*1837–1905). The leading slaver in Central and East Africa in the latter part of the nineteenth century, Tippu Tip was well known to the British and the Belgians – whom he served in the Congo in an official capacity – and counted David Livingstone*, Henry Morton Stanley*, and Emin Pasha* among his acquaintances. Based at Nyangwe (in what is today the Democratic Republic of the Congo), Tippu Tip ran an Omani slaving empire that transported thousands of slaves to the east coast of Africa for shipment to the Persian Gulf and the Gulf of Oman. In 1891, he retired to Zanzibar, where he died, probably of malaria, fourteen years later.

Further Reading

R.W. Beachey, ed. (1976). *A Collection of Documents on the Slave Trade of Eastern Africa* (London, Collins)

Leda Farrant (1975). *Tippu Tip and the East African Slave Trade* (London, Hamilton)

Togoland. Located in West Africa and today part of Ghana*, Togoland came into British hands during the First World War* when its German occupiers since 1884 were swiftly defeated by a combined Anglo-French force. Made a League of Nations mandate under British supervision, Togoland became a United Nations Trust Territory after the Second World War*, and in 1956 voted to join the Gold Coast* upon its independence from Britain, which occurred the next year, as the new state of Ghana.

Further Reading

F.M. Bourret (1960). *Ghana: The Road to Independence, 1919–1957* (Stanford, Stanford University Press)

Kosi Kedem (2007). *How Britain Subverted and Betrayed British Togoland* (Accra, Governance and Electoral Systems Agency)

Tokelau (see Gilbert and Ellice Islands)

Tonga. A South Pacific archipelago lying near Samoa, the 169 islands of the Kingdom of Tonga were first visited by a well-received Captain Cook* in 1773. Known for a time thereafter as the Friendly Islands, British missionaries arrived by the end of the eighteenth century, but it was not until 1900 that Tonga became a British Protectorate, a status maintained until 1970 when Tonga became independent as an autochthonous monarchy (possessing its own monarch) within the Commonwealth.

Further Reading

I.C. Campbell (2001). *Island Kingdom: Tonga Ancient and Modern* (Christchurch, Canterbury University Press)

Noel Rutherford, ed. (1977). *Friendly Islands: A History of Tonga* (Melbourne, Oxford University Press)

Transjordan (see Palestine)

Transvaal. An area of southern Africa beyond the Vaal River and south of the Limpopo River settled by the Afrikaners during the Great Trek*, the Transvaal looms large in the history of the British Empire in Africa. Settled in the 1840s in what then put it out of reach of the British to the south and east, the Transvaal (South African Republic as it was then called) was annexed by Britain in 1877, regaining its independence in 1881 after the First Boer War*. Four years later, the discovery of gold there put immense political, economic, and immigration pressure on the Transvaal's understanding of itself as an Afrikaner bastion, and under the premiership of Paul Kruger* it led the way in the fight with the Orange Free State* against the British in the Second Boer War*. Upon the War's conclusion in 1902, the defeated Transvaal Republic was made part of British South Africa, which in turn led to its membership in the Union of South Africa* in 1910. The Transvaal continued to exist in its old geographical form until 1994, when the post-apartheid South African government re-made the country's provincial structure.

Further Reading

Alan P. Cartwright (1978). *The Old Transvaal, 1834–1899* (Cape Town, Purnell)

John Laband (2005). *The Transvaal Rebellion: The First Boer War, 1880–1881* (New York, Longman/Pearson)

Treaty Ports. The means by which British commercial penetration of China was achieved, the Treaty Ports began with the Treaty of Nanking* in 1842 and continued formally until 1943. Shanghai and Hong Kong* became the most important British Treaty Ports in the nineteenth century, and the centre of the opium trade. Other ports, such as Canton, open to western trade, were also important, although less so. Britain dominated China's commercial trade by the end of Victoria's reign and only in the 1920s in the aftermath of the First World War* did Britain and other western countries begin to surrender their privileged trading position. Shanghai was retained until 1943, however, and Hong Kong*, which had become a Crown Colony in 1843, remained under British control until 1997. Politically, the Treaty Ports became a source of outrage and shame for nationalist Chinese and helped to power the revolutionary movements of the twentieth century.

Further Reading

Chan Lau Kit-Ching (1990). *China, Britain and Hong Kong, 1895–1945* (Hong Kong, Chinese University Press)

Wm. Roger Louis (1971). *British Strategy in the Far East, 1919–1939* (Oxford, Oxford University Press)

Trinidad and Tobago. Located in the southern Caribbean just off the coast of Venezuela, English contact with the two islands was made when they were visited by Sir Walter Raleigh in 1595. Long held by the Spanish, they also came under Dutch and French control. The British began to bring them under the Crown during the Napoleonic Wars, but not until 1889 were they given colonial status. After the failure of the Federation of the West Indies*, Trinidad and Tobago became independent in 1962. In 1976, the country chose to remove the British monarch as its head of state, but remained within the Commonwealth.

Further Reading

Selwyn D. Ryan (1972). *Race and Nationalism in Trinidad and Tobago: A Study of Decolonization in a Multiracial Society* (Toronto, University of Toronto Press)

Kelvin Singh (1994). *Race and Class: Struggles in a Colonial State, Trinidad, 1917–1945* (Mona, Jamaica, University of the West Indies Press)

Tristan da Cunha (see Saint Helena)

Tucker, Alfred R. (1849–1914). A Church of England Bishop of Uganda*
for almost twenty years, Tucker's episcopate covered the period during
which the British Empire in East Africa was busy delimiting the region
in competition especially with Imperial Germany. Born in 1849 at
Woolwich near London, Tucker was a talented painter – later he would
paint hundreds of East African scenes – and sold his first picture at the
age of fourteen. Eventually, he decided to give up the life of a professional
painter, however tenuous, matriculated at Oxford*, and ultimately was
ordained in the Church of England. In 1882, he earned his BA and soon
thereafter was ordained deacon and made curate in a parish in Clifton,
near Bristol. He then went to a church in Durham. During these years
Tucker's latent interest in missions – he had joined a missionary society
while at Oxford – increased. In 1890, he offered himself to the Anglican
Church Missionary Society for service in Uganda. He arrived there only
to find 'a volcano on the verge of an eruption.' What he meant was that
from the late 1870s, as both British Protestant and French Catholic missionaries had begun to arrive in Central Africa, intense rivalries had grown,
both between Europeans and among the local Baganda people themselves.
This competition was exacerbated by the paper partition of Africa that
had begun in 1884, when the great powers met in Berlin to decide the
territorial fate of most of the continent. Uganda, they had determined,
lay within the British sphere. But what the British held on paper, they did
not necessarily hold on the ground, and in the context of their toothless
occupation, Uganda roiled with rumour and strife. The minimal British
presence in Uganda, apart from that supplied by Bishop Tucker, was maintained by the Imperial British East Africa Company*, whose point man
was none other than the intrepid Captain Frederick Lugard*. Both Tucker
and Lugard would return to England to plead that Uganda be put under
Crown rule. In 1894, the new Prime Minister and Gladstone's* successor,
Rosebery, did just that. The Imperialists' forward policy – which Gladstone
had opposed – won the day. Back in Uganda, Tucker was both relieved
and overjoyed at the news and remained bishop until 1910, becoming, in
a sense, an 'Imperial missionary.' In retirement, he wrote a memoir of his
episcopate, which concludes with a ringing endorsement of the 'Pax
Britannica.'

Further Reading

Arthur P. Shepherd (1929). *Tucker of Uganda: Artist and Apostle, 1849–1914* (London, S.C.M. Press)

Alfred R. Tucker (1908). *Eighteen Years in Uganda and East Africa* (London, Edward Arnold)

Turks and Caicos Islands. A British Overseas Territory in the Caribbean, the Turks and Caicos consist of two groups of islands that were first effectively occupied by British settlers from Bermuda in the late seventeenth century. Held for a time by the French during the American War of Independence, the islands were also a favourite haunt of pirates well into the nineteenth century. In 1799, Britain annexed them as part of the Bahamas. In 1848, they became a separate colony, but in 1873 they were made administratively part of Jamaica*, a state of affairs that lasted until 1959. During this period, the Canadian government suggested that they become part of its Confederation, but the idea was rejected by the British. In various forms, however, the idea continues to flare up occasionally in Canadian politics to this day. Internal self-government was achieved in 1973.

Further Reading

Paul G. Boultbee (1991). *Turks and Caicos Islands* (Oxford, Clio Press)

Amelia Smithers (1995). *The Turks and Caicos Islands: Lands of Discovery* (London, Macmillan)

Turner, J.M.W. (1775–1851). The most famous of British Romantic landscape painters, Turner's works depicting Imperial scenes are among his best known. Born in London, he entered the Royal Academy at just fourteen and would exhibit there frequently throughout his life. *The Battle of Trafalgar* (1806 and 1822) and *Slave Ship* (1840) speak to the central Imperial themes of sea-power and slavery explored by Turner. His most enduring and popular work on Empire, *The fighting Temeraire tugged to her last berth to be broken up* (1838), is a highly evocative meditation on Empire's essentially transitory nature.

Further Reading

James Hamilton (2003). *Turner: the Late Seascapes* (New Haven, CT, Yale University Press)

Sam Smiles (2007). *J.M.W. Turner: the Making of the Modern Artist* (Manchester, Manchester University Press)

Tuvalu (see Gilbert and Ellice Islands)

U

Uganda. Initial British encounters with this East-Central African country were by explorers and missionaries. In 1885, a Church of England missionary, James Hannington, was murdered by the traditional ruler (King or Kabaka Mwanga II) of Uganda's dominant Baganda tribe. Shortly thereafter, a large group of Bagandan converts to Christianity were murdered, known later as the Uganda Martyrs. Political anarchy ensued, and eventually a combined lobby of missionaries* and the Imperial British East Africa Company* pressured the Gladstone* government to make Uganda a British Protectorate, both to restore order and to stave off German incursions around the Great Lakes. Gladstone himself resisted such overtures, and soon resigned, forced out by the Liberal Imperialists led by Lord Rosebery*, who would serve briefly as Prime Minister. In 1894, his government extended a Protectorate to Uganda, followed two years later by the beginning of the Uganda Railway* from Mombasa inland. Uganda was raised to colonial status in 1914. Breathtakingly beautiful – the 'pearl of Africa,' in Churchill's words – it achieved self-government in 1961 and independence the following year. Its post-independence history has been marred by misrule, especially that of the criminal regime of Idi Amin*.

Further Reading

David Apter (1997). *The Political Kingdom in Uganda: A Study in Bureaucratic Nationalism* (London, Frank Cass)

Michael Twaddle (1993). *Kakungulu and the Creation of Uganda, 1868–1928* (London, J. Currey)

Uganda Railway. A railway built by the British government to connect the coast of British East Africa* with Lake Victoria in the interior, the Uganda Railway was begun in 1896 and completed in 1901. Running for about 500 miles from Mombasa to Kisumu, it cost the enormous sum of £5 million and employed thousands of indentured labourers from India*. Dubbed the 'Lunatic Line' by some because of its expense and the lore surrounding its construction – including the two man-eating lions of Tsavo which were reputed to have killed as many as 130 workers before being shot – the Uganda Railway opened up the highlands of the colony to white settlement. Subsequently, branch lines were built, providing a network of connections throughout East and Central Africa and helping to create an economic nexus, which included servicing the burgeoning safari industry.

Further Reading

Clarence B. Davis, Kenneth E. Wilburn, Jr, and Ronald E. Robinson, eds (1991). *Railway Imperialism* (New York, Greenwood Press)
Charles Miller (1971). *The Lunatic Express: An Entertainment in Imperialism* (New York, Macmillan)

Ulundi, Battle of. The culminating battle in the Anglo-Zulu* War for regional paramountcy in colonial South Africa*, Ulundi saw an overwhelming British victory, which broke the military power of the Zulu nation. The battle took place on 4 July 1879 near the Zulu capital city of Ulundi. The shadow of the great Zulu victory at Isandlwana* in January hung over the British in the lead-up to Ulundi, but their position had been buoyed by the stellar defence of Rorke's Drift and then reinforced by the arrival in Natal* of thousands of additional troops. Commanded by the embattled Lord Chelmsford (Sir Garnet Wolseley* was en route to supersede him), some 17,000 British troops squared off against as many as 50,000 Zulu impis, the entire Zulu Army, under the command of Cetshwayo*. The battle opened about 9:00 a.m. Half an hour later it was all over. More than 1,500 Zulu lay dead, with perhaps as many wounded, cut down by the superior weaponry of the British, firing from an impenetrable square and supplemented by cavalry. British casualties were less than a hundred. The victory was complete, and for Chelmsford it offered vindication for the earlier disaster at Isandlwana.

Further Reading
John Laband (1988). *The Battle of Ulundi* (Pietermaritzburg, Shuter & Shooter)
Ron Lock and Peter Quantrill (2005). *Zulu Vanquished: The Destruction of the Zulu Kingdom* (London, Greenhill)

Unilateral Declaration of Independence (UDI). Issued in 1965 by the government of Rhodesia (Zimbabwe*), declaring its independence from Britain. After failing to come to an agreement with Britain about constitutional power sharing between the white minority and black majority in Rhodesia's future, the Prime Minister, Ian Smith*, and his Cabinet took a step that was rejected immediately as illegal and unconstitutional by the British government, the United Nations, and most of world opinion. Under UDI, Rhodesia became a republic in 1970, but remained a *de facto* international outlaw until 1979 when, after years of internal warfare, the country reverted briefly to colonial status as the 'British Dependency of Rhodesia.' The next year, after multi-racial elections, full independence came to Rhodesia as the new Republic of Zimbabwe.

Further Reading
Robert Blake (1978). *A History of Rhodesia* (New York, Knopf)
Martin Meredith (1980). *The Past is Another Country: Rhodesia, UDI to Zimbabwe* (London, Pan)

Upper Canadian Rebellion. A violent and failed episode in the history of constitutional reform in Upper Canada (Ontario*), the 1837 rebellion was led by the disaffected journalist and politician, William Lyon Mackenzie*. In taking up arms against the colony's ruling oligarchy, Mackenzie represented a weak strand of radical colonial politics, which was crushed easily. But his complaints against the 'family compact' were substantial, and Westminster had already begun to respond to charges that the government of Upper Canada was corrupt. Much of Mackenzie's dissatisfaction stemmed from the issue of land ownership. Crown reserves and clergy reserves were plentiful and mostly left un-worked. They had the effect of lowering the value of settled farms, many of which, however, were on marginal, isolated land and therefore were inefficient. Another complaint of the growing population of Upper Canada – which included a large number of American immigrants of various Christian denominations such as Baptist and Methodist – was that they saw no good reason for the Church of England's privileged position in the colony. Mackenzie rallied many of these people to the cause of reform and became an outspoken critic of the government, to the point of calling for its replacement by a republic modelled on the United States. In December 1837, and after being inspired by the events of the Lower Canadian Rebellion*, Mackenzie took the precipitous step of marching an armed but motley force of some four hundred farmers and sympathizers into the colony's capital, Toronto, from the north. Mackenzie was no army commander, however, and the force was easily broken up. A small force of rebels from the western part of the colony attempted to help Mackenzie, but they too broke and ran when confronted by government troops. Mackenzie and a small band of cohorts fled to the US border where, on Navy Island in the Niagara River, they proclaimed the Republic of Canada. By mid-January 1838, however, they were forced off the island by British troops. Some, including Mackenzie, escaped to the US. Others were imprisoned, and two rebels were executed. The British government responded to the rebellion by sending Lord Durham* to investigate the state of affairs in Canada. His Report recommended the union of the two Canadian colonies, and ultimately the implementation of responsible government*.

Further Reading

Gerald M. Craig (1963). *Upper Canada: the Formative Years, 1784–1841* (Toronto, McClelland & Stewart)

Colin Read and Ron Stagg, eds (1985). *The Rebellion of 1837 in Upper Canada* (Toronto, Champlain Society)

V

Vanuatu. An island archipelago in the South Pacific, some 1,000 miles east of Australia* and 300 miles north of Fiji*, it was long contested by various European powers. In the 1880s, an Anglo-French naval commission was established, which evolved into the condominium of the New Hebrides in 1906. The islands became important strategically during the Second World War*, the Allies using them as a jumping-off point for the assault on Japan. After the War, incipient nationalism grew into demands for self-government and then independence. In 1980, Britain and France both granted full sovereignty to the Republic of Vanuatu, which remained as a member of the Commonwealth.

Further Reading

William F.S. Miles (1998). *Bridging Mental Boundaries in a Postcolonial Microcosm: Identity and Development in Vanuatu* (Honolulu, University of Hawai'i Press)

Howard van Trease (1987). *The Politics of Land in Vanuatu: From Colony to Independence* (Suva, University of the South Pacific)

Vereeniging, Treaty of. Signed on 31 May 1902, the Treaty formally ended the Second Boer War*. Negotiations took place in Vereeniging, a small town in the Transvaal*. Participants included Kitchener* and Milner* for the British and Smuts* and Botha* for the Boers. Signed in Pretoria, the Treaty ensured the continued sovereignty of the Crown, but provided for the eventual granting of self-government for the Transvaal (South African Republic) and the Orange Free State*, which was achieved in 1906 and 1907 respectively; the payment of reconstruction aid in the amount of £3 million; the use of Dutch (later Afrikaans) in the schools and courts of law; and no requirement for the Boers to discuss the issue of enfranchisement of the majority black population until a later date. This provision became the lasting marker of the Treaty, and was not resolved until full multi-racial elections were held in South Africa* in 1994.

Further Reading
David Smurthwaite (2002). *The Boer War, 1899–1902* (London, Hamlyn)
Peter Trew (1999). *The Boer War Generals* (Stroud, Sutton)

Victoria (1819–1901). Queen from 1837 and Empress of India from 1877, Victoria reigned over the Empire as it grew close to its maximum territorial and population size. Her approach to the Empire was conservative and maternal. She never visited any of Britain's colonies, although she was well-informed of their politics, and in events like the proclamation announcing the passing of East India Company* rule to that of the Crown in India* in 1858 and the naming of Ottawa as the capital of the Province of Canada* the year before, she took an active part in some aspects of Imperial rule. Disraeli resorted to flattery in making her Empress of India, which was celebrated in India with the first Durbar* in 1877, but her interest in British rule in India was genuinely keen, and she later acquired a Hindu manservant, Abdul Karim, the 'Munshi,' who taught her rudimentary Hindustani. She showed her Tory instincts in a fierce concern for the welfare of General Gordon* in the Sudan* in 1884–5, and with it her scorn for Gladstone* and the Liberals. In 1887, the Golden Jubilee of her reign was in large part a celebration of the Empire, as was the Diamond Jubilee ten years later.

Further Reading
Walter L. Arnstein (2003). *Queen Victoria* (New York, Palgrave Macmillan)
Juliet Gardiner (1997). *Queen Victoria* (London, Collins & Brown)

Victoria (Australia). The most densely populated and urbanized state in Australia*, the Colony of Victoria was created in 1851 when its territory was separated from New South Wales*. A gold strike the same year at Ballarat and Bendigo transformed its economy, and by the end of the century Victoria had become the financial centre of Australia. Its capital, Melbourne, was by then the largest city in the Empire after London, and its streets were lined with a magnificent array of Victorian buildings, including the University of Melbourne, established in 1855. Victoria became a state in the Australian federation in 1901.

Further Reading

Weston A. Bate (1978). *Lucky City: The First Generation at Ballarat, 1851–1901* (Melbourne, Melbourne University Press)

Deryck M. Schreuder and Stuart Ward, eds (2008). *Australia's Empire* (Oxford, Oxford University Press)

Victoria Falls. Located on the Zambezi River between Zimbabwe* and Zambia*, Victoria Falls (known locally as Mosi-oa-Tunya, 'the smoke that thunders') was seen first by a European when David Livingstone* encountered it in 1855 on his trek across Africa. A height of 360 feet and a width of about one mile make it one of the world's largest waterfalls. Livingstone later returned to the Falls with John Kirk, making a detailed survey of it during the Zambezi Expedition in 1860. Afterwards, the Falls became one of the best-known natural sites in British colonial Africa, and to this day remains one of the top tourist destinations on the continent.

Further Reading

David Livingstone (1858). *Missionary Travels and Researches in South Africa* (New York, Harper)

D.W. Phillipson, ed. (1975). *Mosi-oa-Tunya: A Handbook to the Victoria Falls Region* (London, Longman)

Vimy Ridge. Site of the most famous battle in Canadian military history, Vimy Ridge was located near Arras on the Western Front in the First World War*. Held by the Germans in what had proved to the British and the French to be an impregnable position, on 9 April 1917 the four divisions of the Canadian Corps fighting together for the first time undertook a well-coordinated and successful attack on Vimy, which rose above the plain to a height of some one hundred feet. Fierce fighting ensued and over the course of five days the Canadians drove the Germans from the Ridge. Some 3,600 Canadians were killed in the assault. The battle was a signal victory for the Allies and confirmed the Canadians as accomplished soldiers. For Canada, Vimy Ridge became a byword for military prowess and pluck, contributing to a sense of nationhood and the development of a national mythology. In 1936, a soaring monument was completed at Vimy, a testament to the battle and to the lives of the 60,000 Canadians killed in the war.

Further Reading

Ted Barris (2007). *Victory at Vimy: Canada Comes of Age, April 9–12, 1917* (Toronto, Thomas Allen)

Pierre Berton (2001). *Vimy* (Toronto, Anchor Canada)

W

Waitangi, Treaty of. Signed in 1840 between the British and a group of Maori* chiefs from the North Island of New Zealand*, the Treaty established Crown rule while recognizing the Maori as British subjects with property rights. The year before, the Colonial Office* had decided that New Zealand should become a settler colony and sent Captain William Hobson* to effect its formal transfer to the Crown. As newly appointed Lieutenant Governor, he drew up a treaty which, after much discussion, was signed by about forty Maori chiefs and representatives initially, and then a short time later by a further five hundred or so. Hobson then proclaimed British sovereignty over the whole of New Zealand and constituted it as a colony separate from New South Wales*, with which it had been linked originally. At the time of the Treaty's signing, and for well over a century afterwards, there was minimal protest from the Maori. Beginning in the 1960s, however, and in train with post-colonialism, the Treaty came under intense historical and legal scrutiny, which continues to this day.

Further Reading
Peter Adams (1977). *Fatal Necessity: British Intervention in New Zealand, 1830–1847* (Auckland, Auckland University Press)
Claudia Orange (1989). *The Story of a Treaty* (Wellington, Allen & Unwin)

Wakefield, Edward Gibbon (1796–1862). A leading Victorian colonial theorist and advocate, Wakefield was notorious in his younger days as a chancer and kidnapper, having spent three years in Newgate Prison for abducting a fifteen-year-old girl whom he had peremptorily made his second wife. Independently wealthy thanks to the riches of his deceased first wife, Wakefield took up the cause of prison reform and, more latterly, colonization. He was closely involved in schemes to populate New Zealand*, Australia*, and Canada* with the 'excess' population of Britain. In Canada, he also undertook the role of hand-picked advisor to Lord Durham*, who was charged by the British government with recommending a new constitutional arrangement in light of the Upper and Lower Canadian Rebellions* of 1837. Wakefield's role was unofficial, however, as his sullied reputation was unacceptable to the government, but his role in information gathering and in helping to draft the Durham Report leading to the eventual implementation of responsible government* was important. Later, he became a key figure in the New Zealand Company, the Colonial Reform Society, and the Canterbury Association, through which he championed the main tenet of his theory of colonization, which was to keep the price of land high so as to finance the growth of colonies through property sales, which would also ensure, he believed, that such new settlements would maintain a tone distinctly higher than that found in the convict-dominated colonies of Australia. He served briefly in the provincial assembly of New Zealand, where he was a strong advocate of responsible government, before falling ill. His last years were spent as an invalid and he died in Wellington.

Further Reading

Philip Temple (2002). *A Sort of Conscience: the Wakefields* (Auckland, Auckland University Press)

Edward Gibbon Wakefield (1973). *The Founders of Canterbury* (Folkestone, Dawsons)

Wallace, Edgar (1875–1932). A prolific London-born novelist, journalist, playwright, and screenwriter, Wallace's vast output included a dozen 'African novels' published between 1911 and 1928. Many of these featured a British district officer (DO), R.G. Sanders, who came to embody all that was seen to be good and right about Imperial administration. The first of the series, *Sanders of the River* (1911), was an instant commercial success. Its portrayal of DO Sanders as eminently trustworthy and supremely resourceful while upholding King and Empire in faraway Nigeria*, planted an indelible image in the popular mind of the DO as the human face of British Imperialism. Made into a film of the same name in 1935, *Sanders* proved to be a critical influence on the inter-war generation of recruits to the Colonial Service. While the novel and film are of no more than antiquarian interest today, Wallace himself remains known if only because of the continued popularity of *King Kong*, of which he was both co-creator and screenwriter of the original film, which came out in 1932, the year he died.

Further Reading

Margaret Lane (1932). *Edgar Wallace: the Biography of a Phenomenon* (London, Heinemann)

Edgar Wallace (1911). *Sanders of the River* (London, Ward, Lock)

War of 1812. A War fought between Britain and the United States, it lasted for three years until 1815; Canadian territory became one of the prime sites for its execution. Animosity left over from the American War of Independence coloured Anglo-American relations well into the nineteenth century. Tension between the two countries was exacerbated by the Napoleonic Wars, especially when Britain attempted to impose trade restrictions on neutral countries, which had a deleterious impact on US trade with France. Moreover, the US accused Britain of the impressment of American sailors into the Royal Navy, as well as offering support to Native Indians who were against American westward expansion. Matters came to a head in June 1812, when the US under President James Madison declared war on Britain. Two months later, the Americans sought to strike a blow against the British by invading Upper Canada across the Niagara frontier, but the attack was repulsed. For the next two years the War was fought on land, on the Great Lakes, and in the Atlantic. American opinion was split on the War, and the British were much more concerned with the climax of the Napoleonic threat in Europe than they were with the Americans, but the battle was joined and in the end both sides accounted for some 20,000 casualties. By 1814, a stalemate had set in and weariness afflicted both troops and governments, and in December the Treaty of Ghent was signed, which signalled the end of the War. Some, however, did not hear of it immediately and the fighting continued, especially in the American South at New Orleans and in what became Alabama. The Treaty did little more than confirm the stalemate, however. The War had changed nothing substantial between the two countries and the grievances that had led to it were not addressed. But it did give a boost to American patriotism, confirming its independence. Even more clearly, the War made plain Canada's* rejection of American continentalist aspirations and affirmed its desire to remain within the British Empire.

Further Reading

Jon Latimer (2007). *1812: War with America* (Cambridge, MA, Belknap Press of Harvard University Press)

Mark Zuehlke (2006). *For Honour's Sake: the War of 1812 and the Brokering of an Uneasy Peace* (Toronto, Alfred A. Knopf Canada)

Welensky, Sir Raphael 'Roy' (1907–91). A Rhodesian politician and champion of white rule, Welensky served for seven years as Prime Minister of the Federation of Rhodesia* and Nyasaland*. Born in Salisbury, Southern Rhodesia (now Harare, Zimbabwe*) to Jewish-Afrikaner parents, he moved north as a young man to work on the railways, eventually becoming an engineer. He was also a champion boxer, which brought him some degree of local fame. In 1938, he gained election to the legislative council of Northern Rhodesia*. Utterly against the prospect of black majority rule in the region and determined to maximize its economic prospects, he championed the idea of a federation of the Rhodesias, which was achieved in 1956 and was also to include Nyasaland. He became its Prime Minister later that year and was subsequently knighted. Always an uncomfortable constitutional arrangement, however, the Federation's demise was hastened by the independence under black rule of Northern Rhodesia (Zambia*) and Nyasaland (Malawi*), and it collapsed in 1963. From then until 1980, Welensky lived in Salisbury, where he worked first to inhibit the government of Ian Smith* from invoking UDI*, and failing that to bring about the normalization of relations between Rhodesia and Britain. The establishment of Robert Mugabe's* Zimbabwe in 1980 convinced Welensky to re-locate to Britain, which he did the next year, living in retirement in Dorset for a decade until his death.

Further Reading

Roy Welensky (1964). *Welensky's 4000 Days* (London, Collins)

J.R.T. Wood (1983). *The Welensky Papers: A History of the Federation of Rhodesia and Nyasaland* (Durban, Graham)

Wellesley, Richard Colley, 1st Marquess Wellesley (1760–1842). Governor-General of India from 1798 to 1805, Wellesley was a key administrator in expanding the Imperial reach of the East India Company over a large part of the sub-continent. Born in Ireland and educated at Eton and Christ Church, Oxford*, he inherited the title 2nd Earl of Mornington (in the peerage of Ireland) in 1781 and three years later gained election to the House of Commons. He served in the Cabinet of Pitt the Younger, who appointed him to the Indian Board of Control, from whence he was made Governor-General. Strongly anti-French as it concerned their remaining position in India, he worked for their complete ouster, which was achieved by 1803. His younger brother, Arthur Wellesley, who would later gain fame as the Duke of Wellington, was his military advisor and used his service in India as a primer for his subsequent campaigning against Napoleon's troops in Spain and elsewhere. Richard Wellesley later served as British Ambassador to Spain, as Foreign Secretary, and as Lord Lieutenant of Ireland.

Further Reading

Iris Butler (1973). *The Eldest Brother: The Marquess Wellesley, The Duke of Wellington's Eldest Brother* (London, Hodder & Stoughton)

P.E. Roberts (1961). *India Under Wellesley* (Gorakhpur, Vishvaridyalaya Prakashan)

Western Australia. The largest state in the Australian* federation, it extends over the western third of the continent for some million square miles. The seafaring Dutch visited its coastline early in the seventeenth century. British settlement began at King George Sound (Albany) in 1826, and three years later at Swan River (Fremantle and Perth). Self-government was granted in 1890, a decade that also saw a gold rush centred on Kalgoorlie, spurring considerable immigration to the region and economic development. Fiercely independent, Western Australia entered the new national federation reluctantly in 1901.

Further Reading

Kay Forrest (1996). *The Challenge and the Chance: The Colonisation and Settlement of North West Australia* (Victoria Park, WA, Hesperian Press)

C.T. Stannage, ed. (1981). *A New History of Western Australia* (Nedlands, University of Western Australia Press)

Westminster, Statute of. An Act of the British Parliament proclaimed in 1931, this was the single most important document in the gradual effective independence of the Dominions*: the Commonwealth of Australia*, the Dominion of Canada*, the Irish Free State*, the Dominion of Newfoundland*, the Dominion of New Zealand*, and the Union of South Africa*. It built on the provisions of the Balfour Declaration* of 1926 and the Imperial Conference* of the previous year, making clear the legislative autonomy of each country's Parliament and precluding the right of the British government to make law for any of the Dominions unless asked specifically to do so by the Dominion in question. The Statute of Westminster did not have any effect on the legislation that had established the constitutions of the Dominions, however, and various residual powers remained with the British Parliament that would only be removed at length, as in the Canada Act of 1982 and the Australia Act of 1986. In political, if not strict constitutional, terms, the old Dominions date their 'independence' from 1931.

Further Reading

Frederick Madden and John Darwin, eds (1993). *Select Documents on the Constitutional History of the British Empire and Commonwealth*, vol. VI, *The Dominions and India Since 1900* (Westport, CT, Greenwood Press)

K.C. Wheare (1953). *The Statute of Westminster and Dominion Status*, 5th edn (London, Oxford University Press)

Wilberforce, William (1759–1833). The leading campaigner against the Atlantic slave trade* and against slavery, Wilberforce spent forty-five years in the House of Commons, for most of which he was a dogged reformer.

Born into wealth in Yorkshire, he was educated locally and in suburban London before going up to Cambridge, where his many friends included William Pitt the Younger. Elected to Parliament in 1780, in short order he became a staunch supporter of Pitt's minority government. Shortly thereafter, Wilberforce's latent religiosity was roused and he experienced a conversion to evangelical Christianity, from which he never departed. Henceforth he directed his energies toward the improvement of social morality and then, beginning with a major speech in Parliament in 1789, to a concerted campaign against the slave trade. The vicissitudes of the French Revolutionary and Napoleonic Wars and Westminster politics intervened in the campaign, but finally in 1807 British participation in the slave trade was outlawed. In the years that followed, Wilberforce sought progressive social change through the application of conservative Christian principles, including the gradual abolition of slavery. At first abolitionism's leader, he later became its figurehead when ill-health and failing eyesight restricted his activities. Considered rightly a moral giant in his own time, just days before his death in July 1833 he was informed that Parliament's passing of an abolition bill was imminent. It did so later that summer and the Slavery Abolition Act was proclaimed the next year, abolishing slavery throughout the Empire.

Further Reading

Roger Anstey (1975). *The Atlantic Slave Trade and British Abolition, 1760–1810* (London, Macmillan)

William Hague (2008). *William Wilberforce: The Life of the Great Anti-Slave Trade Campaigner* (London, Harper Press)

Wolfe, James (1727–59). Commander of the British forces that defeated the French at Quebec* in 1759, setting in train the conquest of New France, Wolfe was killed during the famous action that took place on the Plains of Abraham* just outside the walls of the city. Born into a military family in Kent, he began his career as a marine before transferring to an infantry regiment. He served on the European continent as well as in Scotland against the Jacobites, and in 1758 was sent to North America to participate in the Seven Years' War*. As a brigadier-general, Wolfe was instrumental in defeating the French at Louisbourg, their vital fortress on Cape Breton

Island, in June 1758, and as a reward was chosen to lead the British against the New France stronghold of Quebec the next year. In the summer of 1759, he fashioned a lengthy siege capped by a surprise amphibious landing on 13 September, and in a short but intense battle the French were defeated. He died just as it was reported that the French had broken and were fleeing the battlefield. The victory and subsequent conquest of New France confirmed his legend, later captured famously by Benjamin West in his painting, *The Death of General Wolfe* (1770).

Further Reading

Stephen Brumwell (2006). *Paths of Glory: The Life and Death of General James Wolfe* (London, Hambledon Continuum)

Robin Reilly (2001). *Wolfe of Quebec* (London, Cassell)

Wolseley, Garnet J., 1st Viscount Wolseley (1833–1913). To his contemporaries the quintessential Victorian soldier of Empire who saw service in a number of theatres including India*, Canada*, and Africa, Wolseley was born in Ireland* and commissioned into an infantry regiment at the age of eighteen. Service in Burma*, the Crimean War, the Indian Mutiny*, China, and then Canada* followed. Promoted colonel in 1865, he was appointed Deputy Quartermaster-General in Canada two years later, and in 1870 led the expedition to Red River* to put down the rebellious Métis and enforce Canadian sovereignty over what shortly became the province of Manitoba*. A stint in London was followed by command of the Ashanti* expedition in Africa's Gold Coast* in 1873–4. The Ashanti campaign made Wolseley's reputation and he was promoted major general and fêted widely at home. Much of the rest of his career was connected to Africa. He was sent to Natal* as Governor and then later commanded the British forces in the Anglo-Zulu War, returning to Britain in 1880. The British occupation of Egypt* from the summer of 1882 was confirmed with the Wolseley-commanded victory at Tel el-Kebir over Urabi Pasha* in September. Promoted general and awarded a barony, Wolseley then led the expedition to Khartoum to relieve General Gordon*, arriving two days late in January 1885. Made Viscount Wolseley not long afterward and then field marshal, he continued to be a prominent figure in the British military, appearing also in popular culture as 'Major-General Stanley' in the Gilbert and Sullivan comic opera *The Pirates of Penzance* (first performed in 1879). Never as well loved as Lord Roberts*, or as nobly heroic as General Gordon*, his death just before the First World War* was significant in that it marked the symbolic end of Victorian-era Imperial soldiering.

Further Reading

Halik Kochanski (1999). *Sir Garnet Wolseley: Victorian Hero* (London, Hambledon Press)

Joseph H. Lehmann (1964). *All Sir Garnet: A Life of Field-Marshal Lord Wolseley* (London, Jonathan Cape)

Woolf, Leonard (1880–1969). A noted Cambridge-educated author, publisher, and civil servant, and perhaps known best as the husband of Virginia Woolf, he became a leading anti-Imperialist whose experience as a member of the Ceylon Civil Service from 1904 to 1912 convinced him that economic and commercial advance alone defined contemporary British Imperialism, and therefore he must be its foe. He pointed to Joseph Chamberlain*, Colonial Secretary, as one of the key figures in using Imperial power toward economic ends, arguing that he and his colleagues 'accepted the principle of policy that the power of the State should be used upon the world outside the State for the economic purposes of the world within the State.' In support of his position he wrote various books and articles, including *Empire and Commerce in Africa: A Study in Economic Imperialism* (1920) and *Imperialism and Civilization* (1928). He also was active within the Labour Party, for a time serving as secretary of its advisory committee on inter-national and colonial questions. His views became widely known but not widely accepted, and were later critiqued strongly by Robinson and Gallagher*, among others.

Further Reading

Victoria Glendinning (2006). *Leonard Woolf: A Biography* (Toronto, McClelland & Stewart)

Christopher Ondaatje (2005). *Woolf in Ceylon: An Imperial Journey in the Shadow of Leonard Woolf, 1904–1911* (Toronto, HarperCollins)

X

Xhosa. A prominent indigenous tribal people located in South Africa*, the Xhosa were encountered by the British in the early part of the nineteenth century in the Cape Colony*. Pushed steadily back through frontier wars with the Boers and colonial expansion, the Xhosa reached a crisis point in the 1850s when a cattle-killing movement – symbolic of the deep fissures in Xhosa society caused by contact with Europeans – led to a period of great political instability and famine. The distinctive 'click' of the Xhosa language was mastered by the Revd Henry Hare Dugmore, a Wesleyan Methodist missionary who arrived from England as a ten-year-old with his family. In 1860, he translated the Bible into Xhosa, a first for the language. By the latter part of the century, the majority of the Xhosa working population were waged and migrant labourers, which in succeeding generations would lead to high membership in trade unions and strong political demands. The best-known member of the Xhosa today is Nelson Mandela*.

Further Reading

Elisabeth Anderson (1987). *A History of the Xhosa of the Northern Cape, 1795–1879* (Rondebosch, University of Cape Town)

Alan Lester (2001). *Imperial Networks: Creating Identities in Nineteenth Century South Africa and Britain* (London, Routledge)

Y

Younghusband, Sir Francis E. (1863–1942). One of the distinctive characters of Empire, Younghusband was a soldier and explorer who became a public figure, as well as a mystic. Born in British India*, Younghusband was raised there and in England. Educated at Clifton College, Bristol and then at the Royal Military Academy, Sandhurst, Younghusband was commissioned into the 1st King's Dragoon Guards in 1882 and posted to India. While on leave a few years later, the adventurous soldier went exploring in Manchuria, in the process crossing the Gobi Desert and charting a new route to India through the Mustagh Pass to Kashmir. Made a member of the Royal Geographical Society* and awarded its Gold Medal as a result, in 1889 he was sent on expedition to the Hunza region of far western China, which also was attracting the attention of Russia. The Anglo-Russian Great Game* was on and Younghusband became an enthusiastic participant in it as a member of the Indian Political Service in the 1890s. In 1902, the Viceroy of India, Lord Curzon*, made him Commissioner to Tibet and he promptly led an expedition there, the result of which was the ancient kingdom's effective occupation. He had overstepped his remit, however, but in 1904 he was knighted and then lived for a time as Resident in Kashmir before settling permanently in England. His later years were taken up with, among other things, the presidency of the RGS and advising the Mount Everest Committee in the early 1920s, as well as with much writing on mystical themes. His early Christianity had by then given way to a pantheistic, eastern-style religiosity manifest in the aspiration for world religious unity made plain in books such as *The Heart of Nature* (1921) and *World Fellowship of Faiths* (1935).

Further Reading

Patrick French (1997). *Younghusband: The Last Great Imperial Adventurer* (London, HarperCollins)

Anthony Verrier (1991). *Francis Younghusband and the Great Game* (London, Jonathan Cape)

Yukon Territory. An area of 186,000 square miles in north-west Canada, the Yukon came into permanent contact with whites through the Hudson's Bay Company (HBC)* in the 1840s, although Sir John Franklin* had reached its Arctic Ocean shoreline in 1825. Historically part of Rupert's Land, the Yukon came under Canadian control in 1870, when the HBC lands were purchased by the federal government to become the Northwest Territories*. Self-government for the Yukon followed fairly quickly, as did the impact of the Klondike* gold strike beginning in 1896, when thousands of prospectors arrived in this hitherto remote part of the continent. Mining, oil, the Alaska and the Dempster Highways, and tourism shaped the twentieth-century history of the Yukon. An elected council was established in 1908, the harbinger of semi-representative government that would characterize the Territory's politics henceforth.

Further Reading

Kenneth Coates (2005). *Land of the Midnight Sun: A History of the Yukon* (Kingston, ON, McGill-Queen's University Press)

Morris Zaslow (1971) *The Opening of the Canadian North, 1870–1914* (Toronto, McClelland & Stewart)

Z

Zambia. Located in South-Central Africa, the first Briton to encounter the territory that would later become Zambia was David Livingstone*, whose trans-Africa trek brought him to what he named the Victoria Falls* in 1855. In 1888, the British South Africa Company (BSAC)* negotiated mineral rights for what became known as North Western Rhodesia from the local Lozi king. North Eastern Rhodesia's mineral rights were won in battle against the Ngoni. In 1911, the two regions were united as Northern Rhodesia and administered by the BSAC. In 1923, Crown rule commenced. Copper mining and agriculture dominated the colonial economy. After the Second World War*, regional unification through the Federation of Rhodesia and Nyasaland* was attempted, but it failed and led to a sustained campaign for self-government and independence. In 1964, Northern Rhodesia became the Republic of Zambia, with Kenneth Kaunda* as its first President.

Further Reading

Andrew Roberts (1979). *A History of Zambia* (New York, Africana)

Andrew Sardanis (2003). *Africa: Another Side of the Coin: Northern Rhodesia's Final Years and Zambia's Nationhood* (London and New York, I.B.Tauris)

Zanzibar. A storied, clove-scented island off the east coast of Africa and today part of Tanzania*, Zanzibar became a British Protectorate in 1890 after a long struggle against the Sultan of Oman's slave trade-fuelled control of the island, as well as the rival Imperial interest of Germany. David Livingstone* and others had used Zanzibar as the starting-point for various

African expeditions, and the Royal Navy found it a convenient harbour for its protracted nineteenth-century campaign against the Omani slave trade. Beginning in 1913, British Residents were assigned to Zanzibar, a system kept in place until independence in 1963. The independence period was marred by a bloody uprising, which saw the ending of a constitutional monarchy and the installation of a republic in 1964. A merger with Tanganyika* quickly followed, forming the United Republic of Tanzania, of which Zanzibar is a semi-autonomous region.

Further Reading

Norman R. Bennett (1986). *Arab versus European: Diplomacy and War in Nineteenth-Century East Central Africa* (New York, Africana)

Abdul Sheriff (1991). *Zanzibar under Colonial Rule* (London, J. Currey)

Zimbabwe. Located in southern Africa, Zimbabwe's British colonial period began in 1888 when Cecil Rhodes* and the British South Africa Company* obtained mining rights in the region north of the Limpopo River from the local king, Lobengula* of the Ndebele. Additional mining rights were obtained and in 1894 the 'Pioneer Column' arrived at what they named Salisbury (today's Harare), intent on establishing a new colony. Named Rhodesia the next year, the local Shona and Ndebele peoples resisted the alienation of their land by the initial group of administrators, but their revolts were put down with military force, and beginning in 1897 white settlement commenced in earnest. Known as Southern Rhodesia from 1911, the colony became self-governing in 1923. The unsuccessful Federation of Rhodesia and Nyasaland, together with the enfranchisement and nation-alist demands of the black majority and Britain's sympathy with them, prompted Southern Rhodesia's decision to issue a Unilateral Declaration of Independence (UDI)* in 1965. In the years of turmoil that followed, black independence groups such as the Zimbabwe African National Union (ZANU) and the Zimbabwe African People's Union (ZAPU) fought to bring the white minority regime of Ian Smith* to an end. In 1978, Smith relented and signed an accord paving the way for multi-racial elections, which were held the next year. That autumn in London, the Lancaster House confer-ence met over a span of three months in order to reach terms that would allow for the peaceful independence of what was now called Zimbabwe-Rhodesia. Early in 1980, elections were held. ZANU, under the leadership of Robert Mugabe*, won the elections. He became Prime Minister and then later President, the position he has occupied ever since. Zimbabwe was the last major British African colony to achieve independence, but after initial stability and relative prosperity the country has endured years of criminal misrule, which continues up to today.

Further Reading

Paul Mosley (1983). *The Settler Economies: Studies in the Economic History of Kenya and Southern Rhodesia, 1900-1963* (Cambridge, Cambridge University Press)

T.O. Ranger (1985). *Peasant Consciousness and Guerilla War in Zimbabwe: A Comparative Study* (London, J. Currey)

Zulu. During the late nineteenth century, a fierce warrior people in competition with both Boer and Briton in Cape Colony* and Natal*, the Zulu had emerged as a powerful nation under Shaka, beginning about 1816. During the 1830s, they resisted Boer expansion in Zululand, but in 1838 they lost the signal battle of the Great Trek*, Blood River. Afterwards, they lived in constant tension with the Boers, a tension exacerbated by the British in the 1870s. Under Cetshwayo*, the Zulu sought to resist British attempts to take over their homeland, successfully defeating them at Isandlwana*, before being vanquished later that year at the Battle of Ulundi*. Zulu political sovereignty was effectively destroyed by these events, and for much of the twentieth century they endured extreme political repression at the hands of the South African state before rising again in the aftermath of the ending of apartheid*.

Further Reading

John Laband (1997). *The Rise & Fall of the Zulu Nation* (London, Arms & Armour Press)

Stephen Taylor (1994). *Shaka's Children: The History of the Zulu People* (London, HarperCollins)

Bibliographical Note

The historiography of the British Empire is immense and comes in a number of styles including survey, monograph, area or thematic study, atlas, and biography. For each of the over 400 entries in this handbook two bibliographic entries have been included and, with few exceptions, these inclusions tend to offer targeted explications of the given entry. The purpose of this Bibliographical Note, therefore, is to provide coverage of the major surveys of British Imperial history that are not necessarily captured by the entry bibliographies and which can be used as a point of embarkation for anyone studying the field at large, especially for the first time.

The most comprehensive historical examination of the British Empire yet undertaken is *The Oxford History of the British Empire* (Oxford University Press, 1998–9). Written under the editorial supervision of Wm. Roger Louis, the original five volumes of the series, together with a number of subsequently published cognate volumes, is the standard work on British Imperial history and will stand for the foreseeable future as indispensable to anyone undertaking a serious study of the subject.

Single-volume histories of the Empire are many. Some are written by professional historians, others by popular writers, but together they have created a large corpus of work in which virtually every jot and tittle of the British Imperial experience has received an accounting. A good place to begin is with an old chestnut, A.P. Thornton's *The Imperial Idea and Its Enemies* (Macmillan, 1959). A historian and writer of singular virtuosity, Thornton's signature polemical work repays reading even half a century after its publication. *The Rise and Fall of the British Empire* (Little, Brown,

1993) by Lawrence James is magisterial in scope and written for a broad readership, narrating the trajectory of the Empire as grand history. So too, is Niall Ferguson's *Empire: The Rise and Demise of the British World Order and the Lessons for Global Power* (Allen Lane, 2002), although his interpretation of the history of the Empire, as the subtitle makes clear, is intentionally didactic. Less commanding in tone, but written with a surer hand nonetheless, is Trevor Lloyd's *Empire: A History of the British Empire* (Hambledon and London, 2001). At just 245 pages there is not a better relatively brief history of the Empire available than Lloyd's, although Bernard Porter's *The Lion's Share: A Short History of British Imperialism* (Longman, 1996) comes close, especially on the nineteenth and twentieth centuries. A recent entry in the category is Piers Brendon's *The Decline and Fall of the British Empire, 1781–1997* (Jonathan Cape, 2007), which gives a close treatment of the Second Empire. Brendon owes much to *The Decline, Revival and Fall of the British Empire* (Cambridge University Press, 1982), written by John Gallagher and presented originally as the Ford Lectures of 1974. Excellent too is John Darwin's comprehensive *The Empire Project: The Rise and Fall of the British World System, 1830–1970* (Cambridge University Press, 2009). Darwin is one of the best historians of the Empire at work today, and this book is his magnum opus. Strong on the reinvigoration of the Empire after the loss of the American colonies is C.A. Bayly's *Imperial Meridian: The British Empire and the World, 1780–1830* (Longman, 1989). Very useful too is Sarah Stockwell's edited volume, *The British Empire: Themes and Perspectives* (Blackwell, 2008), as is David Cannadine's eclectic, at times almost whimsical, *Ornamentalism: How the British Saw Their Empire* (Oxford University Press, 2001). Bernard Porter's *The Absent-Minded Imperialists: Empire, Society, and Culture in Britain* (Oxford University Press, 2006) offers a broader analysis of much the same theme. Finally, for sheer scope and readability, the trilogy by James (Jan) Morris – *Heaven's Command: An Imperial Progress*; *Pax Britannica: The Climax of an Empire*; and *Farewell the Trumpets: An Imperial Retreat* (Faber and Faber, 1968–78) – remains a marvelously accessible entrée into British Imperial history.

Visualizing the geographic reach of the Empire is made easy by atlases and illustrated histories, three fine examples being the *Atlas of the British Empire: The Rise and Fall of the Greatest Empire the World has ever Known*

(Facts on File, 1989), edited by C.A. Bayly; *The Cambridge Illustrated History of the British Empire* (Cambridge University Press, 1996), edited by P.J. Marshall; and *Mad Dogs and Englishmen: A Grand Tour of the British Empire at its Height, 1850–1945* (Quercus, 2009), by Ashley Jackson. Encountering the Empire through other means, such as collections of published documents, is made readily available by the two volumes (so far) of the *Archives of Empire* (Duke University Press, 2003), edited by Barbara Harlow and Mia Carter.

Owing principally to Edward Gibbon, the 'Decline and Fall' motif for empire is timeless. In this category there are a number of entries on the British Empire. David Adamson's *The Last Empire: Britain and the Commonwealth* (I.B.Tauris, 1989) is a good place to start. So too are John Darwin's *The End of the British Empire: The Historical Debate* (Blackwell, 1991), and Wm. Roger Louis's *Ends of British Imperialism: The Scramble for Empire, Suez and Decolonization* (I.B.Tauris, 2006). Other essential books in this regard include John Keay's *Last Post: The End of Empire in the Far East* (John Murray, 1997); Ronald Hyam's *Britain's Declining Empire: The Road to Decolonisation, 1918–1968* (Cambridge University Press, 2006); and Peter Clarke's *The Last Thousand Days of the British Empire* (Allen Lane, 2007).

If Gibbon's motif is timeless, so too, it would seem, is empire itself. This is the subject taken up by John Darwin in *After Tamerlane: The Rise & Fall of Global Empires, 1400–2000* (Allen Lane, 2007). A superb encapsulation of 600 years of worldwide imperial history, it provides an arresting reminder of the permanence of imperialism as an organizing feature of human society and for the ongoing structure of international relations.

Index

Napoleonic Wars, 43, 75, 104, 110,
122, 172, 217, 230, 261, 275,
279
Nasser, Gamal Abdel, 74
Natal, 53, 181
Nauru, 181–182
Nehru, Jawaharlal, 27, 121, 129,
182–183
Nelson, Admiral Horatio. *See*
Nelson, Horatio, 1st Viscount
Nelson
Nelson, Admiral Lord. *See* Nelson,
Horatio, 1st Viscount Nelson
Nelson, Horatio, 1st Viscount
Nelson, 2, 183–184, 229, 267
Netherlands, 165
Nevis, 9, 228–229
Newbold, Sir Douglas, 184–185
New Brunswick, 41, 185, 206, 212
Newfoundland, 41, 49, 57, 186
Newman, John Henry, 76–77
New South Wales, 14, 28–29,
186–187, 190
New Zealand, 33, 49, 57, 59, 77,
79–80, 86, 87, 91, 100–101, 114,
169, 182, 187–188, 189, 209,
235, 273, 274
New Zealand Company, 274
New Zealand Constitution Act,
187
Nigeria, 11–12, 39–40, 45, 51,
80–81, 96, 103–104, 108–109,
110, 162, 188, 206, 209, 226,
274

Nile, Battle of the, 75, 184
'Ninety-two Resolutions', 204
Nisbet, Frances (Fanny), 229
Niue, 189
Nkomo, Joshua, 244
Nkrumah, Kwame, 11–12, 20, 94,
189–190, 204
North Borneo. *See* Sabah
Northern Territory, 190
Northwest Company, the, 115, 159,
190, 236
North-West Frontier Province, 191
Northwest Rebellion, 218, 221, 232
Northwest Territories, 192, 284
Nova Scotia, 29–30, 41, 192
Nyasaland. *See* Malawi
Nyerere, Julius K., 7, 193, 255

O

Obote, A. Milton, 7, 195–196
OFS-Sotho War, 177
Oldham, J.H., 196
Omani slave trade, 18
Omdurman, Battle of, 142–143,
197
Ontario, 41, 197–198
Opium Wars, 114–115, 127,
198–199
Orange Free State, 199–200
Ottawa, 32–33, 34
Ottoman Empire, 5
Outram, Sir James, 200
Oxford, University of, 201